The Media Commons

D1614968

THE GEOPOLITICS OF INFORMATION

Edited by Dan Schiller, Pradip Thomas, and Yuezhi Zhao

A list of books in the series appears at the end of this book.

The Media Commons

Globalization and Environmental Discourses

PATRICK D. MURPHY

UNIVERSITY OF
ILLINOIS PRESS
Urbana, Chicago, and Springfield

Printed and bound in Great Britain by
Marston Book Services Ltd, Oxfordshire

1 2 3 4 5 C P 5 4 3 2 1
∞ This book is printed on acid-free paper.

Cataloging data available from the Library of Congress.
LCCN 2016044999
ISBN 978-0-252-04103-7 (cloth: alk.)
ISBN 978-0-252-08253-5 (paper: alk)
ISBN 978-0-252-09958-8 (ebook)

For Monet, Andrea, and Kadie

Contents

Acknowledgments   ix

Introduction   1

1   Earth Discourses: Theorizing the Environment
for Global Media Studies   17

2   Endless Growth: Neoliberalism and Global Media's
Promethean Logic   41

3   Neo-Malthusian Entertainment:
The Limits of Green TV   71

4   Battle of the Blogosphere: Monsanto versus the World   95

5   Amazonian Indigenous Green: Media and
the Ecologically Noble Savage   117

Conclusion: Earth Discourses and the Question
of Agency in the Media Commons   145

Notes   157

Bibliography   161

Index   181

Acknowledgments

It is with great pleasure that I acknowledge those who have helped me through the researching and writing of this book. To start with, Temple University's School of Media and Communication has been the perfect site through which to work on this project. Nancy Morris, Fabienne Darling-Wolf, and Tom Jacobson all provided great advice and offered important suggestions on the key issues, especially regarding that amorphous notion called "globalization." I am especially thankful to Barry Vacker for our conversations about dystopian and utopian narratives in the media, and his enthusiasm for the project. Melissa Meade and Diantha Vliet provided me a steady stream of ideas and information while working as my research assistants. Nicole McKenna, Howard Rice, Debbie Marshall, Rochelle Davis, Caitlin Gamble, and Dawn Ramos, in ways that they are most likely not even aware of, all showed me support and encouragement at crucial times. I could not have completed this book without the exceptional support of Dean David Boardman, Senior Associate Dean Deborah Cai, and Senior Vice Dean for Finance and Administration Don Heller, who all, in different ways, made sure I had the time and space to work on the book despite our heavy administrative load. I have been very fortunate to work in such a supportive and collegial environment.

Work on this project was seeded during my tenure at Southern Illinois University Edwardsville, so I would be remiss not to thank my good friends and former colleagues, Gary Hicks, Elza Ibroscheva, Isaac Blankson, John Kautzer, Dave Kauzlarich, Hannah Reinhart, and the former dean of the College of Arts and Sciences, Kent Neeley. On the other end of things, my 2016 Semester at Sea trip provided an especially rich and diverse community of colleagues and experiences to help think through and refine the book in its later stages. I am thankful to Victor Luftig, Simon Hudson, Colleen Cohen, Rob Huesca, Chandra Ranade, Scott McCoy, Loki Pandey, Annapurna Pandey, Mark Bill, and Zoe Bulaitis for their friendship and the interdisciplinary dialogue we engaged in while at sea.

Many other people contributed their efforts to this book in significant ways. I am very grateful to Andres Hansen, Libby Lester, Stephen Rust, Nancy Morris, Marwan Kraidy, Antonio La Pastina, Phaedra Pezzullo, Zixue Tai, Miya Christensen, Patrick Burkart, Radhika Parameswaran, and the anonymous reviewers for reading chapter drafts and providing critical feedback during various stages of the manuscript's development.

I have been fortunate to have the guidance and friendship of Marwan Kraidy at the University of Pennsylvania's Annenberg School of Communication, and Troy Able at Western Washington University's Huxley College of the Environment. Since our graduate school days at Ohio University, Marwan has been and continues to be my chief sounding board for all things related to media and globalization. He read the manuscript with curiosity and, as always, asked intellectually provocative questions that drove me to deepen my analysis. On the more environmental side of things, I am indebted to Troy, who introduced me to the interpretive school of environmental policy analysis many years ago, and whose conversations with me about environmental policy and power, riskscapes and environmental racism have been inspirational.

I would especially like to acknowledge the generosity of key informants at Discovery Channel, Treehugger.com, Monsanto, the BBC Media Action, and others who have asked to remain anonymous. I am also indebted to former Discovery Chief Operating Officer Peter Liguori, Marketplace's Steve Zwick, and the World Resources Institute's Rachel Petersen. Without the assistance of these individuals, many of the more interesting and illuminating aspects of this book would be missing.

At the University of Illinois Press I owe thanks to my editor Daniel Nasset, whose patience, guidance, and enthusiasm for the book was vital during the long journey to its completion. Likewise, my deep appreciation and thanks goes to my copyeditor, Julie Gay, who was exceptionally responsive and detail oriented. I am also thankful to the Geopolitics of Information series editors Dan Schiller, Pradip Thomas, and Yuezhi Zhao for their feedback and direction, and for adding this book to their important series.

Portions of chapters in this book were published previously in "Putting the Earth into Global Media Studies," *Communication Theory* 21 (3): 217–38.

More personally, this book has many sources of inspiration, the earliest of which stem from a childhood filled with direct experiences with nature. At a young age my parents, Timothy Murphy and Georgia Springer, encouraged me to explore my surroundings, from Virginia's Blue Ridge Mountains, Central Mexico's dry and agave-strewn landscapes, and Western Pennsylvania's densely forested yet industrially scarred Appalachian hills. I am deeply thankful for my mother's light-handed guidance toward these existential sites of discovery, and my anthropologist father's insistence on making sense of "the ways things work" from a more culturally grounded perspective. I am also thankful to my brothers, Timo and Daniel, with whom I have long shared a love of the outdoors, marked in my mind's eye with the early experiences of roaming the banks of the acid-choked red rivers and streams of our youth to graduate in later years to fishing the crystal-clear trout waters of the Ozarks. Without this sense of shared experience and adventure, I doubt I would have developed the eco-conscious curiosity that I possess today, at least certainly not enough to undertake the writing of such a book.

Finally, my wife Karla has been unfailingly supportive of me in my work and for that I am immensely appreciative. And to my daughters Kadie, Andrea, and Monet, to whom I have dedicated this book, I am exceptionally grateful. During periods when I was absorbed by the project and seemingly in a state of perpetual distraction and absentmindedness, my family responded with an endless supply of warmth, humor, and, above all, love. Thank you for that wonderful gift.

Introduction

In an era of concern over global climate change it is understandable that when the relationship between the environment and human practice is talked about, the discussion typically falls on issues such as carbon emissions, mass species extinction, acidification of the ocean, and so forth, not on apparently less urgent topics such as the link between media messages and the social imagination about the environment. Certainly there is good reason for this focus on the impact of human activity on Earth's ecosystems: with expanding, fertilizer-induced "dead zones" in the coastal seas, the deforestation of vast swaths of rainforest lands for soy or palm oil production, increased "megafires" in Australia, Russia, and California, and rapidly melting glaciers of the Andes, Alps, Greenland, and Mt. Kilimanjaro, there is no shortage of concrete environmental canaries in the global mine. Such dispersed, regionalized symptoms illustrate in dramatic fashion the truly global scope of the unfolding environmental saga the planet is experiencing.

However, they also reveal a "politics of the Earth" (Dryzek 2005) generated by a shifting web of policy, economics, culture, and ecological dilemmas made salient via conflicts among corporations, consumers, and communities. Therefore, to appreciate fully how human practice has contributed to the environmental challenges we now face requires a consideration of how discourse-rendering institutions across the globe have mediated public culture. By virtue of their ubiquitous presence in everyday life, commercial and social media deserve special attention, as they are central resources through which audiences conceptualize their understanding of the natural world as well as a means through which citizens respond to Earth's unfolding ecological crisis.

Indeed, within the global move to market economies that has taken place over the past four decades, private media and promotional communication have established complex, integrated networks that serve to shape, frame, and deliver many of the underlying ideas about the environment that individuals and communities experience not only in the "developed world" but also in the increasingly media-saturated Global South.

As various scholars have observed, these integrated media systems promote the pursuit of wasteful cultural practices and ecologically unsustainable lifestyles by presenting an imaginistic and informational confluence of codes of excess and disposability (Babe 1995; Budd, Craig, Steinman 1999; Comor 2008; Lewis 2012). In recognizing this core global pattern, however, it is also necessary to understand that messages about the environment within the global media landscape are by no means monolithic and are often quite contradictory. For instance, what prominent environmental studies scholar Chet A. Bowers (2006) has called "the myth of endless technological progress and equally endless advances in the capacity to consume" (87) has been confronted in some interesting ways through environmentally progressive themes emerging in media fare around the world. This practice is adduced in everything from its presence as a subtext in Brazilian telenovelas and Japanese anime to the central theme of Australian eco-makeover reality shows and Al-Jazeera's "Fragile Planet" series. These themes also emerged with force in a range of internationally distributed animated films like *Spirited Away* (2002), *Happy Feet* (2006), and the global 3D blockbuster, *Avatar* (2009). In 2006 even MTV, the global champion of youth consumer culture, went temporarily "green," inviting Noble Prize winner and environmental guru Al Gore to give the "keynote address" at its annual video awards. And of course the internet has become home to a wealth of eco-driven fare; some of it, like *The Meatrix*, has reached international audiences with paradigm-shifting messages.[1] In 2010 DC Comics even had Superman quoting Thoreau while walking—not flying—across America to reconnect to the earth (Straczynski 2010).[2]

Though encouraging, such eco-friendly trends and attempts at environmental consciousness raising are nevertheless part of globally interlaced media spheres dominated by a broader corporate model of information and entertainment designed to normalize commodity hunger. Even the family film *Wall-E* (2008), Pixar's scathing critique of consumer excess and environmental abuse, served as a launching point for the cross-media marketing of merchandise that will end up in dumps. More troubling yet are the implications of an environment merely commoditized through "branding" campaigns, media events, and multiplatform messaging, elaborated increasingly under the banner of "corporate responsibility" designed to cultivate positive public perception, not necessarily eco-consciousness (for example, Exxon's distribution of "sponsored educational materials" to public schools after the Valdez oil spill; *Forbes* magazine's naming ExxonMobile "green company of the year" for 2009; Coca-Cola's iconic polar bear Christmas advertising campaign developed in partnership with the World Wildlife Fund).

Yet the problem with making sense of environmental issues is not just tied to the networked yet oddly contradictory media spheres that audiences inevitably find themselves trying to negotiate to get a better purchase on the state of the global commons. Rather, it is the fact that *what to actually do is itself a point of contention*, as the range of competing and in many cases co-evolving ideas have a rich and global history. Long before the Lorax spoke for the trees or Wall-E went about cleaning up a post-tipping-point Earth—or, for that matter, before Rachel Carson stopped hearing singing birds or the ecotage antics of Edward Abbey's *The Monkey Wrench Gang* inspired Earth First!—voices ranging from eco-political interlocutors of the sublime to Malthusian guardians of the planet's limits have argued, in quite different ways, for a defense of the natural world and its resources. Indeed, imagining human relationships with nature can be traced back to the books of Genesis and Revelation in the Bible, which produced both pastoral and apocalyptic environmental narratives (Garrard 2004; White 1967), and elements of "conservationism" can be found from the eleventh to fifteenth centuries in societies ranging from Islamic Egypt, the Venetians, and Germanic states, to India, China, and Japan, as well as the Incas and Aztecs in the Americas (Miller 2007).

Meanwhile, even in the shadow of global climate change, some contemporary thinkers continue to be committed to advancing the cornucopian notion that for humans on planet Earth, things are actually getting better despite what the media (viewed as today's public myth tellers) are reporting to audiences. For instance, in *The Skeptical Environmentalist: Measuring the Real State of the World*, Danish political scientist Bjørn Lomborg (2001) famously argued that our general view of the environment is shaped by "The Litany" of our ever-deteriorating environment delivered through entertainment and news media, helping to make the catastrophic familiar. According to Lomborg, The Litany goes something like this:

> Our resources are running out. The population is ever growing, leaving less and less to eat. The air and the water are becoming ever more polluted. The

planet's species are becoming extinct in vast numbers—we kill off more than 40,000 each year. The forests are disappearing, fish stocks are collapsing and coral reefs are dying.

We are defiling our Earth, fertile topsoil is disappearing, we are paving over nature, destroying the wilderness, decimating the biosphere, and will end up killing ourselves in the process. The world's ecosystem is breaking down. We are fast approaching the absolute limit of viability, and the limits of growth are becoming apparent. (4)

The persuasive power of The Litany, Lomborg asserts, rests on its omnipresence to the point that it has almost become "reassuring." But, he warns, there is just one problem: "this conception is simply not keeping with reality," as things are actually getting better, not worse for most of the planet's inhabitants as life expectancy, human welfare, and prosperity are on the rise (2001, 4–6).

As these disparate lines of thought underscore, human history has not produced an agreed-upon understanding of what noted American ecologist Garrett Hardin (1968) metaphorically labeled "the commons," since ideas about the earth's care and treatment are linked to a range of moral, aesthetic, and political questions that are further complicated by the fact that the terms of particular debates are shifting and contested, often reframed by contextual circumstances and recast in relation to emerging technologies. Is preserving a rainforest from loggers or protecting a mountaintop from miners as important to communities or citizens when the economy is suffering and people are searching for ways to make ends meet? Should native peoples be permitted to continue to hunt, fish, and harvest materials from protected lands because of cultural rights and traditions while others are bound to follow restrictive conservation laws? Are genetically modified seeds an innovative response to climate change and population growth by increasing crop yields while requiring fewer pesticides and fertilizers and less water, or are they, as GM critics assert, the stuff of an agricultural biotechnology industry engaged in biopiracy and peddling a Pandora's box of enviro-hazards capable of stripping ecosystems of their biodiversity?

Such tensions and antagonisms are found at the heart of almost any environmental debate, and looking at how we define and talk about them typically has considerably more to do with how citizens respond to them than the actual underlying science of any given issue. Understanding the political, cultural, and institutional dimensions of this dynamic is therefore crucial because, as communications scholar and former Sierra Club president Robert Cox (2013) succinctly puts it, ideas about the environment have consequences since they "actively shape our understanding, create meaning, and orient us to a wider world" (20–21). As with other subjects negotiated within the public sphere, people draw from symbolic constructions about the environment to create meaning and guide social practice. Thus, ideas privileged by knowledge systems chart the direction through which this interplay between culture and politics unfolds. Eco-critic Greg Garrard (2004) provides a useful illustration of this dynamic, arguing, "A 'weed' is not a kind of plant, only the wrong kind in the wrong place. Eliminating weeds is obviously a 'problem in gardening,' but defining weeds in the first place requires a cultural, not horticultural, analysis" (5–6).

The purpose of *The Media Commons: Globalization and Environmental Discourses* is to consider, as a defining characteristic of globalization, how such definitions about the environment are shaped, privileged, and altered by contemporary media systems. In short, how is a "weed" identified, and how do such definitions cast "the problem"? These two interrelated questions are pursued through the mapping of how distinct, competing, and/or oppositional, even antagonistic, environmental discourses are "enunciated" (to borrow from Foucault) in different ways through today's expanding media spheres. To do so, this book draws on a range of theoretical traditions, analytical tools, and empirical materials to inform the study of how, as discursive sites of power and representation, media and communication networks serve as systems of knowledge that mold our environmental consciousness. Below I explicate the theoretical, analytical, and empirical entry points.

A Discourse Approach to Media, Globalization, and the Environment

One of the impetuses for writing this book has been to help direct the discussion about media and globalization toward environmentalism. A review of the media studies literature reveals an absence of work that has directly pursued this objective. While there has been some important scholarship by political economists on media economics and consumption that is certainly necessary to help inform the study of media, globalization, and the environment (Babe 1995; Budd, Craig, and Steinman 1999; Comor 2008), this literature has either tended to lean toward issues of public policy without engaging the cultural complexities of media and globalization or has attempted to decipher globalization's relationship to consumer culture without sufficiently considering the links between the environment and media culture.

Meanwhile, in key texts that have influenced the conceptualization of globalization and culture within global media studies (for example, Appadurai 1996; Darling-Wolf 2015; Featherstone 1990; Garcia Canclini 1990, 2000; Hannerz 1996; King 1997; Kraidy 2005; Pieterse 2015; Said 1993; Straubhaar 1991; Tomlinson 1999), there is little to no treatment of the environment. So, while the field of global media studies has produced rigorous interrogations of key globalization issues such as cultural imperialism, dependency, cultural identity, cultural hybridity, global flows, postcolonialism, representation, the social imagination, and so on, there is a pervasive silence when it comes to questions concerning the environment.[3]

Fortunately, there is a wide range of sources from other fields and intellectual traditions from which global media researchers can productively draw to help make sense of how the environment has been conceptualized and to guide analysis. For instance, within the field of rhetorical criticism, concepts such as ethos, pathos, logos, and persona have been employed to develop a tripartite model of environmental discourse analysis based on ethnocentric (nature as resource), ecocentric (nature as spirit), and anthropocentric (nature as object) renderings (Herndl and Brown 1996). More recent work has also provided insight into how "image events" serve as a form of transformative environmental politics (DeLuca 2006). Closely aligned to these theoretical interventions is the work of eco-critics, who have produced a rich body of literature on the range of environmental visions presented through recurring tropes (for example, "wilderness," "pollution"), narratives (such as jeremiad and apocalypse) and metaphors (a place apart, tipping point, mother earth, and so on) in art, literature, and media (Corbett 2006; Garrard 2004; Heise 2008). Historians, geographers, and anthropologists have likewise produced scholarship on the capacity of environmental representations to shape public consciousness, tied in significant ways to place, performance, and gender in relationship to the production and maintenance of cultural identities (Escobar 1998, 2008; Gold and Revill 2004; Merchant 1989). Finally, communication scholars, particularly those concerned with environmental risk, have generated a strong corpus of work on how environmental issues are covered and thus framed by the news media, and how environmental pressure groups and others have learned to use these practices to find their own public voice (for example, Allan, Adam, and Carter 2000; Anderson 1997; Boyce and Lewis 2009; Cox 2013; Depoe and Condit 1997; Hansen 1991, 1993, 2010; Lester 2010; Lester and Hutchins 2013; Maher 1996; Peeples and Depoe 2014).

These areas of criticism, inquiry, and analysis converge, in that all understand the symbolic treatment of the environment as a means through which the public's perception of the natural world is affected by orienting it toward some ideas and away from others. They provide useful analytical tools and historical frames of reference for how particular rhetorical arrangements can reveal continuing oppositions, or what Cox (2013) labels "environmental antagonisms" (for example, human health versus industry; environmental justice versus nature as "a place apart"; conservation versus preservation) that shape how we conduct our everyday lives as consumers and citizens, practice and digest the lessons of science, or inform the policymaking of the state and the politics of corporate "social responsibility." This vast literature offers indispensible lenses through which to examine what actors are involved in the sponsorship of particular environmental constructions and the interests they serve.

While I draw substantially from all of these pools of scholarship, the main thrust of this book's theoretical orientation is guided by the analytical devices and distinctions developed by the "interpretive school" of environmental policy analysis (Abel and Stephan 2008). The theoretical framework I put forward is especially informed by John S. Dryzek's book *The Politics of the Earth: Environmental Discourses* (2005), which I argue presents media scholars with a useful way to examine how ideas about the human relationship with the environment are presented and circulated across various media spheres around the globe.

Dryzek sees discourse as "a shared way of apprehending the world. Embedded in language, it enables those who subscribe to it to interpret bits of information and put them together into coherent stories or accounts" (9). This rendering of discourse as social navigation owes much to the work of Michel Foucault in that it is based on the assumption that if discourses of the powerful are successful, they bind the contours of agreement and dispute within a given historical context. They therefore surface as naturalized and self-perpetuating in ways that serve to legitimate the links between knowledge and power. Accordingly, one measure of a powerful discourse is that its underlying principles "do not need conscious articulation" because they become "so ingrained and taken-for-granted that it would never occur to anyone to mention them" (Dryzek 2005, 51). In this respect Dryzek's understanding of discourse follows closely Foucault's position that discourses do more than just designate things (codes, for example) because they are produced through "practices that systematically form the objects of which they speak" (1972, 49). However, whereas Foucault largely saw subjectivity as governed by discourses in which individuals move, thus shaping what is allowed, forbidden, and obliged (1972; see also Barrett 1991), Dryzek (2005) argues that while discourses are powerful, "they are not impenetrable" (22).

This explains why competing discourses can coexist and even coproduce each other, and therefore how dominant discourses can be challenged and modified.

It is through such departures from Foucault's conceptualization of discourse as the site of power that gives Dryzek's work a more "open" inflection. That is, there is greater emphasis placed on the range, disintegration, and reemergence of various discourses as shaped and reconfigured through political and civil arrangements that experience fissures, periods of stress, reconciliation, settling, and appropriation. This focus allows Dryzek to assert that though a particular discourse may emerge as dominant during any temporal moment, this emergence does not mean that it simply erases all others. Rather, a range of discourses may be present at any given time, competing and complementary, that shape the contours of hegemonic culture and affect its transformation and disintegration.

In my view, it is precisely this elaboration of discourse as a complex and even potentially contradictory site of power, agency, and contestation that makes the lessons from interpretive school of environmental policy analysis an attractive theoretical launching point for the investigation for how environmental issues are presented and circulated across various media spheres around the globe. Through this lens, emphasis is on how discourse is primarily a way to seek out and identify *how political power is encased in particular knowledge systems and packaged in cultural story lines.* And as Foucault and others have shown, and as Dryzek forcibly argues in his own scholarship, how the discursive threads produced and recycled through institutions, networks, and communities tells us something about underlying assumptions surrounding "natural" relationships and the motives of the agents that produce them. It is through their very range and inflection that competing discourses reveal the ideological and cultural struggle at play, particularly in the form of agency. By following this investigative path, media scholars interested in pursuing environmental questions can develop more purposeful and urgently needed research on how power, agency, and representation are tied to different institutions, social arrangements, and historical processes around the world.

Sites of Inquiry and Empirical Materials

Critical theorist and social activist Andrew Ross (1994) reminds us, "ideas do not emerge out of a social vacuum," and, in fact, it is useful to recall that the rise of modern (Western) environmentalism "has been concurrent with the globalization of the economy; both share the common discourse of transnational interests" (14). With this observation in mind, in the chapters that follow I focus on specific media industries, practices, and histories that can tell us something about the ways in which economic globalization and environmentalism have been and continue to be intertwined. I place investigative emphasis on how environmental discourses have been formed and reformed within the contemporary process on globalization by social context, institutional alignments, and the discourse-rendering practices of commercial and social media networks—or what I am calling in this book "the media commons."

While not a singular site, the metaphor of the media commons is useful because it implies interconnections and overlaps that have the look and feel of something experientially "local" and immediately accessible but yet is subject to a mixture of external and internal pressures (global, regional, national, local). Within this "space," of central interest is how commercial and social media condition ideas about the environmental through the articulation of agency (who has the power to act). Trying to make sense of this process therefore involves identifying and analyzing the structures and practices in relation to the regimes of truth that media produce through recurring tropes, key terms and metaphors, and converging storylines. The institutional examinations and case examples the book provides pursue this chore through the identification and interpretation of Earth discourses as follows: media's institutional encasements and evolutionary trajectories (chapter 2), "green" genres and corporate decision making in global television networks (chapter 3), multiplatform branding strategies and representation (chapter 4), and local-global ecological intervention as tied to symbolic power and the (Western) environmental imagination (chapter 5). These treatments reveal much about the social arrangements that produce, as well as the sponsors of, particular discourses by shedding light on their underlying assumptions (for example, the place of nature), motives (such as self-interest vs. public interest), and articulation of agency within the media commons.

Since media systems are typically understood to be cultural, economic, and/or political institutions, and not environmental, my investigation of the rendering of Earth discourses in the media commons required an interpretive, multifold approach that considered structural arrangements as well as institutional practices and text production. Drawing partially from the approach outlined by Fairclough (1995, 33–34), this consisted of:

- Institutional analysis—I looked closely at the wider changes in society and culture in terms of how structures of ownership, economic policies, commercial initiates and partnerships, and state agendas and communication policy produced the conditions for the production of particular Earth discourses.

- Fieldwork and interviews—As a means to consider the institutional and cultural practices that produce environmental discourses, I conducted abbreviated field site visits and made observations at media production facilities and community media centers. I also gathered data through conversational interviews with media workers and others involved in the production of environmental discourses, both in situ and via Skype. [4]
- Textual analysis—I paid attention to the "texture" of particular visual effects, images, and their transformation over time. This involved cataloging of programs, which I pursued primarily through the intertextual analysis between genres and the interpretation of discursive strategies by identifying key terms and images, metaphors, reoccurring tropes, and the articulation of agency.
- Observation of media events and exhibitions—I attended media events and exhibitions (2011 and 2012 NATPE conventions in Miami) and cataloged promotional efforts (such as websites, blogs, social media, commercial displays, and graffiti) as a means to measure how media discourses are situated and reproduced in wider social, cultural, and institutional contexts.

Beyond the identification of this analytical framework and sites of inquiry, I feel compelled to mention that my interpretive process unfolded in fits and starts. As a media ethnographer who has for the past twelve years taken on administrative roles in two different institutions, my ability to conduct extensive fieldwork has been more limited that I might have liked. As a result, the empirical materials and interpretations I present herewith had to be gathered and made from alternative investigative practices and "passing" ethnographies (Couldry 2003). Nevertheless, I was fortunate to have had access to many willing participants, rich (albeit condensed) field visits, and diverse research sites to move the project productively forward. The same could be said of the writing process. As for a timeline, from 2008 to 2016, the investigative and interpretive process was seeded and nurtured in St. Louis, Missouri, wrestled through in Mexico City during family Christmas visits, recharged during multiple Ozark fishing trips, teased out in teaching assignments in La Paz, Bolivia, and Dublin, Ireland, and continued through completion in Philadelphia. Most recently, I found further inspiration during my spring 2016 participation in the University of Virginia's "Semester at Sea" program, which gave me the opportunity to visit China, Japan, Hawaii, Vietnam, Myanmar, India, Mauritius, South Africa, Ghana, Morocco, and England, expanding my understanding of the range and complexity of environmental attributes of the media commons. And to my utter horror, it also supplied me with three and a half months of witnessing firsthand the inescapable trail of plastic and other life-suffocating waste in the Pacific, Indian, and Atlantic Oceans, which served as further motivation to complete the book.

It is my hope that the lessons from the interrogations I perform in this book are something that can make media's role in the production of the environmental imagination more salient, and as such a means through which to imagine better, more eco-conscious and environmentally responsive media models. With that said, the analysis presented in these pages presents an admittedly limited and partial view inasmuch as it primarily maps things from the perspective of "core," not the "periphery," nor does it delve deeply into more horizontal networks of information sharing and advocacy—projects that are urgently needed and that others have already begun to explore (see, for example, Lester and Hutchins, 2013). Nevertheless, while I acknowledge these limitations and partialities, I share the book's case examples hoping that they may inspire further investigation of how our global media have produced particular environmental discourses and whose interests they serve.

The Environment

Finally, within my analysis of the environmental discourses in the media commons, it should be noted that my treatment of "the environment" is understood in the broad terms outlined by Cox (2010), which is "a wide range of concerns, from wilderness, air and water pollution, and toxic wastes to urban sprawl, global climate change, and quality of life where people live, work, play, and learn" (58). In terms of aligning this project in relation to some vision of ecologically based advocacy, I am in agreement with Heise (2008), that scholarship should be animated by an environmental imagination grounded in the rights and well-being of the nonhuman world as well as a formulation of environmental justice premised primarily on systems and territories understood to encompass the planet as a whole as opposed to a specific place-based rendering (10).[5] This book is an investigation of where things stand and how they got that way; that is, how media have been used, both deliberately and not, to shape, frame, and indeed manufacture how audiences see, and by extension respond to, the environment.

Overview of Chapters

Chapter 1 maps out Dryzek's excavation of the ontological underpinnings and political implications of what he calls "Earth discourses." The work of Dryzek and others from the interpretive school of environmental policy analysis offers not only a path through which the forces that shape public debate and frame government and corporate environmental positions become more readily seen and open for interrogation, but also an almost seamless connection to media-related concerns of power, agency, and their institutional encasements. Of primary interest is how the emergence of the "Promethean discourse," an environmental discourse tied to abundance, limited government, and innovation, has been conversely related to the "Limits discourse," which is grounded in the construct of scarcity and the "commons" and related metaphors, and how the debate between the two has spawned a range of other, alternative environmental discourses.

Chapter 2 presents an analysis of how neoliberal reforms initiated in the late 1970s and continued into the new millennium provided the perfect edifice for the resurrection of the Promethean discourse. Surfacing first prior to the Industrial Revolution as an unarticulated discourse grounded in westward expansion and the conquest of wilderness, the commercially based global media system that was spawned at the end of the twentieth century became the perfect vehicle for the Promethean discourse to regain its hegemonic status. Because of its grounding in the notions of competition, abundance, and perpetual growth, the Promethean discourse gained purchase through the global spread of neoliberalism—a political-economic philosophy anchored in the principles of "strong private property rights, free markets, and free trade" (Harvey 2005, 2)—which together were articulated through the commercial media system's elaboration and privileging of consumer capitalism.

To consider how the discourse has "gone global," the chapter charts changes in structural networks, policy, and relationships of capital in commercial media that favored the Promethean discourse's reemergence. It also explores how the development of privately owned, commercially operated media systems, from transnational media corporations (TNCs) in "the West" to smaller but still highly influential private media systems in Latin America, Asia, Eastern Europe, Africa, and the Middle East, have led to the rise of global consumer culture, even as many nations were undergoing democratic reform. There is also a focus on how the World Trade Organization (WTO), which was created in 1995, was charged with facilitating the "opening of markets" by administering multilateral trade agreements, removing protectionism, and setting a global agenda for privatization and liberalization. In bringing these various transformative forces and agendas into focus, the chapter illuminates how this reshaping of media systems around the globe began to create the perfect circumstances for citizens to self-identify as media audience members and consumers and, by extension, tacit agents of Promethean ontology and its market-oriented vision of environmental stewardship.

Chapter 3 considers the resurgence of Survivalism on cable and public TV and how it has introduced a new generation of media audiences to the Limits discourse. The focus is on the structural considerations within cable and public TV and on identifying the discourse's defining characteristics and symbolic constructions through specific genres and recurring themes. The chapter traces two trajectories: "After Earth"/"Nature's Revenge" themed programming and more pedagogically designed "Green lifestyle TV" in internationally networked cable and public TV channels like Animal Planet, BBC, NatGeo, SyFy, History Channel, Discovery Channel, and others.

The chapter concludes by arguing that the revised rendering of the Limits discourse within the media commons shifts emphasis away from overpopulation and carrying capacity, primary concerns in the Limits discourse of the 1960s and 1970s, placing it instead on how human activities have had a transformative effect on Earth's ecosystems. This shift can be charted in how the revised version of the Limits discourse has surfaced through the recurring presence of certain images (post "weather event" landscapes, abandoned cities, refugees, zombies, mutant animals, return to wilderness, and the like), metaphors (such as apocalypse, tipping point, ecological footprint), and environmental antagonisms (health of the commons vs. business-as-usual growth). However, television's ability to translate the underlying concerns of a "new" Limits discourse has been at best limited, as character-driven, eco-entertainment and event programming that provides little actionable information has thrived, while a more instructive eco-conscious toolkit approach of green lifestyle television has largely failed.

The focus of chapter 4 is on the media-intensive efforts of biotech giant Monsanto to re-brand itself from a chemical company to a food company. The chapter charts how the multinational agricultural biotechnology corporation has pursued this brand-identity shape-shifting through a highly interlaced, multiplatform media strategy involving advertising campaigns, social media, online magazines, "webisodes," employee blogs, and other online content. Monsanto's media-based image-altering strategy is motivated as a way to respond to its many critics—from citizen-based groups in India, where, evoking Gandhi, ecofeminist Vandana Shiva has called for a "seed

Satyagraha," and in Mexico, the birthplace of maize, where native seed activists have mobilized to discredit the company and challenge its efforts to commoditize food production.

At the center of this inquiry is how Monsanto has used the trope of "sustainability" to craft a proactive profile that is responsive to the challenges the planet is facing. Through my analysis of these efforts, I argue that the company's vision of sustainability is being elaborated through a blending of the urgent and foreboding discourse of Survivalism with the more entrepreneurial Promethean discourse. However, Monsanto also further complicates this articulation of environmental sustainability by selectively employing key terms from problem-solving discourses as a means to provide cover for its Promethean moorings. Foregrounding the issue of environmental agency, the chapter concludes with an assessment of what kinds of imagined relationships with the environment the company privileges through its media operations, and how these have been crafted as a means to combat those who have challenged Monsanto's vision of food production and "responsible" environmental stewardship.

Chapter 5 examines the significant place of the Amazon and its indigenous residents in global environmental imagination. Drawing from the cultural-survival efforts of the Xavante, the Kayapó, and the Paiter-Suruí, I trace how indigenous rights and Western environmentalism have shaped each other. At the core of analysis is how these indigenous communities have elaborated different communication strategies—from image events to the adoption of new media technologies—to pursue cultural survival and self-determination from the 1970s until the present. The chapter considers how, through the different periods of Amazonian activism, indigenous actors have been both framed by and drawn from the notion of the "Ecologically Noble Savage"— an iconic construction within the Western environmental imagination that defines native peoples as "natural conservationists" who live in harmony with the earth. The political currency of this rendering, as part of a broader Amazonian imaginary within the media commons, has informed the creation of alliances between indigenous communities and Western eco-conscious actors to "save the rainforest." While these partnerships have benefited both the "First World" and "Fourth World" actors involved, they have often been built on false assumptions and divergent agendas and thus have changed substantially over the years. This shifting ground has produced very different environmental discourses over the past forty years, moving the place of native Amazonians from one of confrontational eco-conscious cultural activists aligned with Green Radicalism to the shared market-based, scientifically validated indicators consistent with Ecological Modernization.

The Media Commons: Globalization and Environmental Discourses concludes by digesting the main issues explored in the book and what they tell us about how the mediation of ideas about the Earth might shape and constrain environmental action. The core argument is that the global media landscape that materialized at the end of the twentieth century and that continues to evolve in the new millennium presents an overriding Promethean discourse about the environment. This Earth discourse has become dominant because it is thematically consistent with global media systems' privileging of free-market ideology and because it has been enabled, in no small part, by the ideological underpinnings of neoliberalism—an economic philosophy that has had largely negative global environmental consequences. In short, the global media system has become a core mediator in the global media commons, and it is guided by a Promethean ontology that assumes that growth is perpetual and that the market will solve any and all environmental problems.

However, Earth discourses are nevertheless coproduced. So, while acknowledging the hegemonic status of the Promethean discourse in the media commons, I argue that even powerful discourses are not immune to challenges or closed to complementary partnerships. Rather, discursive coproduction provides openings in ways that distinct, alternative, and even antagonistic environmental discourses coexist. But as the case examples I provide demonstrate, this apparent "openness" is double edged. On the one side, they reveal how alterative discourse can gain a foothold in the public sphere to incite change and transform ecological thought, while on the other, underscore how alternative discourses can become diluted, drawn into and revised to fit into the broader, commercially driven global-media landscape. This duality suggests that the contemporary media commons is currently defined by some very troubling, non-ecologically responsive normative trends as well as some signs of hope and possibility.

1

Earth Discourses

Theorizing the Environment for Global Media Studies

For much of the world, today's primary guiding environmental discourses can be traced to industrialism. In his seminal book, *The Politics of the Earth: Environmental Discourses*, John Dryzek (2005) identifies these as Administrative Rationalism, Democratic Pragmatism, Ecological Modernization, Sustainable Development, Green Radicalism, Survivalism, and the Promethean discourse. For the purposes of this book's focus on media and globalization, the last two of these are perhaps most important to discuss first at length because as foundational "big picture" discourses historically counterposed to one another, they have informed the development and trajectories of all other discourses by establishing the parameters of debate about the limits of our planet's carrying capacity and the capacity of innovation, particularly in the hands of the free-market economy, to respond to today's environmental challenges.

The (Unarticulated) Promethean Discourse

Chief among the Earth discourses debated and dissected within the interpretive school of environmental policy analysis is what has been called the "Promethean discourse." This discourse takes its name from the Titan of Greek mythology who was celebrated for tricking Zeus by stealing fire and giving it to humans, thereby greatly increasing the human ability to reshape the world for their own needs. Through this sense of creativity and inventiveness, followers of the Promethean school of thought envisioned a world of unlimited possibilities and abundance (see, for example, Lomborg 2001; Simon and Kahn 1984).

This discourse built on a previously existing "cornucopia" mentality (which also serves as its key metaphor), whereby the commitment to growth and material well-being was founded on the notion that earth's resources were designed to be exploited for the good of society. Hence, from early on there was little reason to explicitly articulate this discourse, as its underlying characteristics were naturalized by political and economic agendas. Dryzek notes:

> For several centuries, at least in the West, the dominant Promethean order had been taken for granted. The Industrial Revolution produced technological changes that made materials close to home (such as coal and later oil) into useful resources. At the same time, European colonial expansion opened up new continents and oceans for exploitation. Capitalist economic growth became taken as the normal condition of a healthy society. (2005, 51–52)

Significantly, "scarcity," as eco-critic Greg Garrard (2004) observes, is understood within this cornucopian vision as an "economic, not an ecological, phenomenon, and will be remedied by capitalist entrepreneurs, not the reductions in consumption urged by environmentalists" (17). This reframing of scarcity rests on the Promethean argument that human welfare (for example, life expectancy, access to resources, falling food prices, clean water) has qualitatively increased in measureable ways as a result of population growth (Simon and Kahn 1984). "More people on the planet," Garrard writes, "means more resourceful brains, more productive hands, more consumption and therefore more economic growth" (17). Following this line of reasoning, extraction of the earth's bounty was seen as unproblematic because the Promethean discourse drew its strength from a political climate constituted by loosely defined yet ideologically dense notions, such as "progress" and "growth"—which, as I will discuss further in chapter 2, were discursively translated during the Cold War into things like "modernization" and "development."

But even before the Industrial Revolution, the deployment of such terms was central to the imperatives of colonialism and Western expansion, animating policies of "discovery" and the military practices tied to them. In fact, for most of the early American, Canadian, and Australian experiences, "wilderness" was defined in direct contrast to the "culture" of Europe, and following the Book of Genesis, nature was conceptualized as separate from and subordinate to humans (Christoff and Eckersley 2013; White 1967)— conceptualizations, it is worth noting, quite distinct from those of the native peoples who already populated those regions long before the Europeans arrived. Moreover, during much of this history of intervention, acquisition and control over resources had a distinctly Eurocentric character, as it was built on "regimes of truth" whose discourses were "encased in institutional structures that exclude specific voices, esthetics, and representations" (Shohat and Stam 1994, 8). Through this historical process, "progress" and the like evolved as "root metaphors" of change, and via their reproduction over time, they became naturalized, taken for granted, and commonsensical, thus forming what social ecology scholar Chet A. Bowers (2000) has argued to be "the basis of thinking and acting in many areas of cultural life" (27). Interestingly, one could find this dynamic across societies with a diverse range of political ideologies, from Marxism and socialism to fascism and liberalism—a commonality that "might surprise their adherents, more conscious of their ideological differences than of their industrialist commonalities. But all these ideologies long ignored or suppressed environmental concern" (Dryzek 2005, 13).

Dryzek (2005) posits that the underlying Promethean ontology is founded on a specific set of principles and absences. The guiding principles include small government, competition's stimulation of innovation, and agency as the domain of economic actors (such as Adam Smith's "invisible hand of the market"). The ontological absences, which are in many ways equal to or even of greater importance than the principles, include the notion that natural resources are not created by nature but rather through human transformation of nature. This central notion is linked to the perspective that natural resources are just matter, and so ecosystems and nature itself do not exist. Rather, resources are located and tapped only when they are needed, so there is no reason to worry about quantity or reserves. These ontological points of departure combine to form a discourse that there are no real environmental limits, and that human innovation expressed in markets, energy, technology, and prices will solve any problems we encounter. In this way, the Prometheans deal with potentially troubling issues (water shortages, for instance) or unanticipated consequences (pest and disease adaptation to genetically engineered crops) as opportunities for innovation and technological advancement stimulated by the open market and pursued through self-interest. In essence, no matter how finite Earth's resources seemed to be or how complex the problems that emerge, human ingenuity, innovation, and technology will always find or create new energy sources and solutions.

While some challenges were mounted against the Promethean hegemony in the early 1900s in the United States, in particular via the preservationism championed by John Muir and conservationism espoused by Gifford

Pinchot, the ontological moorings of the Promethean discourse, which fed on the climate of extraction and exploitation that defined industrialization, continued to enjoy great acceptance in both modern states and developing nations after World War II, so it became difficult to evaluate or even question the basic tenets laid out by the Prometheans (Dryzek 2005). This began to change radically in the late 1960s and early 1970s as the environmental costs of "progress" and "growth" became more visible and thus a point of increased scrutiny within the public sphere. The result was greater public focus on the care and treatment of the earth and by extension mounting political pressure on industry with regard to its activities and responsibility for cleaning up its act. Not inconsequentially, it was also in the 1960s–1970s that images of Earth were first made available to the public, thanks to the orbital flights of John Glenn and Yuri Gagarin and later the Apollo missions. Not only did these images frame the planet as a strikingly beautiful, small, and delicate place but, as they emerged at the dawn of a nuclear age, the pictures fed a growing sense that humans in fact possessed the capacity to destroy their own planet (Christoff and Eckersley 2013; Heise 2008; Vacker 2012).

It is hard to overstate how these images shaped the thinking of the time. As Heise (2008) points out, the environmental movement appropriated images of Earth for the first Earth Day in 1970, and "neither McLuhan's notion that the world had turned into a global village nor Lovelock's Gaia hypothesis of the Earth as a single superorganism can be dissociated from its impact" (22–23). The blowback facilitated a change in the discursive tide stronger that anything that Muir or Pinchot, during their attempts to refashion the public consciousness about the environment in the early 1900s, might have envisioned. On the one hand, the Promethean discourse, which prior to this time was so powerful and taken for granted in the West that it didn't require deliberate articulation, now demanded a deliberately manufactured defense. On the other hand, with the realization that Earth was indeed a finite, fragile, and interconnected system, the possibility for alternative visions of the environment was opened up. Within this temporal moment the Promethean discourse suddenly found itself vulnerable to critique, under siege from counterdiscourses as diverse as conservationism and Sustainable Development and to reform environmentalism and radical ecologism (Dryzek 2005). Such discourses surfaced in relation to the imagery of the environmental apocalypse and a new sense that "the environment" was a real, living thing, which in turn spawned debate about things like cultural rights, freedoms, and human responsibility.

Survivalism: The "Limits" Discourse

Preeminent among these different ways of seeing and talking about the environment has been the "Limits" discourses, or what Dryzek calls "Survivalism." Counterposed to the Promethean emphasis on creativity and inventiveness, Survivalism focuses on Earth's limited carrying capacity as population growth exceeds resource availability. This discourse is moored in the 1960s–1970s discussion within academia on population growth and natural-resource depletion (Hardin 1968; Lovelock 1972, 1979), and in particular the publication of such works as Paul Ehrlich's *The Population Bomb* (1968) and the Club of Rome's *The Limits to Growth* (Meadows et al., 1972). These texts resuscitated a Malthusian concern for the planet's limits by outlining dire predictions and presenting disconcerting scenarios about the demise of nature. Concern over the relationship between humans and the natural world especially gained traction within the public sphere with the publication of Rachel Carson's seminal *Silent Spring* (1962), the book that many credit with starting the contemporary environmental movement. Carson's work revealed the powerful negative effects that humans could have on the biosphere if our practices, even those designed to make life better, were left unquestioned. Her book, when considered within the context of the 1969 release of the Apollo 8 "Earthrise" photo taken by astronaut William Anders from the moon and the iconic "Blue Marble" photo taken by the crew of the Apollo 17 in 1972, underscored R. Buckminster Fuller's (1969) assertion that planet Earth was like a spaceship with finite resources and in need of constant maintenance. Combined, these publications and photos generated a tsunami of scholarship and reporting.

This moment of political and ecological convergence also inspired a wave of films and television programs that helped stir public interest about human activity and the limits of nature while announcing, at least in North America, the dawn of the contemporary environmental movement. Echoing the academic and political conversations during the 1960s and 1970s, the narrative of ecological collapse occupied a strong presence in Hollywood films (*The Planet of the Apes* [1968], *The Omega Man* [1971], *Silent Running* [1972], *Frogs* [1972], *Soylent Green* [1973], *Chinatown* [1974]). These films were grounded in dystopian tales of population growth, pollution, resource scarcity, and environmental degradation (Hochman 1998; Ingram 2000). By the late 1960s in Canada and the United States, commercial television and animation had also become homes for environmental themes that were explicitly aligned with mainstream environmentalism (*Twilight Zone, Our Vanishing Wilderness, The Lorax, The Bear That Wasn't*) (Starosielski 2011). Moreover, the apocalyptic narratives of overcrowding, industrial waste, and mass extinction in these films and animation also transferred Cold War terminology onto environmental scenarios as the weight of human excess, it was thought, would "blow up" the commons (Heise 2008, 26)—a point of analysis that has been well documented by a number of film scholars (see, for example, Brereton 2005; Hochman 1998; Ingram 2000).

While proponents of Survivalism in this era placed emphasis on the relationship between exploding populations and overconsumption, one of the important discursive threads was also the recommendation of drastic, even draconian measures to respond to the looming environmental challenges. One of the early texts that helped establish this position was Garrett Hardin's seminal essay "The Tragedy of the Commons" (1968), wherein Hardin provided a scenario of a pasture open to all—one of the key metaphors of Survivalism. Within this space, "herdsmen" come to graze their cattle. Hardin argued that, as one might expect, each herdsman would try to keep and graze as many cattle as possible. This arrangement works for many years because various factors (tribal warfare, disease, poaching) keep the numbers of cattle and herdsmen relatively low. However, eventually there comes a time when social stability begins to increase the number of both. It is at this moment that the inherent logic of the commons "generates a tragedy" (1244). Hardin explains that, as rational beings, each herdsman begins to ask how he might add to his herd to maximize his gain. The guiding question for the herdsman is "What is the utility *to me* of adding one more animal to my herd?" This question, and how it is acted on collectively by the (now growing number of) herdsmen, leads to "one negative and one positive component." These are:

1. The positive component is a function of the increment of one animal. Since the herdsman receives all the proceeds from the scale of the additional animal, the positive utility is nearly +1.
2. The negative component is a function of the additional overgrazing created by one more animal. Since, however, the effects of overgrazing are shared by all the herdsmen, the negative utility for any particular decision-making herdsman is only a fraction of -1. (1244)

From this scenario Hardin concludes that "freedom in a commons brings ruin to all" (1244).

Through his rather bleak metaphor, Hardin presented a direct challenge to the cornucopian assertion that human innovation and creativity would allow

Earth's inhabitants to overcome any problems involving resource depletion. In his opinion, "it is fair to say that most people who anguish over the population problem are trying to find a way to avoid the evils of overpopulation without relinquishing any of the privileges they now enjoy. They think that farming the seas or developing new strains of wheat will solve the problem—technologically" (1243). To Hardin, advocating a technical solution to the problems of the commons demands "little or nothing in the way of change in human values or ideas of morality" (1243) and as such was ultimately a means through which to avoid more difficult ways of addressing resource control. Indeed, one of the unspoken constructs anchoring the Promethean faith in technological innovation as the answer to our global ills was Adam Smith's "invisible hand"—the notion that

> an individual who "intends only his own gain" is, as it were, "led by an invisible hand to promote . . . the public interest." . . . The tendency "assumes that decisions reached individually will, in fact, be the best decisions for the entire society. If this assumption is correct it justifies the continuance of our present policy of laissez-faire in reproduction. If it is correct we can assume that men will control their individual fecundity so as to produce the optimum population. If the assumption is not correct, we need to reexamine our individual freedoms to see which ones are defensible. (1245)

Hardin, like other writers within the Limits discourse (Ehrlich 1968; Ophuls 1977; Ostrom 1990), is clearly not in favor of just letting the market flesh out some sort of innovative, technological response that merely shifts the problem to production. The Limits scholars are interested in more philosophical questions at the center of the issue, namely, "What is the maximum good for all?" It was, at least to Hardin, an unresolvable question in need of a seemingly impossible solution because people cannot agree on what is "the maximum good" from our resources, from our environment, and for local quality of life because to do so means we must define *what is good*. As Hardin noted, "To one person it is wilderness, to another it is ski lodges for thousands. To one it is estuaries to nourish ducks for hunters to shoot; to another it is factory land" (1244).

Despite some of its more compelling arguments about environmental exhaustion and individuals pursuing material interests, and its potentially powerful effect on policymaking, the Limits discourse was not necessarily well received, due in part because of where some of its chief proponents ultimately took their arguments: as a matter of stewardship over croplands, fisheries, grasslands, forests, and the like, the maximum good should not be left to the democratic decision making of decentralized communities motivated by localized concerns and special interests. Rather, if developing countries were unwilling to devise ways to control population growth and care for the greater good, then developed nations, Hardin (1977) argued, should form ecological "lifeboats" afloat in what would then otherwise be a sea of global misery. Another solution is Ophuls's (1977) call to manage the commons via "ecological mandarins"—a corps of eco-experts selected by a centralized government to establish a comprehensive plan (Dryzek 2005, 39). Though some Survivalists have offered more democratic, less authoritarian prescriptions, and others (most notably, Nobel Prize winner Elinor Ostrom [1990]) have tried to find a more balanced way of theorizing the commons, the Limits discourse is by and large a "big picture" discourse that sees agency as the domain of scientists, administrators, and other elites.

* * *

Given Survivalism's "big picture" emphasis on centralized control over resources and elite decision making as sites of agency, it is perhaps no surprise that a number of alternative discourses have surfaced that advocate much more collective and managerial problem-solving approaches to environmental stewardship. Indeed, as rivalry and conflict hold center stage in the Limits discourse, in many ways the alternative discourses described below have been a rejection of the Limits discourse's apocalyptic vision and authoritarian solutions, in concert with opposition to the Prometheans' oddly unproblematic, cornucopian ecological horizon. Instead of the bleak visions of the Survivalists or the blind optimism of the Prometheans, the alternative discourses are animated by much more pragmatic and morally grounded visions of environmental stewardship, ranging from the professionalized oversight of public resources for "the greatest good" and partnerships among science, industry, and government to far less hierarchical, more community-based governance of the commons and even more radical, paradigm-shifting ontologies.

Democratic Pragmatism

One of the more noteworthy of these is Democratic Pragmatism, a discourse that Dryzek (2005, 99) characterizes as based on interactive problem solving reconciled with the status quo and institutional structure of liberal capitalist democracy. As much of the world has moved toward free-market capitalism and democracy in the last few decades, this Earth discourse has been able to take advantage of some structural tendencies to gain traction. Taking its bearings from pragmatist philosophy (John Dewey, William James, and Charles Pierce are examples), Democratic Pragmatism treats environmental affairs as "ripe for tentative problem-solving efforts in which a plurality of moral perspectives is always relevant" (Dryzek 2005, 100). This sense that environmental issues present "opportunities" suggests an allegiance with the Promethean compass, but in fact the point of departure of the Democratic Pragmatists is focused squarely on securing legitimacy through public consultation, consensus building, and administrative flexibility. In this way it also distinguishes itself from the bleak and rigid Survivalists and related elite-led, problem-solving discourses like Administrative Rationalism (discussed later in this chapter).

One key characteristic of Democratic Pragmatism is that it has been shaped directly by its practice of governance not just by its philosophical orientation, especially in the realms of environmental-impact assessment, policy dialogue, and deliberation. As Dryzek (2005) explains it, public consultation is now a "necessary accompaniment to environmental policy development in many countries" (102). Here he provides a series of examples: In 1970 the Nixon administration established the U.S. Environmental Protection Agency in part as a means through which to reach out to the public to help draft environmental policy. Later in the 1970s Sweden, Austria, and the Netherlands consulted citizens about the development of nuclear power. Also in the late 1970s a Canadian case involving government protection of indigenous groups interests provided opportunities for public testimony and dialogue to shape a more participatory decision-making process concerning a proposed arctic oil and gas pipeline. In 1990 the Australian government sponsored policy dialogue as a mechanism to engage in sustainable development planning with national environmental groups and industry representatives regarding forests, fisheries, tourism, energy, mining, and the like. In 2003 the United Kingdom created "GM Watch," a government initiative designed to gauge public perceptions about the risks and benefits of genetically modified crops and foods. Though sometimes public consultation is merely symbolic, these cases demonstrate that public comment can have a real imprint on environmental policy.

This kind of participatory engagement in environmental issues is possible because Democratic Pragmatism emphasizes "governance" over "government" (Dryzek 2005, 108–9). That is, opportunities for participation in interactive problem solving are open for interests both within and outside government, which translates into policy elaboration not as a matter of formal government (such as adherence to constitutions, centralized authority, and formal division of responsibility) but rather as the result of interactions enabled through networks. It is worth noting that this difference lies in direct opposition to the exercise of hierarchical authority envisioned by the Survivalists to contend with environmental resource control.

Significantly, this conceptualization of participatory, networked governance over rigid government dovetails in some rather compelling ways with Castells's assertions about the flows and exchanges of information. Central to Castells's (2000) scholarship is the observation that the interlaced structure of contemporary media that emerged in the mid-1990s created the potential for interactive networks to extend "the realm of electronic communication into the whole domain of life, from home to work, from schools to hospitals, from entertainment to travel" (394). As Castells argues, the race to develop the most advanced and responsive media systems became paramount for North America, Europe, Japan, and several countries in Latin America. The state in all of these cases was motivated to create avenues through which communication technology could be used as a means to achieve hypermodernity, cultivate power, and pursue commercial interests, but the primary agents behind this initiative were private, not governmental.

The interpretive school of environmental policy analysis only hints at these developments, but it is apparent that because networks are decentralized and flexible, they can accommodate different perspectives and engender collaborative problem solving among different social actors, such as citizen groups, NGOs, and corporations, and thus have the potential to foster public-private partnerships that otherwise might not develop. Indeed, the blogosphere and social media have become particularly ripe "sites" for such networks to take shape. However, these very attributes also open up opportunities for private interests to appropriate the collaborative possibilities of Democratic Pragmatism (for instance, through technologically enabled surveillance techniques involving individuals and group membership). The larger point is that within networks, flows condition both consumption and production, and so whether opportunistic or more organic/authentic, many of these kinds of elaborations are traceable to specific actors within networks and, as such, their interests.

What is less easily discernible is whether or not interactive policymaking is, by definition, good for environmental stewardship. Dryzek (2005) asserts that, though social networks may be "open" and therefore offer the potential for a truly "public" public sphere, because of their apparent piecemeal nature there is no assurance of appropriate feedback from all sectors. "That liberal democracy and governance networks are self-organizing systems (as is the capitalist market) does not mean they are adequate in light of ecological criteria" (111). Additionally, Cox (2013) points out that despite many of its positive attributes, environmental communication grounded in collectivity and consensus building can also be hobbled by "groupthink" shaped by communal pressures to conform to place-based decision making that exempts the local from more national or global standards. Therefore, whether welcomed or not, negative feedback is needed to help transcend or confront problem solving weighted too much by hyperlocal, egoistic concerns or decision making colored by concessions made in order to avoid contentious issues. This is difficult but not impossible, as Democratic Pragmatism defines by its very nature public interest within plural terms. The problem that challenges the authentic exercise of Democratic Pragmatism, however, is that "politics in capitalist democratic settings is rarely about disinterested and public-spirited problem solving in which many perspectives are brought to bear with equal weight" (Dryzek 2005, 117). Indeed, one of Castell's (2000) most important arguments is that networks shift power, often in ways that are not easily identifiable because participation appears so "open" to those who can shape information traffic and thus cultural flows. For example, consider the influence that citizen groups such as Citizens United and political action organizations (especially so-called Super PACs) have had on public debate in the United States through "citizen" channels or "grassroots" organizing.

These characteristics make media by default a main political arena in the practice of governance and therefore central to both the utopian possibilities and dystopian failures of Democratic Pragmatism. With this in mind, it is worth thinking through two of Castells's quieter yet immensely significant observations, both of which I elaborate further in later chapters but which beg some seeding now. First, he posited that during the hypercompetitive period of the late 1990s, when various interests were jockeying for position to influence the direction of media policy and innovation, the ability of business to control the initial stages of development of multimedia systems allowed corporate interests to acquire a structural advantage that "will have lasting consequences on the characteristics of the new electronic culture" (397). In Castells's view—and the past three decades have certainly provided ample evidence from around the world to support this—the development of this electronic culture is therefore not so much guided by health, education, or other social goals but rather by prevailing business strategies and their ties to the ideology of the "leisure society." Second, within the multiplatform, converged media universe, it will continue to be the "ability to differentiate a product that yields the greatest competitive potential" (399) that will chart the direction of who gets to participate in the global mediascape, and to what extent.

The implications of this networked mediascape for Democratic Pragmatism are quite mixed. Obviously the challenge for finding democratic "voice" and engendering collaboration and consensus building are limited by the fact that the control over media content is tied directly to financial and technological resources—something that media conglomerates have and are able to build on via horizontal and vertical integration synergies, yet which even the best-equipped NGO, community group, or independent "green" interest group must constantly struggle to maintain. However, even taking into account the severe limitations of this uneven playing field, the new media technological landscape still allows for groups to pursue interactive problem solving by establishing a cultural, and by extension political, presence. Indeed, just as today's media landscape provides openings for "prosumer" agency for fans, gamers, and bloggers of commercial entertainment fare (Jenkins 2006), citizens may likewise find agency by engaging in environmental advocacy and debate through blogging and social networking (citizen journalism, YouTube channels, accountability campaigns, microvolunteering) and the elaboration of media-related public events (protests, boycotts, sit-ins, public hearings) (Cox 2013).

Administrative Rationalism

One of the primary and earliest "problem-solving" discourses to emerge is what Dryzek (2005, 75–98) has coined "Administrative Rationalism." Far less concerned with normative principles of participation and collaboration than Democratic Pragmatism, at the center of this discourse is the notion that resources should be managed in ways to assure they remain renewable and produce efficient and sustainable yields for the greatest number of beneficiaries. This underlying philosophy surfaced as the platform of a "conservation movement" at the beginning of the twentieth century in the United States, which was a response to the environmental abuses of the Industrial Revolution. Led by forester Gifford Pinchot, who had spent part of his youth traveling and being educated in Europe and so was familiar with Europe's efforts to repair its environment after years of resource exploitation without management, conservationism evolved as a professionalized strategy for natural-resource stewardship.

Though similarly animated by the desire to confront the overuse and abuse of natural resources like forests, lakes, and rivers (unlike his rival John Muir's focus on wilderness preservation, which was guided by the idea that nature was sublime and thus had its own value outside of human needs [Oravec 1981]), Pinchot's conservation movement "had no interest in wilderness preservation, environmental aesthetics, or pollution reduction" (Dryzek 2005, 76). Rather, it was charged with securing, as Pinchot himself put it, "the greatest good for the greatest number of people"—an agenda he thought would be best pursued by following the lessons of science and exercised through the creation of management bureaucracies, not shared governance. The key to institutionalizing such an agenda was therefore the development of a professional class of environmental decision makers who, because of their superior understanding of the goals and practices of conservation, were able to set policy that guided the sustainable use of renewable resources.

These roots in conservationism make administrative rationalism an "ethnocentric" discourse in that it regards the environment as a resource to be managed for the benefit of human welfare (Herndl and Brown 1996). Indeed, despite Muir's staunch ecocentrism, even the conservation movement's eventual valuation of his more transcendental ideas about nature became grounded in the assertion that access to wild places had a restorative function for the human spirit, especially for alienated urbanites (Garrard 2004). The embrace of these ideas thus injected conservationism's utilitarianism with a particularly anthropocentric rendering of Muir's sublime. But beyond this cursory recognition of aesthetics, during the course of its history Administrative Rationalism has been defined primarily by its focus on policy and its institutions and methodologies elaborated to serve the public interest.

Because of this evolution of ideas about nature's "administration," Administrative Rationalism can be identified by its assumptions about "natural relationships," which are played out in the following way: nature is subordinate to human problem solving, people are subordinate to the state, and experts and managers control state decision making about environmental stewardship. Though Dryzek (2005) is careful to note that these assumptions are not articulated with the confidence and forthrightness of human domination over nature of the Prometheans, it is a discourse nevertheless that advocates, in no muted sense, that environmental problem solving should be left to "the experts" (87). As such, it can be recognized through and indeed is constructed by the activities and decision making of experts and managers empowered by an administrative state and in line with the goals and functions of liberal capitalism.

Ecological Modernization

Ecological Modernization is a policy discourse that, in the words of Dutch political scientist and urban planner Maarten Hajer, "recognizes the ecological crisis as evidence of a fundamental omission in the workings of the institutions of modern society" (1995, 3). The discourse's point of departure is that environmental degradation is a structural problem that requires a coordinated intervention to bring about change. But unlike the case of Administrative Rationalism, cultural authority in Ecological Modernization is not tied solely to or even primarily to the state's experts for policy and planning. The emphasis is instead placed on cooperation between government, scientists, and industry, stimulated through the creation of incentives for business to take a leadership role in designing and implementing environmental solutions. According to Hajer (1995), the discourse relies on "the language of business" and operates "within the boundaries of cost-effectiveness and administrative efficiency" as an approach to environmental policymaking that "actually constitutes a challenge for business" (31). That is, rather than being a threat to the existing system of free-market capitalism by calling for wholesale structural change, it asserts a need for coordination and cooperation between business and government based on technological innovation, science, and expert-led guidance in the form of think tanks and creative corporate leadership. In this respect, Hajer observes, Ecological Modernization avoids the sorts of "social contradictions that other discourses might have introduced" and suggests that there is a "techno-institutional fix for the present problems" (32).

Responses to ecological dilemmas, then, are pursued through tactics and practices involving procedural integration and energy efficiency, which benefits industry. The resulting institutional climate is thus open to, as opposed to adversarial toward, industry in that it requires industry to serve in the creation of generative strategies for resource management and policymaking. As Dryzek (2005) sums it up, "The key to ecological modernization is that there is money in it for business" (167). Central to this discourse is therefore the self-interest of business, namely the savings associated with working toward greater efficiencies and waste reduction, and the connections that businesses can build on by moving toward addressing instead of denying the environmental concerns of consumers.

As this description suggests, Eco-Modernization surfaces as both a policy strategy "based on a fundamental belief in progress and the problem-solving capacity of modern techniques and skills of social engineering" and as an economic ideology anchored in adjustments to processes of production and consumption (Hajer 1995, 33–35). It distinguished itself from the Promethean discourse in that whereas the Public Prometheans flatly dismiss ecological concerns while calling for deregulation, innovation, and discovery, the Eco-Modernists appropriate ecological issues as a means to chart and justify a path of progress requiring techno-scientific management and industrial partnerships. This attempt to reconcile environmental challenges with economic development situates Ecological Modernization within the confines of exiting institutional structures while calling for new normative commitments. To do this, the discourse draws on what Hajer (1995) notes are "some rather credible and attractive story-lines." These include: "regulation of the environmental problem appears as a positive-sum game; pollution is a matter of inefficiency; nature has a balance that should be respected; anticipation is better than cure; and sustainable development is the alternative to the previous path of defiling growth" (65). Moreover, as the discourse is anchored in questions tied to the relationship between consumption and production, it operates with the unannounced assumption that its primary audience is composed of discerning consumers as opposed to active citizens.

These storylines and silent assumptions are grounded in the perspective that past efforts to respond to environmental problems were typically reactionary (remedial) as opposed to anticipatory and progressive. The current Eco-Modernist storylines are therefore meant to situate a new, more responsive set of concepts, ideas, and categories through which to address environmental conflict and position actors. For Eco-Modernists "the key to effective action is therefore to anticipate and prevent unwanted environmental ramifications of production and consumption decisions" (Dryzek 2005, 169–70). By definition this framing of action requires that the various agents of Ecological Modernization (whom Dryzek identifies as business, government, scientists, reform-oriented environmentalists) work together to guide and monitor environmental stewardship, which, because of how it is conceptualized, is a matter of balancing environmental protection with economic prosperity. One of the guiding metaphors Dryzek uses to represent this balancing act is the "tidy household" wherein efficiency is maximized and waste is minimized (2005, 171).

Based on these characteristics, it is perhaps not surprising that one of the criticisms levied against Ecological Modernization is that it inherently ignores the question of ecological limits because its framing of the environment is ultimately tied to how to treat nature as a human resource (and therefore, like Administrative Rationalism, an ethnocentric discourse). This tendency can be seen in both its "weak" application via the "emphasis on technological solutions to environmental problems" and to a lesser extent in its potential for "strong" application in policy and practice, characterized by what Hajer calls a reflexive self-awareness over economic and political decision making (a "reflexive modernity") coupled with "concern with international dimensions of environment and development" (Dryzek 2005, 173–75).[1] However, despite the shortcomings and limitations of technocratic planning and unfulfilled promise of reflexive modernity, Eco-Modernism has found success in shaping cleaner and greener practices in a number of settings, such as the Netherlands, Finland, Japan, Sweden, and, especially, Norway and Germany (Dryzek 2005; Hajer 1995[2]).

In terms of its place within the global mediscape, over the past few decades this discourse has quietly but quite strategically moved to the center of various multinational corporations' increasingly media-intensive, multiplatform "social responsibility" branding efforts, and it has played a part in how carbon-trading offset credits are imbued with market-friendly cultural capital—a point of analysis I examine in chapter 5.

Sustainable Development

Because of its ties to IGOs (such as World Bank, UNESCO, UNICEF) and NGOs (World Wildlife Fund and WaterKeeper are two examples), perhaps the most globally recognized Earth discourse has grown to be "Sustainable Development." Sustainable Development is closely associated with *Our Common Future* (1987), a report published by the World Commission on Environment and Development, led by Norwegian Prime Minister Gro Harlem Brundtland, which argued for an integrated, longitudinal pursuit of "economic growth, environmental stewardship, population stabilization, peace, and global equality" (Dryzek 2005, 148). The discourse is founded on the notion that, through coordinated efforts, natural systems and human systems can productively coexist through intelligent, collective planning and decision making. It is an environmentally hopeful discourse in that, while it recognizes limits and scarcity, there are opportunities to stretch the boundaries of these pressure points and find ways to develop practices through which many in the global commons can benefit. Indeed, the discourse's origins grew out of the claim that while economic development is required to satisfy the needs of the world's poor, the development aspirations of the world's peoples "cannot be met by all countries following the growth path already taken by the industrial countries, for such actions would over-burden the world's ecosystems" (Dryzek 2005, 153).

Even though the discourse has been given serious consideration through global governance and policymaking since the 1980s, especially following the publication of the Brundtland-led report, it continues to operate discursively as an oddly ambiguous theory, as opposed to an applied, transformative plan of action. The problem is linked to its discursive elasticity, which has made it overly pliable and thus vulnerable to the private and state interests that are only superficially "green" or to groups that used it to recast environmental antagonisms in terms that privileged their positions and agendas. Paradoxically, this elasticity is also one of its strengths, which is that agency is open to being networked through its location at various levels, from local interests nested in specific biological-social settings to larger, more superficially attached state and nongovernmental actors, as well as growing connections to corporations.

With operating assumptions that include growth, cooperation, and distributive justice—"goals" that give sustainable development the feel of a target as opposed to a discourse—Dryzek (2005) argues that finding Sustainable Development as an adopted path in a given place or a practice mapped out through policy is a rather elusive exercise. It is therefore perhaps more useful to understand it as a "discourse that will inspire experimentation," not unlike "democracy," in that its meaning is constructed situationally through "social learning, involving decentralized, exploratory, and variable approaches to its pursuit" (158). However, the way nature is treated within Sustainable Development also suggests that it has an underlying "we can have it all" perspective, and so it is subordinate to human needs and has value in terms of its capacity to fuel social improvement (157). This places the discourse into the ethnocentric category, but because of its shape-shifting contextual flexibility, it can also appear to align with anthropocentric articulations. In this respect we may find fragments of it, hints and suggested directions for a normative recipe for the common good, making it a discourse ripe for the ecological imagination of mediamakers and the representations they produce for a green horizon, but without necessarily prescribing a clear path for where these renderings should take us.

Green Radicalism: Environmental Justice and Ecofeminism

Less convinced of the possibilities of simply altering existing structures and practices of governance via administrative or consultative problem solving we find manifested variously in Administrative Rationalism, Democratic Pragmatism, and Sustainable Development, or necessarily going along with the marriage of corporatism and environmental policymaking of Ecological

Modernization, is the discourse of "Green Radicalism," which Dryzek (2005) splits into "green consciousness" (changing the way people think), and "green politics" (changing social structures). Taken as a whole, Green Radicalism can be defined as a means through which to pursue environmental alternatives for living, and so it is typically the operating discourse of choice for any movement that aspires to take environmental action against the grain of the status quo. This means it is home to a wide range of ideologies and political organizations. These include environmental justice, a movement focused on environmental risk, particularly as it affects the poor and ethnic minorities; ecofeminism, an environmental philosophy anchored in the assertion that ecological problems are rooted in androcentrism; animal liberation, a movement/philosophy that asserts the rights of all sentient beings against human exploitation; antiglobalization, a movement based on concern for global justice in the face of corporate control of labor and natural resources; ecological citizenship, a kind of ecological philosophy involving the citizens' commitment to environmental stewardship and obligations to future generations; and the green consciousness of "deep ecology," which privileges biocentric equality (that all living things have equal value) and self-realization, represented most notably in the work of novelist Edward Abbey (*The Monkey Wrench Gang*) and poet Barry Lopez. What these disparate movements and ideologies have in common is a commitment to creating a green public sphere by taking on unresponsive institutions and their recalcitrant practices and the thinking that supports them through resistance, agitation, social movements, or in some cases more forceful measures, such as ecotage (Dryzek 2005).

ENVIRONMENTAL JUSTICE

As a school of thought emerging out of Green Radicalism's focus on social change ("green politics"), Environmental Justice is the principle that "all people and communities are entitled to equal protection of environmental and public health laws and regulations" (Bullard 1996, 493). As a movement it has been described as "dedicated to justice in the distribution of environmental goods and decision making" (Sandler and Pezzullo 2007, 1). These two definitions underscore that at its core Environmental Justice is a discursive sphere of struggle for recognition and political agency enmeshed in issues of risk, pollution, protection, health, and sustainability. As a discourse, the environmental questions it raises and activities through which it has been shaped (lobbying, boycotts, sit-ins, demonstrations, blogging, and the like) have historically been anchored in racial, social, and economic factors implicated by the prevalence of toxic industrial waste dumps in poor and ethnic communities within the United States, although increasingly it has taken on a considerably more global scope because of a growing sense of shared experiences with corporate polluters. For instance, the 2009 documentary film *Crude* follows a David-versus-Goliath story involving a class-action lawsuit brought by indigenous and poor communities in the Ecuadorian Amazon against Texaco/Chevron for its environmental abuses. Dubbed the "Amazon Chernobyl," the catastrophe's issues of human rights and environmental contamination feature largely in the film, which profiles citizen mobilization, the moral bankruptcy of big oil, collusion between state and corporate interests, media influences and the public sphere, and clashes between local culture and transnational interests.

Unfortunately, *Crude*'s tale of environmental abuse, neglect, and marginalization is quite consistent with the experiences of countless communities in the United States, where the Environmental Justice movement began. Because environmental degradation of minority and low-income communities by industrial practices became so commonplace and disproportionate, the Comprehensive Environmental Response, Compensation, and Liability Act, or the "Superfund Law," was established in 1980 to clean up contaminated sites and provide a registry for hazardous substances that endangered public health. This law, along with the increased localized activism and organization of those involved in Environmental Justice, allowed the movement to achieve greater prominence. Moreover, the federal government established National Environmental Justice Advisory Council (NEJAC) and the Interagency Working Group on Environmental Justice (IWG) to help implement Environmental Justice goals (DeLuca 2007). As Kevin DeLuca notes, members of these bodies have defined such goals to be "achieved when everyone, regardless of race, culture, or income, enjoys the same degree of protection from environmental and health hazards and equal access to the decision-making process to have a healthy environment in which to live, learn, and work." (29).

But while largely celebrated as a recognition of the environmental rights of previously disempowered communities, for many aligned with deep ecology, Ecofeminism, and other camps within Green Radicalism, Environmental Justice addresses issues not so much in terms of equality tied to environmental stewardship as it does the needs of people. In his 2007 essay "A Wilderness Environmentalism Manifesto: Contesting the Infinite Self-Absorption of Humans," DeLuca digs deep into this charge, asserting that environmental justice activists have largely been successful in shifting the focus of the environment from wilderness to human self-interest (for example, human health and habitat)—a move that represents, he laments, a "retreat from speaking for the trees to once again speaking for people, just like everyone else" (33). DeLuca is rightfully concerned that this shift goes hand in hand with (a misapplication of) postmodern positions that nature is but a cultural construct imbued with racist, sexist, and classist elements. Moreover, the grounding of nature in humanism creates a space for a highly flexible and potentially problematic notion of cultural rights to morph into a brutally political tool—one where, for instance, the "right to work" or "ancestral practices" trump environmental preservation.

ECOFEMINISM

A different, but somewhat overlapping approach to how Environmental Justice performs Green Radicalism is Ecofeminism. With its focus on liberation and the logic of domination embedded in androcentrism, Ecofeminism dovetails quite well with issues traditionally associated with the women's movement, such as empowerment, equality, and political agency, as well as "female virtues related to care, empathy, intuition, connection, and cooperation" (Dryzek 2005, 197). This position stands in stark contrast to the cornucopian privileging of the "rational economic subject" whose self-interest fuels innovation (Garrard 2004, 26) while also separating it from the autocratic elements of Survivalism. There is also, as Merchant (1989) has explored at length, an inherent tension with the "scientific revolution" at play here, as feminine sensibilities bring to environmentalism greater possibilities for the integration of human and natural ecosystems by emphasizing cyclical, reproductive processes and decentralized, nonhierarchical forms of organization.

This nonmechanistic, more organic framework may not presently have enough discursive force to completely undermine the normative (cornucopian) valuation of progress through technological innovation, but globally speaking its political echo through environmental activism is worthy of attention, especially as it may be gaining some ground. For instance, among its most prominent champions is physicist-philosopher Vandana Shiva, who has long advocated for the wisdom of feminine, cultural, and nature-based "ways of knowing" over the science and technology. Shiva (1991, 2005) argues not only that technological change primarily serves the interests of those who control it rather than the social values of those who are asked to adopt it, but also that it shifts power from common rights to private-property rights.

> In the narrow view, science and technology are conventionally accepted as what scientists and technologists produce, and development is accepted as

what science and technology produce. Scientists and technologists are in turn taken to be that sociological category formally trained in Western science and technology, either in institutions or organisations in the West, or in Asian institutions mimicing the paradigms of the West. These tautological definitions are unproblematic if one leaves out people, especially poor people, if one ignores cultural diversity and distinct civilisational histories of our planet, which has created diverse and distinctive cultures. Development in this view is taken as synonymous with the introduction of Western Science and Technology in non-Western contexts. The magical identity is development = modernisation = Westernisation (2740).

The recognition of unquestioned Western "truths" and how they shape the normative boundaries of environmental thought is the terrain through which Shiva and other Ecofeminists of the Global South have oppositionally positioned their activism. The organic, nurturing philosophy underlying this kind of approach to environmental politics has particular resonance in the developing world, as agriculture is still often primarily the domain of women and bound by longstanding local practices and community networks. Moreover, in many ways it is aligned with how other ecologically driven political movements conceptualize sustainability, justice, and peace in that it directly challenges the normative ideas of ownership and private property championed by corporate globalization (Shiva 2005).

Finding Discourses

For scholars of media and globalization, the question becomes how to identify and map out how these discourses are being presented and, by extension, how they might be shaping the environmental imagination. As Dryzek (2005) notes, if one merely accepts the Promethean perspective, then concerns about environmental stewardship and questions about the limits of the Earth are irrelevant, and all people need to do is leave things alone, as innovation, entrepreneurship, and the market will produce the responses needed to tackle any impending crisis. Clearly, there is plenty in the daily global media diet of many of Earth's inhabitants that suggests that this is not only a reasonable direction to take but an incredibly attractive and fulfilling one as well—a point taken up in chapter 2 herewith. But the other discourses lead us, along with peoples' actual experiences with climate-change-related environmental events (rising seas, drought, wildfires, floods, tornadoes, invasive species, and so forth), in very different directions by pointing out, in distinct ways, how and why we need to reevaluate and transform our political and economic systems, as well as cultural practices, in order to contend with the litany of ecological pressures facing the planet. These different ways of imagining the environment are at times fairly transparent, as the recent string of end-of-times films produced in Hollywood, Bollywood, and even Nollywood evidence, and even more so on cable and public TV, as they leap off the screen in biblical proportions by relying on well-worn survivalist tropes and iconography (the topic of chapter 3). But not all stories involving the commons are so apocalyptic, as what is more often the case is that environmental jeremiads come in the form of vague hints and subtle turns and references, calls for community-based problem-solving skills, or green "prosumerism" designed to engage citizen-consumers as participants in an Earth-friendly cultural turn or to situate a very different logic of natural relationships.

Given how densely these discourses are often bound together, making sense of them sometimes seems too complex or even contradictory to penetrate, so it is useful to return to Dryzek's (2005) question of what, within each discourse, is given the capacity to act ("agency"), and (for the purpose of this book) how it is articulated within specific media landscapes around the globe. To cite a previous example in this discussion, in much of the world where waves of industrialism and neoliberalism have shaped policy, the hegemonic Earth discourse is Promethean—an environmental discourse grounded in the notions of competition, innovation, and abundance. Here, agency is the domain of economic actors; networked media institutions render this agency through a combination of key images and master terms such as growth, progress, and innovation aligned with free enterprise. Other discourses place emphasis elsewhere, such as agency anchored in the shared governance and community problem solving of Democratic Pragmatism or in the place of race, class, and gender in some camps of Green Radicalism. Table 1 provides a useful summary of the Earth discourses detailed in this chapter and reveals the various typology of metaphors, motives, and related assumptions.

As this typology suggests, whether commercially driven, led by the state, or animated by more citizen-based interests, deciphering what discourses are prominent across a range of different social contexts and media institutions and content can illuminate the interplay between economic interest, political power, and environmental justice in ways that can expose the links between corporate agendas, the materialism of class conflict, issues of resource depletion and community rights, and cultural memory. From this theoretical point of departure, a critical approach to the study of environmental discourses can

Table 1. Media and the Politics of the Earth

Discourse (Dryzek)	Key terms and metaphors	Agents, structures, motives	Place of nature
Survivalism (Limits)	Resource exhaustion, overpopulation, scarcity, environmental despoliation, the apocalypse, wilderness, pollution, human excess, pandemics, migration, security, risk, the commons, The Lifeboat, Spaceship Earth, a place apart, tipping point, enviro collapse	*Elites*; hierarchy and control; motivation, site of contention between self-interest and collective interest	Global vision of nature, focus on limits/scarcity, rivalry and conflict
Promethean	Perpetual growth, innovation, markets, technology, competition, discovery, entrepreneurship, trends, cornucopia	*Everyone*; free market; self-interest tied to material well-being	Nature is only brute matter
Administrative Rationalism	Conservation, unitary, scientific, cost-benefit	*Experts and managers*; social hierarchy; public interest	Nature is subordinate to human problem solving
Democratic Pragmatism	Citizens, voice, shared governance, equality, policy, public sphere, cooperation and competition, liberal capitalism, networks, town hall	*Representatives*; civic/legal; self-interest and public interest	Equality among citizens; mostly silent on nature
Ecological Modernization	Connection to progress, efficiency, precautionary principle, risk society, reflexive modernity ("strong" eco-modernization), tidy household	*Experts, technocrats, environmentalists as partners*; business, government, science and technology; public good and industry efficiencies	Marriage of environmental protection and economic prosperity subordination of nature, limits downplayed
Sustainable Development	Social progress, growth, social change, development, public good, responsibility, sustainability, renewable energy, cooperative	*Local, state, and transnational*; public sphere; actors motivated by public good	Nature as capital, subordinate to human needs; stewardship connected to progress
Green Radicalism (Environmental Justice; Ecofeminism)	Culture, autonomy, local, risk/health, toxic waste, empowerment, activism, race, class, gender, NIMBY, passion, emotion, intuitions, spirituality, Mother Earth, Gaia, the seed	*Community and individual actors*; community/residents; cultural and human rights	Equality among people; agency of nature downplayed (Enviro Justice); Nature has agency, too (Ecofeminism)

Table adapted from Able and Stephan 2008; Dryzek 2005.

therefore excavate how environmental issues are handled through institutional arrangements and the control and presentation of cultural metaphors and symbols that massage public perception and thus exert political power. Here the interpretive chore for media scholars rests squarely on interrogating the broader tapestry of converging storylines and antagonisms by identifying the root metaphors, key terms and master images, and other rhetorical devices that imbue discursive agency *in relation to the institutions, systems, and communities that produce them* (Cox 2013; DeLuca 2006; Dryzek 2005; Garrard 2004; Heise 2008; Herndl and Brown 1996). Such investigative foci allow us to develop a better sense of how we and others conceptualize the environment and by extension how we repress, engender, appropriate, or even diffuse issues such as environmental stewardship through competing and contradictory media messages. To initiate such an approach toward what might best be understood as an investigation of the politics of the environmental imagination, it is thus necessary to establish under what political and economic conditions Earth discourses have surfaced, what systems and actors have served and are serving to chart their trajectory, and finally, *cui bono*—a task I take up in the remaining chapters in this book.

2

Endless Growth

Neoliberalism and Global Media's Promethean Logic

After defeating Jimmy Carter in the 1980 Presidential election, Ronald Reagan, in one of his first housekeeping chores, ordered the removal of the solar panels President Carter had had installed on the White House roof. Though primarily a symbolic gesture, few of Reagan's moves could have been more emblematic. While forward thinking, Carter's panels were devices linked to protectionist policies and fears of scarcity anchored to a Limits mentality—something the new administration of optimism wanted nothing to do with.

Looking back, it is clear today that such symbolic indicators were unambiguous signs of something bigger taking place, a tidal shift from prudent narratives of resource depletion, environmental despoliation, and overpopulation to a more enterprising and, eventually, "globalizing" discourse of innovation, progress, and abundance the free market could produce and deliver. Initially, this shift back to a Promethean horizon was slow, as the post-1960s emergence of alternative notions about the Earth suggested that politics, policy, and law responded to environmental limits in carefully considered ways, creating in the process an atmosphere of dialogue, cooperation, and environmental enlightenment. This was a period when governments in the West introduced more protectionist policies, created administrative departments, and elaborated international environmental regimes, putting the issue of the environment at the forefront of public attention. However, with the growing influence of the ideas of libertarian economists (like Friedrich Hayek and Milton Friedman) and with the rise of Prime Minister Margaret Thatcher in the United Kingdom and President Reagan in the United States in the late 1970s and early 1980s, these policies and administrative bodies became sites of contention, with many of the more protectionist environmental initiatives reconditioned by the new models of privatization and trade (see Anderson and Leal 1991; Laferrière and Stoett 1999; Okereke 2008; Vogler 1995). Subsequently, most challenges to the Promethean discourse, particularly those of the Survivalists, soon found themselves ushered to the margins or, later, like the voices within Green Radicalism, Environmental Sustainability, or Administrative Rationalism, selectively appropriated by environmental policymakers and their pro-growth backers.

In many ways the neoliberal reforms initiated in the 1970s and 1980s, which accelerated through the 1990s and into the new millennium, provided the perfect host for the Promethean discourse to emerge from its semi-dormant state. Surfacing first prior to the Industrial Revolution as a discourse grounded in colonial expansion and the conquest of wilderness, the initial wave of the Promethean discourse did not require articulation because its cornucopian assumptions about limitless nature, human ingenuity, and endless growth were taken for granted (Dryzek 2005). However, given the challenge of the limits of "the commons" that emerged with force in the 1960s and 1970s, breathing new life into the Promethean order now required not only the direct defense by its backers (such as industry and governments) but also a promotional infrastructure that could systematically condition the public imagination. This reanimation relied on the neoliberal imperative and its primary ideological mode of delivery, the globally networked commercial media systems, to resurface and expand their ranges across regions and within societies, and take root culturally around the world.

The main argument put forward in this chapter is that the power of the global spread of neoliberalism has resided not only in its institutionalization through diverse, regionalized media industries, but also in how that institutionalization has systematically situated the commercial logic of the market and the "liberating" role of consumption in people's lives. As knowledge-rendering institutions, the reengineering of media's architecture under liberalization made the mass delivery of ideas consistent with the Promethean discourse possible because it privileged and amplified definitions of agency that articulated Promethean logic. This in turn fostered the rise of the "entrepreneurial citizen" and "neoliberal subject" by governing populations, as critical theorists Bill Grantham and Toby Miller (2010) bluntly put it (channeling Foucault), "through market imperatives, invoking and training them as ratiocinative liberal actors" within "an enterprise society" (175). In short, during the global neoliberal turn, commercial media spheres were established as the delivery systems of a Promethean discursive regime. This, among other effects, institutionalized consumption and promoted market subjectivities while resurrecting a discourse of entrepreneurship, innovation, and abundance, making participation in consumer society seem normal, timeless, and commonsensical. The result has been the subordination of environmental issues to economic responses by conditioning consumer-based relationships with the environment.

The Promethean-Neoliberal Coupling

So how has this turn back to Promethean logic happened? In some interesting although often imperceptible ways the Promethean-Neoliberal coupling has been articulated through shared ontologies and guiding assumptions. As an environmental discourse tied to industrialization, the Promethean discourse emphasizes competition, and in doing so reveals an affinity for the notion that the market is the best means of organizing economy and society (Dryzek 2005). As an economic philosophy and political ideology, neoliberalism "proposes that human well-being can best be advanced by liberating individual entrepreneurial freedoms and skills within an institutional framework characterized by strong private property rights, free markets, and free trade" (Harvey 2005, 2). Both the discourse and the philosophy find common ground in market libertarianism, which shuns state oversight and protectionism (or at least claims to), and as such, one flows rather seamlessly into the other.[1] Conveniently, through this confluence not only does the Promethean discourse help neoliberalism shape the contours of a global free-market economy (asking questions such as "Why should business curb growth to invest in governmental environmental remediation when it is cheaper simply to externalize risks?"), but also, by virtue of its alignment with the environmental discourse, neoliberalism generally promotes a Promethean view of how the public's relationship with the Earth can be operationalized.

This discursive-philosophical linkage needs to be registered, because it relies on an alignment that was not always present. For instance, prior to the rise of neoliberalism as a political-economic order within modern societies, most Western nations adhered to some form of Keynesian economics, and despite its ties to industrialism, the Keynesian philosophy brought with it an "embedded liberalism" that called on state oversight of industrial activities (Agnew 2005; Harvey 2005). Thus, the state actively intervened and set social standards for things like wages, education, healthcare, and so on. As Harvey (2005) points out, within this model "a social and moral economy (sometimes supported by a strong sense of national identity) was fostered through the activities of an interventionist state" (11). While perhaps uneven, the effect was global in scope, as even international market expansion was defined by embedded liberalism, as was the case in the United States, where from 1945 to 1970 the conceptualization of a "world market" was still profoundly tied to the notion that the national economy was its basic building block. According to Agnew (2005), within this period the idea that markets could "completely [replace] state-based institutions as the basis for international relations was widely seen as a relic of nineteenth-century thinking. A fully liberal agenda—free market, free trade, laissez-faire—was never adopted" (124).

So while the Keynesian economic model may never be mistaken as inherently "green," it nevertheless carried with it the idea that state oversight could be mobilized to restrict commercial interests' misuses and abuses of natural resources. In fact, in the United States and Europe in the 1960s and 1970s the state was becoming more responsive to public concern about the environment and in setting environmental policy. It is illustrative to recall that in 1970 the Nixon administration created the Environmental Protection Agency to prevent pollution, protect public health, enforce environmental laws, and through education and research advance the nation's understanding of environmental issues. While to some extent the purpose of this was to placate at least one segment of an increasingly unruly civil society—namely, those involved in the Earth Day movement—within this context it was also Nixon who was famously (mis)quoted as saying, "We are all Keynesians now" (Reich 2011, 44–45).

But even as environmental governance was becoming more acceptable, by the end of the 1960s a number of important developments surfaced. According to Agnew (2005), these included the inability of U.S. manufacturers to keep up with American mass consumption, the direct investment of U.S. corporations overseas, and the flow of domestic technology and management—developments that would later undermine the guiding Keynesian model of global economy. As Agnew further explains, one of the most important changes was that by increasing trade in manufactured goods and by encouraging foreign investment, the United States unwittingly cracked open the door that would undo its own post–World War II reorganization of the world economy. Western capitalism was driven by an ethos of mass consumption, and the United States positioned itself as the prototype of the consumer society. At the heart of this global initiative was the assumption that economic growth was secured through "ever-increasing consumption for increased segments of national populations" (128).

While this cornucopian turn was largely successful, after the war in parts of the world that were focused on rebuilding and that had many years earlier, not inconsequentially, already adopted a Fordist model of production (Europe and Japan, for example) (Christoff and Eckersley 2013), for various reasons the Second World and Third World were not willing or able to adhere to these new modes of production and consumption. To rectify this problem, searches for "moderate" regimes, the elaboration of "development" plans, and creation of economic agreements were undertaken to facilitate what was perceived as appropriate change. Third World governments were implicated in new international institutional arrangements and "stability" plans, and they were encouraged to accept enormous aid loans to finance expensive infrastructure projects and new technologies (Escobar 1995, 2008; Perkins 2006). Initially, this was managed through bilateral agreements tethered to Western Cold War politics. Though interventionist and involving state interests, in some very real ways these initiatives also seeded a number of what would evolve to be pro-Promethean relaunching points, not the least of which was "modernization."

Here the role of communication loomed large. In fact, Western communication theorists who asserted the primacy of information and technology for the transformation of traditional societies generated much of the development theory designed to guide the modernization of the Third World (for example, Rogers 1962; Rogers and Svenning 1969; Schramm 1964; for an overview see Shah 2011). These scholars built on Lerner's *The Passing of Traditional Society* (1958), which posited that the "media spread psychic mobility" (55). Within the dominant paradigm of this body of scholarship, proponents argued that progress would follow the "increase in expectations" of traditional populations, that individuals learn behavior by observing role models, and communication was considered the best mechanism through which to drive these transformative processes (Waisbord 2001). This strategy reflected the broader modernization theories' premise that underdevelopment could be blamed on Third World cultural traditions, and that those countries needed only set such traditions aside and "follow in the footsteps of the West to achieve economic 'takeoff'" (Shohat and Stam 1994, 17). Indeed, as environmental policy scholars Peter Christoff and Robyn Eckersley (2013) assert, despite the place of state interventionism, the ideological foundation of this new order carried with it a Promethean vision of industrialization and reflected the Cold War language of the "space race." Through this vision, progress took place, "beginning with benighted primitive traditional societies and, after a series of stages including 'pre-take-off' and 'take-off' during which traditional societies disintegrate and heavy industrialization occurs, culminating in a 'period of mass consumption'—with affluent, American-style society as its apogee" (35–36).

This thinking was part and parcel to the chore of rescuing "underdeveloped" countries and transforming them into viable nations able to partake in the material and organizational fruits of the industrialized world. This agenda directly reflected the World Bank's post–World War II "development" mission, which emphasized, among other things, considerable faith in science and technology (Escobar 1988)—things close to the hearts of the Prometheans. Through this period, as both discourse and practice, modernization, progress, and communication emerged as a Third World thematic bundling in the form of development, formally announced to the world via the UN's proclamation the that 1960s were the "Decade of Development."

But by the mid-1970s, high unemployment, coupled with growing rates of inflation ("stagflation") in Britain and the United States, began to discredit the interventionist, demand-side governments associated with Keynesian economics, providing an opportunity for liberal economic theory to move from the margins of policy circles to the center (Agnew 2005). The full shift to market liberalism became most visible in the late 1970s through the 1990s, with an international move away from state interventionism and toward an even greater emphasis on private resource control and entrepreneurial initiative. Laissez-faire was positioned as an "unmitigated good," as stabilizing policies were considered "distortions" whose elimination would provide "only better allocation of economic resources" (Kuttner 2000, 153). In other words, at the very moment when environmental governance was settling in to become an important function of the state, economic forces and free-market ideology were redirecting public policy away from protectionism. Ironically, during this period the move to privatization invited the idea that environmental stewardship and sustainable resource management were not the business of business but rather roles of the state.

While this might sound primarily like a Westphalian ballad, the implications for these developments were truly global, especially when considering that the adoption of neoliberal orthodoxy as an economic philosophy unfolded in a variety of sociopolitical settings: tested first in Chile and Argentina in the 1970s, finding its feet in the United Kingdom and the United States in the 1980s, taking shape in post-apartheid South Africa and in countries formed after the fall of the Soviet Union, in welfare states like Sweden and New Zealand, and finally taking root in developing countries with considerable arm twisting by neoliberalism's chief global enforcers, the IMF and the World Bank, from the 1990s to the present (Harvey 2005; see also Stiglitz 2003, 2012). Even China and Vietnam embraced forms of market-socialism that drew considerably from neoliberal doctrine (Harvey 2005; Ong 2006), and Russia's own transition from communist industrialization to free-market enthusiast has been a move from one type of Promethean order to another (Dryzek 2005; Christoff and Eckersly 2013). Collectively, during this period these "markets" presented a vision of a world economy fundamentally reorganized from that of the 1970s, defining a global economic phase of accumulation and flexible production in which business operations took "the form of core firms (often transnational in scope) connected by formal and informal alliances to networks of other organizations, firms, governments, and communities (also sometimes known as disorganized capitalism)" (Agnew 2005, 141).

Global studies scholar Manfred B. Steger (2005, 2009) has pointed out that, since the late 1980s, this version of globalization has been aggressively peddled by the Global North in a "decontested" (post-Soviet-style communist) ideological landscape. To feed its growth, neoliberal globalization has counted on an expanding commercial media sphere to cultivate consumerist identities by the billions. One finds support for this claim in a 2004 University of Maryland survey of nineteen countries on four continents. Steger notes that this study found that, "even after five years of massive, worldwide demonstrations against 'corporate-globalization,' 55 percent of the respondents believed that globalization was positive for them and their families, while only 25 percent said it was negative (20 percent were unsure). Surprisingly, popular support of globalization was especially high in poor countries of the global South" (Steger 2005, 14).

To fully appreciate how we have arrived at this contradictory place within our collective planetary history requires attention to how, as dominant institutions within the move to market economies across the globe, the media industries have transformed and been used to condition the public imagination. Latin American communication scholar Jésus Martín-Barbero (1993) asserts that media serve as the "architecture" in the form of systems and genres in different regions that articulate countries into the transnational project of neoliberalism. The profile of global media that has surfaced through neoliberalism that I map out in this chapter underscores his assertion, but in ways I argue are profoundly troubling for our environmental future.

Media, Globalization, and the Neoliberal Turn

Internationally, the effects of neoliberal reform on the media industries became increasingly visible in the 1980s and 1990s through changes in structural networks, policy, and relationships of capital (Hallin and Mancini 2004;

McChesney 1999, 2004; Ó Siochrú, Girard, and Mahan 2002). During this period the growth and expansion of media firms was characterized by major mergers, leveraged buyouts, and internationalization, which lead to the rise of transnational media corporations (TNMCs) like Time Warner Inc., the Walt Disney Company, News Corp Ltd., Bertelsmann A.G., and Sony Inc. (Bagdikian 2004; Herman and McChesney 1997). These entities were able to consolidate through a combination of decentralization, market penetration, foreign direct investment, and horizontal and vertical integration strategies (Albarran and Chan-Olmstead 1998; Bettig and Hall 2003; Gershon 1997, 2000). Through these strategies media corporations capitalized on regional and global trends in deregulation and privatization, which, ostensibly at least, altered telecommunication policies to promote competition and eliminate trade barriers. The result was the creation of truly giant transnational media conglomerates with unprecedented control over the production and distribution of information and entertainment through cross-media ownership.

THE UNITED STATES AND WESTERN EUROPE

In the United States, the 1996 Telecommunications Act was a landmark decision that set the tone for many things to come, not the least of which were media enterprise convergence and the exploitation of public domains. The act allowed media companies to establish media product synergies through an almost unending echo effect and thus better penetrate market segments and geographic zones. Indeed, more than ever before the intertwined media channels that the new ownership models produced permitted TNMCs to access, manage, and "sell" audiences to advertisers both in terms of large-scale demographics and smaller, more lifestyle-based audience segments— in essence creating new, more effective ways to procure the "right kind" of consumers for their clients.

Proponents argued that the 1996 act would minimize protectionism and unleash the entrepreneurial spirit to help create more dynamic, competitive markets—all of which met with minimal resistance as American ideals tied to freedom and liberty. However, Robert McChesney (1999, 2005), a U.S. media scholar who has been relentlessly critical of these market-driven arrangements, has written at length about how, within these transformations, democratic participation has come to look more and more like consumer choice as media conglomerates claim to be just "giving people what they want." This trend in consumer democracy continued to gain momentum into the new millennium despite the fact that, with the growth of mega-media corporations and thus fewer sources of information, it became less possible to think of these as real "free" markets. Central to McChesney's charge was that power shifted from consumers to producers when media concentration and conglomeration limited the fare to that which could generate the greatest profits. This "closed loop" is fixed, as consumer choice draws from a menu already provided, allowing the producers to assert that they have "given them what they want" even though the consumers have, rather, selected a choice from what is presented as an open menu responsive to audiences' needs and tastes. The irony here is that the very idea of the "opening up" of mediascapes via liberalization was debated as a means through which to give American consumers better ("freer") access to and greater choice within the market-place of ideas. In short, the promise to deliver more goods and services to the "consumer" via an unbound market is precisely the narrative that assured public consent, acquiescence, and, most important, participation.

The effects of such initiatives were not just seen in TNMC creation and policy changes in the United States. In countries with highly protectionist policies and often state-run public media systems, the "perceived inefficiency of central planning and government-protected monopolies . . . [were] char-acterized by poor financial performance, overstaffing and dependency on government subsidies, . . . [and] poor export performance" served as the "motivation for such . . . regulatory reforms" (Gershon 2005, 20). At the center of concern were polarizing perspectives on the free flow of informa-tion versus cultural sovereignty, points of contention that actually surfaced many years earlier through UNESCO's New World Information and Com-munication Order debates (NWICO) (Pickard 2007). Emerging from these querulous meetings, "free flow" advocates, which were primarily the United States and other Western countries, argued that media content was com-merce, no different than cars or shoes, and indeed the free flow would ben-efit all people in all nations because of its democratizing potential. However, critics of these ideas, typically voices from countries with less technological power and economic influence, asserted that media content was culture, not commerce, and that each country should decide how information should be disseminated. In his book *Communication and Cultural Domination*, Herbert Schiller (1976) put a critical lens on the early versions of these exchanges, arguing how, according to Pickard (2007), "the language of the free flow of information was more a language of oppression than liberation, used by U.S. corporations to rid themselves of regulatory constraints" (133). Despite these concerns and criticisms, or rather perhaps because of them, regional trade agreements involving the media industries were replete with exemptions and side agreements, demonstrating that economic imperatives usually won out over concerns about cultural sovereignty (Galperin 1999a, 1999b, 2000; McAnany and Wilkinson 1996; Wheeler 2000). Nevertheless, the commercial restructuring of media—indeed, in many cases the very creation of media "markets"—exploded in the 1990s.

To help further "globalize" this emerging neoliberal media landscape, the drive to "open markets" was facilitated by the creation of the World Trade Organization (WTO). Launched on January 1, 1995, the WTO was charged with administering multilateral trade agreements and removing protectionism. It is not surprising that this global agenda of privatization and liberalization helped facilitate an unprecedented number of international mergers and acquisitions among transnational media corporations. These developments were seeded during the Uruguay (1986–1994) and later rounds of the General Agreement on Tariffs and Trade (GATT), which involved some particularly intense negotiations between the United States and some European nations, led by France, regarding the liberalization of audiovisual services and related cultural factors (for example, national identity) (Wheeler 2000). However, France's cultural concerns were evidently not enough to stifle Europe's full move to media marketization. For example, Murdock and Golding (1999) reported that in 1996 the telecommunications directorate of European Commission released a Green Paper that "argued forcefully that 'too "heavy" a regulatory framework in [Europe] could result in a migration of economic activity to other regions' with a consequent loss of competitive advantage" (121). The authors underscored that the paper was indeed a "concerted effort" to maximize corporate ambitions, noting that the European Commission later punctuated this position by releasing a statement that "there should be no restrictions on business activities" (Murdock and Golding 1999, 126).

It is important to recognize that the European Commission's agenda to pursue a competitive position against foreign (U.S.) interests was also motivated by more expansive "cultural" considerations—namely, the creation of a strong pan-European market (Wheeler 2000). This effort was tied to the EU's desire to establish pan-European citizen buy-in through greater identification with the European Union. As such, concern over national culture was sometimes sacrificed for a broader European agenda, with alterations in media policies and structures surfacing as key barometers of change. To fully appreciate these shifts, it is useful to understand this agenda in relation to past practice and how it affected what was until then a fairly diverse and disjointed European mediascape. European media scholars Stylianos Papathanassopoulos and Ralph Negrine (2011) note that before the "deregulatory turn" in the 1980s, the most influential European media shared the trait that they placed the public good and the public interest over commercial concerns, as characterized by the TF1 (France), ARD (Germany), RAI (Italy), and, of course, the BBC (Britain) (17–18). These public broadcasters all operated with this charge, and while highly bureaucratic, hierarchically organized, and similarly structured, their political and cultural status was grounded in the specificities of national culture, so their profiles reflected and were responsive to national identities. But with deregulation in concert with the EU's project to "Europeanize" Europe, more European countries moved toward market-driven broadcasting models, adopting advertising-dependent funding structures as state funds were cut. This process led media sectors, such as television, to seek out opportunities for consolidation and integration, creating webs of interest across the European media. Within this context, Papathanassopoulos and Negrine (2011) observed, "Oddly enough, the creation of so many commercial broadcasting systems led to some sort of convergence and greater similarities than had existed previously" (19).

Not surprisingly, the exponential growth of commercial media models in Europe undercut the public media services' ability to maintain their preeminence, profoundly reshaping Europe's media scene. But that does not mean public media simply disappeared under the weight of free-market thinking. For instance, "welfare states" characterized by state interventionism and an ongoing commitment to social responsibility (the Scandinavian counties, for instance) continued to invest in public broadcasting as a matter of public interest, asserting that broadcasting has a social influence that was "too great to be left under the control of private interests" (Hallin and Mancini 2004, 164). Moreover, although perhaps with a bumpy start, the BBC transitioned well under market conditions, surfacing as a skilled creator of high-quality entertainment fare and as an innovative force in multiplatform media spheres. So it is difficult to argue that public media has not continued to be an important actor in Europe. Nevertheless, it is undeniable that the drive toward commercialization diminished the place of public broadcasting in Europe and forced it to reinvent itself in relation to competition and marketization.

These changes created an interesting dynamic within Western Europe and in no small way produced perhaps the defining feature of the region's media profile: the dynamic growth of commercial media systems that took root around the formerly dominant public models—a meshing of public and private media that is now what gives the broader European mediascape its "European" feel. That is, while now primarily defined by "the market," European media writ large nevertheless surfaces as a tapestry of competing ideas and practices, such as consumer demand and public interest, commercial competition and lingering state-run licensing fees, cross-border alliances and ongoing localism, and media consolidation and "triple play" bundling alongside audience fragmentation and lifestyle media. But while acknowledging this complexity and the contradictions within it, it should be understood that the pan-European media sphere that took shape through marketization is clearly a delivery system for a social imagination grounded in capitalist consumption, privileging Promethean-like ideas and motivations such as individual empowerment, competition, private holdings, and entrepreneurship.

EASTERN AND CENTRAL EUROPE

The capacity of the liberal model to penetrate the European public sphere while being shaped by competing ideologies has not just been a Western European broadcasting experience. Eastern bloc countries, emerging from communism and establishing new economies and aspiring democracies, sought inspiration from the West. As various media scholars (Downey and Mihelj 2012; Gross and Jakubowicz 2013; Hallin and Mancini 2004; Papathanassopoulos and Negrine 2011) have noted from the outset, the restructuring of the region's media systems involved financial and political ties to national political parties, but as the process unfolded, it was increasingly steered by commercialization, technological innovation, and globalization, especially in the form of U.S. influence. According to Gross and Jakubowisz (2013), during this period of transition different media reformation formulas surfaced, defined in terms of combining aspects of both communism and capitalism and involving "catch up" efforts that modeled Western media. This model masked elements of old systems while proclaiming an alignment with democracy, and, eventually, through the enthusiastic embrace of economic liberalism by individual rights and responsibilities. While these transitional trajectories gave each country distinct media profiles (as was the case in the West), over time the shared transnational forces pushed Central and Eastern Europe to form a more commercially driven media landscape defined in no unambiguous way as a delivery system for consumer culture.

These structural transformations and the changes in content and flow that followed helped produce a change in discourse that normalized "promotional culture" in Central and Eastern Europe. Eastern European media scholars Nadia Kaneva and Elza Ibroscheva (2013) provide examples of how this took place in various former Eastern bloc countries, where political life, nationalism, and even gender became important discursive sites through which the embrace of market-driven principles became salient. Political campaigning, for instance, morphed into an enterprise of intense activity as consumer advertising principles and practices (jingles, logos, and sound bites, for instance) were quickly applied to political advertising. Here the new advertising industry leaders turned to Western, primarily American consultants to learn the secrets of addressing citizens as consumers and "branding democracy" to stimulate electoral activity, "reaffirming the conflation of consumer choice with political choice" (Kaneva and Ibroscheva 2013, 77–78). The capacity of commercialized media discourses to reshape the cultural landscape also showed up in national identity, as advertising campaigns designed to associate domestically manufactured goods with nationalism became more commonplace. This form of "patriotic consumption" emerged as a strategy for different Central and Eastern European countries to promote themselves as post-communist regional leaders by rearticulating national identity in consumerists' terms (78).

In addition to these discursive threads, gender surfaced as a stunningly salient marker of consumption, as "the discourse of sex became inextricably linked with the discourse of economics" (Borenstein 2008, 88, as quoted in Kaneva and Ibroscheva 2013, 80). This trend mushroomed during the growth of commercial media outlets in post-communist Eastern Europe, as the naked female body became a staple within this new mediascape—a "commodity" now associated with "liberated" post-communist societies. One of the more bizarre examples of how this unfolded is the Czech Republic weather program *Počasíčko* (Czech for "a little weather"), which featured "a naked woman who would present the forecast while dressing appropriately for the day's meteorological conditions" (Kaneva and Ibroscheva 2013, 80). Kaneva and Ibroscheva assert that not only did this commodification of a new kind of Eastern European femininity set up the perfect launching point for cosmetics and fashion and other consumables promoted to manufacture and then capitalize on feminine angst, but it also paralleled the region's growing association with prostitution, sex tourism, and sex trafficking.

Collectively, these discursive adjustments are signposts of a radical change from communist subjectivities grounded in party politics and membership to market-driven subjectivities expressed in consumer versions of ideas like "freedom," "choices," and "liberation"—"civilizing" narratives linked to past memories of shortages, lack of choice, and impeded desires. The production of this kind of subjectivity is a requirement for these new models of consumer culture in social and political life to take root and be reproduced by the citizen-consumers who internalize them. In that sense, it is undeniable that the post-communist media landscape in Eastern and Central Europe helped usher its citizens into the neoliberal-Promethean ontological realm with many of the same defining characteristics and guiding assumptions that it occupies in the Western European and, of course, U.S. public spheres— namely, that agency is liberated via the free market, and that material well- being and innovation are best pursued through self-interest and the entre- preneurial spirit.

LATIN AMERICA

Like Eastern and Western Europe, from the late 1980s through the early 2000s commercialization substantially changed the media topology of Latin America, although with some different dynamics at play. Most noteworthy was the place of media conglomeration in Latin America, as the region was already home to some of the world's most powerful private media firms, with a list of cultural industry leaders that includes Mexico's Grupo Televisa, Bra- zil's Organizações Globo, Venezuela's Cisneros, and Argentina's Clarín. In his study of Latin American television, John Sinclair (1999) observed that while cross media ownership became common worldwide, the "Latin American model," defined most prominently by Globo and Televisa, was stunning in the degree to which the companies were integrated vertically and horizontally "in conjunction with the traditional family-owned patrilineal and autocratic mode of ownership and control," adding up to a presence in virtually all na- tional media sectors and massive export operations (77).

From their inception these privately owned media groups established American-style commercial models for broadcasting, with their political power and public influence rooted in laissez-faire agreements and clientelism established with the state (Fox 1988, 1997; Hallin and Papathanassopoulos 2002; McAnany and Wilkinson 1996; Wilkinson 2007) as well as "de facto deregulation by lack of regulation," as illustrated by the case of Argentina (Galperin 2000, 183). Additionally, these regional media giants enjoyed "ex- tensive ties and joint ventures with the largest media TNCs, as well as with Wall Street investment banks" (McChesney 1999, 12). These cozy relationships with political parties and external interests allowed some, like Televisa and Globo, to achieve near monopoly status and build vast national audiences, especially through entertainment fare, which profoundly shaped national cultures (Hughes 2008; Sinclair 1999; Straubhaar 1982). With these players already firmly rooted in the commercial, political, and public spheres, they were in prime positions to take advantage of the possibilities of economic integration when states sought ways to privatize public services and liberalize their economies. As such, during the early phases of neoliberal reform they were able to extend their influence over national and regional cultures, and even further internationalize their operations (Amaral 2002; Galperin 1999a and 1999b; Lugo-Ocando 2008; Mayobre 2002; Sinclair 1999). In fact, in some cases they even "outpaced institutional reform," as with Televisa, which by the mid-1990s was producing "over 50,000 hours of programming per year . . . more than that which is produced by all the US networks combined" (Sinclair 1999, 75).

But with neoliberalism also came a new set of dynamics, and Latin America experienced the growth of more competitive and diverse media systems. Following the lead of Reagan, Thatcher, the "Washington Consensus," and the WTO, regulatory reforms were widely implemented and fledgling companies soon found openings through which they could insert themselves in what were formally closed markets. In Argentina this took place via the vast privatization of many state interests that were sold or leased to the commercial sector. The country's media landscape was altered radically as deregulation sparked cross-media ownership and invited foreign investment. Here, both established and emergent actors went to work; the newspaper company Clarín, for example, invested in television and other media, and new alliances, such as CEI-Telefonica, a rival media conglomerate, formed through a partnership between U.S. Citibank group and Telefonica de Argentina. According to Vialey, Belinche, and Tovar (2008), the postmilitary junta reduction of state oversight of the media that transpired in the 1990s was a means through which the government could court media owners and forge supportive, pro-neoliberal relationships—a ploy that worked until the market crash of 2001. In Mexico during this period, Televisa had a series of missteps, such as overextending its export operations and trapping itself in an inflexible advertising model that undercut its ability to be responsive to new market pressures and opportunities (Hughes 2008; Sinclair 1999; Wilkinson 2007). TV Azteca, the 1993 outgrowth of a previously state-run television network, surfaced during this time and, in order to capture an audience share, provided much edgier and critical fare than the vacuous programming and lap-dog journalism widely associated with Televisa, along with a much more flexible and less expensive advertising policy.

Interestingly, even though liberalization was undertaken to relieve government of many of its burdens and to create opportunities for big business, throughout most of Latin America this dynamic coincided with an era of democratization (Fox and Waisbord 2002). Within this context the old media regimes and their upstart competitors responded by aggressively pursuing business, not public-service goals or concern for deepening democratic participation, thus perpetuating a broadcasting history defined by a market-oriented version of "progress" (Fox and Waisbord 2002; Hernandez and McAnany 2001). For example, in Mexico the move from a state-shaped to a corporate-controlled public sphere was accompanied by a new articulation of progress. As Mexican cultural critic Carlos Monsiváis (1996) pointed out, the collusion between media and politics allowed proponents of neoliberalism to replace key terms in the national imaginary, such as "nationalism" with "productivity," "revolution" with "modernization." Even entertainment fare, like the "tequila novelas" of the 1990s produced by Televisa and its rival TV Azteca, became discursive tools to positively frame neoliberal principles for media audiences. These texts relied on the highly romanticized, folkloric iconography of haciendas (sites of primary accumulation and extremely exploitative labor relations established before and after Mexican independence) and presented a Mexico unfettered by state oversight and the more egalitarian and public-nationalist principles of the revolution (nationalized public resources and "land and liberty," even for the poor), while ideologically compatible with the free-trade political climate (Chávez 2006). Such programs punctuated Monsiváis's (1996) observation that "in these days of neoliberalism we need to examine the attempts to destroy political consciousness in the name of freedom" (137). Indeed, if one can draw a single broad conclusion about media across Latin America during the deregulatory turn, it would be that through a new, less monolithic mediascape marked by "competition" and "diversity," the presence of the consumer culture merely deepened and expanded.

SUB-SAHARAN AFRICA

Trends in the regions that have experienced some of the most transformative social and economic changes, such as sub-Saharan Africa, Asia, and the Middle East, also bear the unambiguous signs of marketization. This has occurred through the privatization of national broadcasting systems, the proliferation of new media channels, contracts with foreign investors, and the reformation of the role of the press formerly connected to authoritarian regimes. And as is the case with Latin America and Eastern Europe, much of this activity has taken place alongside the dual forces of democratization and consumerism (Algan 2003; Johnson 2001; Juluri 2003; Kraidy 2010; McCargo 2002; McDaniel, 2002, 2007; Nyamnjoh 2013; Onwumechili 2007; Pendakur 1989; Semanti 2007; Sowards 2003). Indeed, through their reformation in these regions, news and entertainment media support the neoliberal notion that market forces are naturally part of the process of democratization and thus serve an important ideological function by cultivating the perspective that freedom and social status are expressed through the consumption of goods. But the change has also involved a mobilized citizenry seeking political agency and voice in concert with a hunger for entrepreneurial opportunities.

For example, during the 1990s in sub-Saharan Africa the "good governance" programs of the IMF and the World Bank called on countries within the region "to create legal frameworks and privatize their telecommunications infrastructures and industries with the goal of making them attractive for foreign investment" (Eko 2003, 202–3). These external pressures to privatize were applied while internal actors in the form of students, trade unions, and educators were also pushing for reforms. The result was a perfect storm of internal and external fronts, which created an atmosphere of change both political and cultural in nature (Blankson 2005; Bourgault 1995; Eko 2003; Kasoma 1997; Sparks 2009; Wasserman 2011). Politically, this atmosphere catalyzed democratization, with a new media climate facilitating the transition by offering openings for new voices to enter the public sphere (Avle 2011; Blankson 2007; Nyamnjoh 2013; Onwumechili 2007; Tomaselli 2000). Culturally, the commercially driven media helped introduce "global culture" into the lives of many Africans through a new wave of cultural expressions and consumer lifestyles, stimulating the creation of syncretic forms such as "hiplife" (Blankson 2005; Oduro-Frimpong 2009, 2014). As a result, throughout sub-Saharan Africa political participation, cultural transformation, and marketization were tethered together via the commercial media's articulation of cultural modernity and political consciousness. The interpretive processes involved to make sense of these changes have surfaced as sites of intense cultural negotiation as the emphasis on individual rights and freedoms at the heart of both liberal democratic theory and consumer culture have often run counter to African realities.

In addition to these dual forces, Africa's liberalized commercial turn has made the region attractive to a new set of players. For instance, China has exercised soft and hard power interventions by investing heavily in sub-Saharan Africa's emerging mediascape. This has been part of its own anti-colonial and anti-imperialist agenda, and has taken place primarily through infrastructural realignment and technological knowledge transfer, leading some to question if these efforts are just another means to foster cultural reproduction and dependence (Banda 2009). The new players, however, have also been African, as "entertainment brokers"—that is, agents from various African countries hired by large production houses—have worked hard to establish pan-African markets for their television productions and thus create attractive audience packages for large corporate sponsors (Thalén 2011).

These pan-African market formations have also fed the continued flow of foreign programming, primarily from the United States and Latin America to Africa via French- and English-language distribution agencies whose missions are to bundle large audiences for national television stations (Touré 2007). This has been pursued in no small part because Africa is now seen as boasting highly attractive markets, with one of the world's fastest-growing populations and private-consumer activity reportedly higher than in India or Russia, particularly with regard to apparel and consumer goods (Hattingh, Russo, Sun-Basorun, and Van Wamelen 2012).

In addition to these investments of soft power, technological transfer, and macrotrends in population and consumption, radio—that most "traditional" of electronic media—continues to be a powerful and accessible force in the lives of Africans and a site of the intense proliferation of advertising and entrepreneurship (Alve 2011; Grätz 2013). Combined, these forces in the wake of neoliberalism have produced a whole class of new African cultural actors, from videographers, journalists and disk jockeys to PR offices, advertisers and producers, sometimes wearing multiple hats, which has fed the growth of a vibrant media ecology and a rising sense of "Afro-cosmopolitanism" (Avle 2011; Grätz 2011, 2013; Musa 2011; Thalén 2011).

These things said, it is important to note that much of this morphing into a more cosmopolitan profile has also taken shape via less formal and more entrepreneurial models and networks of cultural and economic exchange. "Nollywood," the West African video industry that owes its birth to the entrepreneurs and "marketers" (financers, producers, and distributors) of Nigeria's Alaba open-air electronics market, has become what media scholar Jade Miller (2012) calls part of alternative, globally interlaced periphery-to-periphery circuits, with "fewer distinctions between black market, gray market and white market, or between formal and informal, than in dominant global networks" (122). Miller reports that while many within Nollywood aspire to an "American way of doing things," the informal system of production and distribution that has emerged has allowed it to dominate the movie scene, eclipsing the fare of both Hollywood and Bollywood on West African television screens.

As these various developments suggest, the media landscape in sub-Saharan Africa has been composed of formal and informal networks of production and distribution that have profoundly shaped the region's articulation of cultural modernity and expression of political consciousness. While dually conditioned by powerful global interests and exceptionally inventive forms of cultural production, this landscape evokes a media commons that locates agency (for example, political and cultural transformation) in relation to market-based modes of expression, most saliently in the form of growth through entrepreneurship.

INDIA

Given its prominent place in global media production and flows, and the degree in which its mediascape has changed, India is certainly one of the most compelling examples of media transformation under neoliberalism. For much of the early part of the twentieth century Indian audiences relied largely on the British press and radio and Hollywood films for their media diet, and the country remained a "TV laggard" until the mid 1990s, deliberately keeping television experimental until the late 1970s (Shahin 2015; Tunstall 2008). With India's low levels of literacy, as mass media slowly became available to broader audiences, cinema, not the press, took on the most significant role. More than any other, this medium was responsible for shaping Indian national consciousness, especially as more Indian films eventually became available—something that fit more in line with Prime Minister Jawaharlal Nehru's vision of Indian modernity defined by scientific and technological progress than the Gandhian notion that the future lay in self-improvement and gainful activity. These nascent years in media development, like other cultural concerns in India during its break from British imperial rule, were defined more by "modernity" versus "tradition" or "Western" versus "indigenous" (political stand-ins for "colonizer" and "colonized") than debates about "public" versus "private" or "socialist" versus "capitalist" media models (Athique 2012). Moreover, the Nehru administration saw media—film and radio specifically—as instructive in nature and thus didactic tools for shaping a new India by engendering progress and fostering a "scientific temper" (Athique 2012, 38).

Nation building therefore largely drove media policy in India until the 1970s, when Indira Gandhi, Nehru's daughter and political successor, decided to chart a new path by investing in the potential of television as a mass medium. Paradoxically, Gandhi's strategy was to use television as a means to connect with the subaltern classes, envisioned almost exclusively as rural, while neglecting the urban upper-middle classes, even though it was largely only the urbanites that owned televisions. To overcome this geographic limitation, the country invested in satellite technology to reach rural populations. It also invested more heavily in Doordarshan, the Delhi-based public-service broadcaster, with national television broadcasts beginning in 1982 (Kumar 2006; Rajagopal 2000). Interestingly, despite the socialist principles that informed media policy in India, this launch was made possible in part by permitting advertising, thus providing some of the first signs of commercialization of the then still-emerging Indian mediascape (Athique 2012).

When India introduced market-based media models, growth was slow and uneven, taking place first in film (1970s-1980s) and then later in television (1990 and beyond). The two industries would eventually merge and become synergetic, with film feeding the fledgling television industries with content, and television serving as a key promotional medium for film. First, however, political ambitions and language inequities tied to caste and class power, regionalism, and the residues of colonialism molded what aspects of Indian society and culture made their way onscreen and which ones did not. It is not surprising that, given its prominent place in Indian politics and elite society, Hindi was the language of choice for Doordarshan. Through much of the 1970s and 1980s television, like radio, was treated as a state service, giving it, in Jeremy Tunstall's (2008) words, an "obsessively inward-looking gaze," with little information about the outside world (171).

By the end of the 1980s the number of televisions in India increased exponentially, and more entertainment fare such as soap operas started to become popular. The "edutainment" program *Hum Log* (We People) became Doordarshan's first megahit, drawing a giant national audience despite its pedagogical purpose, which was to teach the Indian underclasses about birth control (Singhal and Rogers 1989). Other, even more popular programs followed, such as *Ramayan*, an epic centered on the life of the god-king Ram, which during its run in 1987 reportedly drew ever-increasing audience numbers, climbing from "40 million to 60 million to 80 million viewers per week over a few months" (Rajagopal 2000, 296). Such success drew attention to the idea that there was money to be made by tapping into the neglected commercial potential of this increasingly popular medium, endowing television with a level of legitimacy that it had not enjoyed before in India (Pendakur 1989). These developments, along with the growing availability of VCRs and cable in the 1980s, also helped generate a boom in media-related entrepreneurship, from the rise of neighborhood video parlors to the production of pirated entertainment fare, greatly increasing the capacity of Indian audiences to locate alternative (non-state) media.

But all of this was merely a slow buildup for the 1990s, which was, as with many other parts of the world, a truly intense time of change for India's media industries. This was a period ripe for the emergence of new visions of Indian television as audiences were hungry for something different than the didactic fare of Doordarshan and not particularly interested in more dubbed foreign programming. The ensuing change was profound. From 1991 through 1993

India witnessed the arrival of CNN and Star TV (Hong Kong) via satellite and the expansion of cable offerings, such as Asia TV and Jain TV. During the same time Doordarshan was informed that it would need to become sponsorship driven, migrating from 20 percent reliance on advertising to 80 percent. This led to an explosion of advertising on Indian television, as ad "expenditure quadrupled during 1993–1998 with a compound annual growth rate of 33 percent" (Tunstall 2008, 176).

But the capacity to create something new, particularly for the Indian lower-middle classes, was perhaps best recognized by an Indian toothpaste tube manufacturer, Subhash Chandra. As Athique (2012) explains, Chandra's plan was simple: cut deals to get access to "the back catalogue of the prodigious Indian cinemas" and put them on television. The result was ZEE TV, a Hindi-language private television channel that appealed to 90 percent of the Indian television audience by providing "vulgar Indian popular culture"—a new model of Indian television that ignited the "massive expansion of television ownership into the middle classes during the 1990s" (57–58). Not only did content production explode, but the Zee model drew in other players from Rupert Murdoch and Sony to a slew of Indian investors, instigating a moment of growth that "consisted of over six thousand production houses by the mid-2000s" (59). It also forced transnational companies like MTV and STAR TV to re-create their content for the Indian (primarily Hindi) market (Kumar 2006).

In the wake of these new models, and in hindsight what might seem like the natural progression from the dominance of big-Hindi TV like Zee and Doordarshan, the film-television connection evolved to cater to distinct regional and language audiences. Through this diversification, moving into the new millennium much of India's media landscape was defined by the operations of translocal media networks. These included Sun TV and JJTV, Tamil-language providers, as well as Eandu TV, AsiaNet, Udaya TV, and others that relied on language and ethnic-regional identity to craft relationships with specific audiences (Kumar 2006)—a shift toward "local markets [that] mirrored the meteoric rise of regional language cinemas in South India in the 1960s, and led to a further wave of local competitors" (Athique 2012, 59).

Through these changes the Indian media scene went from oddly monolithic and barren to exceptionally diverse and ubiquitous in a very short period, and suggesting that the days of limited offering, foreign-dominated content, slow growth, and state-led "development" media are part of what must seem like a very distant past for the majority of today's Indian audience members. Or as Tunstall (2008) puts it, "most of present-day India's people—one-sixth of the world's population—have had little or no exposure to made-in-America or made-in-Europe media" (139). But despite its complexity and regional diversity, the commercialized and fragmented media model that surfaced became perhaps the perfect delivery system for new ways of thinking and dreaming about everyday life. For example, according to Kirk Johnson (2001), a researcher who conducted extensive fieldwork in rural India from 1995 to 1996 and in 2000, the presence of television profoundly transformed village life, reshaping social relationships and reframing the cultural imagination by encouraging material accumulation, urban modeling, and associating consumerism with social mobility. Johnson observed, "Things that were once a luxury are now a necessity. Television advertising has made great inroads into village society. From toys to hand cream, from liquor to blue jeans, these products are now perceived as necessities. This spirit of consumerism is rapidly taking over village life and is probably the most significant change one notices upon entering the village" (151). Younger participants in his research seemed the most profoundly effected, one sharing, "People in the village today are very greedy. I even want many things that I can't have. We see many things on TV that we would like to have, and therefore we become greedy" (152). Another study, this one focused on Indian Music television audiences conducted by Vamsee Juluri (2003), found that urban middle-class viewers felt that "commercialization and privatization have made television more accessible and representative" (65) and provided models for mobility and success, while working-class participants thought music television, though pleasurable, presented aspirations for their children, not themselves.

Though fiercely nationalistic since the early days of Indian cinema, it is clear that during India's neoliberal turn its cultural industries, in an attempt to serve audiences that were formerly neglected, became more diverse and inclusive by celebrating a wider range of Indian realities. But through this amplification of Indian media culture, the country's film and television complex, despite its investment of "Indian-ness," became a central site for the cultivation of new dreams, new appetites, new aspirations—in short, new subjectivities tied to growth, competition, and material comfort that in no uncertain terms manifested in stark contrast to the austerity of its not-so-distant Gandhian past.

CHINA

Such a review would be incomplete without the very significant case of China, which is important to consider because while it has clearly emerged as one of the world's largest and most complex media markets, its profile has unfolded within a context of mixed communist and capitalist interests defined through nationalism and regionalism and alternating periods of tight state control and leniency. Chinese media had been operating commercially since the mid-1980s, but given Deng Xiaoping's mantra of "stability above all else" the Chinese government was primarily concerned with national sovereignty and information control and continues to be especially sensitive to the capacity of the media industries to spread information and shape cultural values. Therefore, it should come as no surprise that, like art and culture, the media industries in China are understood by the Chinese Communist Party to be first and foremost the agents of enlightenment and morality, not tools for transgressing cultural boundaries or expanding markets (Zhu 2012). This ideological imperative is what has driven the state monitoring and censorship of commercial, noncommunist media content, with restrictive clampdowns taking place in ebbs and flows over the years through what Tunstall (2008) has characterized as a "bewildering number of different state agencies and government departments" (208).

Nevertheless, in 2001 China entered into the World Trade Organization, a move that was initially considered a sign that China was opening its domestic media market to international competition. With WTO membership several changes in policy immediately followed, such as permitting limited foreign investment in media production; more co-production opportunities for television, films, and animation with local partners; and an increased import quota of foreign movies, among others. So, for those external actors eager to see how this most-sought-after "emerging market" could be tamed, the new, ostensibly more relaxed WTO China seemed like a marketer's dream, and major TNMCs like Sony, Disney, and News Corp quickly sought out ways to expand their empires into China (Li and Dimmick 2005). Partnerships were pursued with regional interests and local power brokers, who were often eager to attract foreign investors. However, as a continuation of the tradition of "making the foreign serve China" (Tunstall 2008, 209), commercial plans and ambitions had to be pursued through relevant government agencies and industry regulators. As corporate strategists quickly found out, their capacity to be realized and sustained was highly contingent upon establishing strong relationships with the state—something that has not always been easy, but ultimately rewarding if the actors understood Chinese authorities' reasons for pursuing partnerships with global media capital (Fung 2008).

Of course, despite the apparent limitations associated with doing business in a country where party-run capitalism steers trade, there were many reasons external media interests were so anxious to penetrate the Chinese market. Most obvious was the matter of sheer numbers. Tunstall (2008) outlines China's media universe in terms of its vastness, noting that it is "unique in having 900 million people who speak a single language, Mandarin" (Tunstall 2008, 191), reporting that "by 2005 China had about 330 million households containing at least one television set" (207). In *Two Billion Eyes: The Story of China Central Television*, Ying Zhu (2012) frames things more globally, albeit directly in relation to the state, asserting that with more than 1.2 billion viewers globally, including millions in the United States, Latin America, and Africa, China Central Television (CCTV), the official mouthpiece of the Chinese Communist Party, reaches the world's single largest audience. And while CCTV suffers from the view that it is merely an apparatus of state ideology, its recent market-conscious efforts to attract more robust audiences have unfolded via the cultivation of "branded" personality news anchors, the development of game shows, women's programming, and other entertainment and lifestyle fare—programming that it would have found inconsistent with its cultural mission in the past (Zhu 2012).

For the growing Chinese middle class and younger Chinese disinterested in CCTV's programming, regional commercial television has become the most attractive option, drawing increasing audience shares. For someone weaned on a Western media diet, much of this programming would be instantly recognizable, ranging from soap operas, historical dramas, and animation to cheaper "reality" fare, such as cooking shows, game shows, variety programs, talent contest shows, "survivor" shows, dating shows, and so on. In some notable cases, these offerings have been stunning in their capacity to draw huge audiences. For instance, because of the size of its audience, *Super Girl*, an *American Idol*-style singing-contest show produced by Hunan Satellite TV, claimed that the cost of advertising on its channel was greater than that on the *National News Bulletin*, CCTV's most expensive time slot (Zhu 2012).

In addition to regional programing, audiences have also migrated to alternative programming via the internet. Indeed, despite considerable state oversight, the internet has been enthusiastically embraced in China for news and entertainment needs, particularly in urban areas (Tai 2006; Wallis 2011). Moreover, along with its celebrated ability to help citizens mobilize ("netizens") and challenge state corruption through increased accountability and transparency (Tai 2015), new media have become key tools for television viewing, from *Downton Abbey* and *House of Cards* to popular and typically counter hegemonic *e'gao* videos (Wallis 2011; Zhu 2012). In addition, the rising popularity of *Weibo*, a microblog similar to *Twitter*, facilitates the audiences' exposure to news topics that CCTV is sensitive to, such as corruption or environmental despoliation. Such emerging vectors of media consumption suggest that private, provincial media in China are capable of challenging CCTV in economic as well as political terms and thus can erode the network's credibility and dominance.

These are some of the various signs that the Chinese media landscape has been transformed by neoliberal globalization, which, true to form in the cultural industries, trades on audiences' desires and manufactured needs. But even as consumer culture moved in full force to take up residence on the televisions, computer monitors, and mobile devices for a generation of Chinese citizens, these transformations have been closely related to state objectives, often in paradoxical fashion. In short, the increase in media's scope and accessibility is the result of the government's decentralization policies, which have essentially dictated that media commercialize since the state dramatically cut subsidies, forcing broadcasters to become self-reliant through advertising revenues (Curtin 2005; Huang 1994; Zhao 2000; Zhu 2012). And while the proliferation of private, competitive media is said to have facilitated the rise in higher standards for investigative reporting, which includes more coverage of environmental degradation, it has also made for what Tunstall (2008) describes as a media climate "aggressively capitalist in the pursuit of audiences and advertisers" (191).

The degree to which these trends encourage the world's largest population to aspire to consumer lifestyles does not bode well for China's environment, which is already highly stressed and degraded. But it does fit into a longer historical pattern of environmental practice, which has been colored by Taoism, Confucianism, Legalism, Buddhism, and Marxist-Leninist thought. Asian studies scholar Elizabeth Economy (2004) observes that while philosophically these traditions may be grounded in a healthy respect for the power and importance of nature, combined they have "hampered the development of modern scientific rationalism" and "[accorded] little value to some of the core elements of effective environmental governance: independent scientific inquiry, a transparent political system, and accountable leadership" (27). Within China's long history, more recent developments, including those described herewith, have exacerbated these tendencies. For instance, just a few years after Mao's death in 1976, Deng Xiaoping declared "To Get Rich Is Glorious," effectively shaking off the vestiges of the Cultural Revolution while advancing in the process a state-supported shift to the market, which encouraged more intense Promethean-hued exploitation of natural resources to enable economic growth. When these traditions and political shifts are understood in conjunction with the marketization of the Chinese cultural industries, the privileging of materially driven lifestyles, and the country's increasing appetite for fossil fuels, the possibility for a balance between commodity hunger and sustainable development in China looks bleak.

"We're all Order Prometheans now"

Environmental communication scholar Julia B. Corbett (2006, 92–93) asserts that there is "no other act—period—that communicates as much about your relationship with the environment as your consumption." The globally networked media landscapes I have described in this chapter make it clear that, despite their distinct evolutionary paths and deepening national and local cultural characteristics, most of the world's entertainment and information industries have become neoliberal institutions and systems in the service of the Promethean discourse. This begs underscoring because much of the recent scholarship in global media studies emphasizes cultural distinctiveness and peculiarities over what American anthropologist Clifford Geertz called "overlapping resemblances" (Kraidy and Murphy 2008). But by focusing on translocal overlaps and the webs of meaning that draw them together (for example, the ways in which the various media systems around the world have embraced a similar underlying celebration of material accumulation and expansion in the form of progress and self-satisfaction), a highly troubling vision of the media commons emerges. In fact, it is a nightmare scenario for those who see things from a Survivalist perspective, as what has surfaced are quite literally interlaced global systems that invite Earth's residents, borrowing from Hardin's metaphor of the commons, to "bring more cattle"—a call increasingly presented in culturally recognizable and thus attractive packages.

Consider, for instance, how, despite its diverse cultural encasements, the structural changes described in the previous sections moved media systems around the world from relative isolation to a more globally interconnected (overlapped) and homogenous landscape of media industries operating on the principles of profit and private ownership. Television in particular bears witness to this paradox of change, as neoliberal globalization encouraged the tendency toward imitation and standardization in concert with cultural hybridization—a development that has perhaps been most visible in the trade of television formats and the "localization" of programming. Programs like *Who Wants to Be a Millionaire?* and *America Idol*, it turns out, could easily be adjusted by domestic programmers to suit local tastes and aesthetic judgments, and thus these shows have been big business around the globe since the early 2000s (Darling-Wolf 2015; Moran 2009; Waisbord 2004). This is not just a matter of "giving people what they want" in cultural clothing they understand but rather is a salient reminder that, despite the diversity and difference in the various systems described above, the commercial imperative is what drives content creation within contemporary global media systems.

As Waisbord (2004) has pointed out, the trade in "pie and crust" formats and the strategies that inform them reveal the growing homogenization of the professional sensibilities of television executives worldwide, cultivated through exchanges of "what works and what doesn't" through annual trade shows, industry trade publications, and other professional exchanges. The creeping normalization of adjustable commercial television models that celebrate competition and choice has become evident even in public broadcasting, as witnessed in the BBC and even China's CCTV, as the logic of the market and audience shares became the necessary terrain through which public TV program development has been elaborated (Waisbord 2004; Chen 2012). These become defensive strategies, as format adaptations are not only open to audience tastes and easy to make, but they also offer production efficiency, minimize risk, maximize advertising, and meet national quotas—all important characteristics when subsidies are drying up and "public" entities are forced to cover their own costs or even generate a profit.

Ironically, within the shifts and shutters to market-based media models, programming formats, and the forces that shape them, the capacity of transnational media trade to look and act "local" and "national" has made neoliberal globalization all the more invisible to national audiences. This is largely because most media around the world now feel culturally rooted, as locally the defining aspects of, for instance, the pan-Arab *Star Academy* or Hunan TV's megahit *Super Girl*, were not so much the formulaic features of the talent competition or the elaborate sets, which are strikingly similar globally, but rather the distinct qualities found in local narratives, song, dance, fashion, contestants' backstories, and use of language, all of which give the shows their local "structure of feeling." This capacity of tapping into identifiable ingredients to make something look and feel "local" while being decidedly "global" allows audiences to embrace programming as their own, punctuating Lebanese media scholar Marwan Kraidy's (2005) assertion that cultural hybridity *is* the logic of late capitalism.

Clearly, this logic builds on the infusion of cultural rootedness and inscribed authenticity, an investment that obscures the overlapping resemblances, at the center of which is the promotion of the free market. From a global view, then, seeing the proverbial forest for the trees is difficult, as the structures and practices of the media systems permit the self-justification of the market either to go unnoticed or to be dismissed as merely one character-istic within the broader flow of representations and promotional activities. So, I am not surprised that we now find ourselves in a world populated by citi-zens—even in the poorest places on Earth—who have been nurtured by a diet of pro-growth, pro-business, pro–private-property, pro-consumption, and pro-pleasure lifestyle models that flow freely from a powerful Promethean-neoliberal confluence fueled by the notion that agency "is for everyone," as long as they are conceptualized as "economic actors" (Dryzek 2005, 59).

In industrialized nations with highly developed commercial media systems and sophisticated advertising industries, this has been performed primarily by appealing to the notion that consuming products leads to fuller lives and that individual identities can be enhanced through the lifestyles one adopts. In the context of looming climate change and mass species extinction, it is therefore ironic but certainly not surprising that fear in the commons is re-lated more to consumer angst and cultural identity than to environmental limits. Meanwhile, the position of the market as the locus of meaning in the Global South and former socialist nations has been become normative, a product of neoliberal globalization's presentation of consumption and the freedom to choose as markers of modern democratic societies.

What both the North and South seem to share is that the accumulation of material goods, experiences, and upscale lifestyles are articulated as in-herently democratic aspirations, as "choice" is an existential expression tied to civil liberties and social mobility. These connections are even present in China, where the market is a pathway to personal empowerment and sover-eignty (Ong 2006). So, despite being mediated by networks driven by business objectives rather than shared governance and accountability, the benefits of the systems now in place are communicated in relation to concepts such as freedom and individual expression because they appear open, responsive, and fruitful (Steger 2009).

In these ways, globally networked media systems are designed to cul-tivate market subjectivities anchored in a neoliberal worldview that em-phasizes individual agency and self-reliance while minimizing social issues like climate change, air pollution, or plastic waste as things to be attended to through smarter, more measured forms of consumption. This discourse tends to reify a highly nonresponsive, status quo, "we are working on it" eco-logical imagination that requires little from the citizen other than to think and act like a consumer adjusting what product or service he or she might select. Indeed, in the end, the media's transnational articulation of the Promethean discourses is not about failing to mobilize public opinion about environmental issues in particular directions, but rather how, as knowledge systems, the global commercial media complex slowly but constantly cultivates a dissolved, even distracted, relationship with the earth, expressed in largely individualistic and passive ways. Thus via its assumption of "more is better," the Promethean-neoliberal social order actually serves to condition an environmental consciousness that is, at best, ecologically ambivalent, as audiences are led to pursue non-invasive actionable solutions (for instance, recycling a once-used plastic bottle, replacing inefficient light bulbs or buying a car with an "eco-boost" engine) within the larger objective of living a more materially comfortable vision of life on Earth.

The following chapters explore the continuing power of the Promethean-neoliberal alignment in relation to competing Earth discourses, and how the media commons has been shaped by this discursive terrain.

3

Neo-Malthusian Entertainment

The Limits of Green TV

In the 1960s and 1970s the narrative of ecological collapse occupied a strong presence in commercial entertainment fare in the West. As explicated in chapter 1, drawing from Paul Ehrlich's *The Population Bomb* (1968), the Club of Rome's *The Limits of Growth* (1972), Rachel Carson's seminal *Silent Spring* (1962), and Garret Hardin's "The Tragedy of the Commons" (1968), in different ways film, television, and animation during this period became important discursive sites for the presentation of Survivalism's concern for the planet's carrying capacity. The dystopian tales of overcrowding, conflict over resources, environmental degradation, and mass extinction in these media also applied Cold War terminology to the anthropocene of unquenchable human needs that would "blow up" the commons (Heise 2008, 26). However, despite the emergence of some television programs and feature films with very powerful environmental messages in the 1980s and 1990s (*The Emerald Forest*, 1985; *FernGully: The Last Rainforest*, 1992; *Captain Planet and the Planeteers*, 1990–96), with the broad adoption of neoliberal policies in the West and elsewhere, market-based thinking that rejected protectionism soon eroded the place of scarcity and nature's demise in the public sphere, moving the Limits discourse from center stage to the periphery.

But Limits entertainment has certainly not disappeared wholly from view during the neoliberal age. On the contrary, despite its now secondary status, in some notable ways audiences continue to find themselves enmeshed in entertainment media with neo-Malthusian visions (Branston 2007; Cubitt 2005; Vacker 2012). Film continues to be a medium of choice for Survivalist storytellers as Western filmmakers have generated a seemingly endless supply of "zombie" movies like *28 Days Later* (2002), *Shaun of the Dead* (2004),

I am Legend (2007), *Zombieland* (2009), and *World War Z* (2013), where the
1970s Cold War anxieties of mass obliteration have been recast in the form
of pandemics, migration, militias, and uprising, digested and reproduced
in the form of virally reanimated "life" and the human communities that
must learn to survive in a new biohazardous world. Big-budget Hollywood
and non-Hollywood productions have also thematically coalesced around
end-of-Earth and "tipping point" scenarios, such as *The Day after Tomorrow*
(2004) and *The Road* (2009), as well as "nature's revenge" cinema like the
Korean film *The Host* (2006), the Australian-made ecotourism nightmare
Rogue (2007), and the beaver-zombie cult favorite, *Zombeaver* (2014). Also
of interest is the emergence of films that articulated alternative discourses
such as Environmental Justice and Ecofeminism, like *Erin Brockovich* (2000),
Children of Mean (2006), *District 9* (2009), *Avatar* (2009), *Even the Rain*
(2010), *Elysium* (2013), and *Snowpiercer* (2013), which in different ways recast "old school" Limits concerns like population growth and conflict over
resources as more explicitly tied to how power is exercised in relation to
class, ethnicity, immigration, and extractivism.

While acknowledging film's presentation of different Survivalist narratives,
its presence on the big screen pales in comparison to how the Limits and more
problem-solving-oriented discourses have taken up residence on cable and
public television. Within expanding networks of global media and the new
possibilities of cross-channel sharing and niche programming, environmental catastrophe, the fear of collapse, and eco-defense strategies have found a
platform like no other. This resurgence of Survivalist storylines along with
more progressive problem-solving fare in Western mediascapes are linked
to a number of converging forces. These range from the increased frequency
of climate-change-related experiences that directly touch people's lives (for
example, drought, wildfires, floods, invasive species) coupled with audiences'
consumption of media "extreme weather" coverage, such as the Indian Ocean
tsunami in 2004, Hurricane Katrina in 2005, "Superstorm" Sandy, and other
eco-disaster events (Leyda and Negra 2015), to contemporary concerns tied
to geopolitics (such as immigration, globalization, and pandemics). They are
also a response to the bestselling book *The World without Us* (Weisman 2007)
and the unexpected success of Al Gore's jeremiad *An Inconvenient Truth*
(2006) and the "tipping point" film, *The Day after Tomorrow* (2004)—works
that represented a touchstone moment in environmental communication
and a shift in popular discourse (Rust 2013). From these real-world events,
box-office surprises, and a bestseller, those in the media industries learned
that environmental catastrophe, the fear of human extinction, and indeed

climate change itself could draw big audiences, sparking an immediate increase in Survivalist-themed and green-hued popular culture.

Like film, cable and public television's investment in entertainment programming that explores the state of the commons has taken many forms. Genres include the robust generation of eco-horror "event" programming, post-apocalyptic dramatic series and "after-Earth" docudramas. Various versions of these kinds of programs have been produced by Animal Planet, the BBC, PBS, NatGeo, TNT, the Discovery Channel Network, SyFy, AMC, the History Channel and others in multiple languages, suggesting that there are sizable and diverse audiences around the globe for end-of-days TV. Also within this context of eco-curiosity, cable and public television have moved into newer discursive terrain, experimenting with the creation of more progressive, "greener" lifestyle programming by turning ecological crisis into an opportunity for direct human action. Much of this programming shares an affiliation with problem solving (for example, Democratic Pragmatism and Sustainable Development) and radical environmental Earth discourses (Environmental Justice, Ecofeminism) and thus has sought to push television beyond merely featuring various versions of the tragedy of the commons and into more action-oriented terrain.

Given the pervasiveness of this wide portfolio of Limits and problem-solving TV programming, this chapter explores the resurgence of Survivalism and more progressive discourses on cable and public TV and how it has introduced a new generation of media audiences to key Limits points of debate (such as human excess, resource exhaustion and conflict, environmental despoliation, overpopulation, pollution) through specific genres. I focus on identifying the discourse's defining characteristics and symbolic constructions through its content in relation to structural considerations within Western cable and public TV. In particular, this involves tracing two trajectories: "After Earth"/"Nature's Revenge"–themed programming and more pedagogically designed "Green lifestyle TV." The chapter concludes by arguing that the revised rendering of the Limits discourse shifts emphasis away from overpopulation and carrying capacity, primary concerns in the 1960s and 1970s, placing it instead on twenty-first-century threats (such as climate change, pandemics, migration, terrorism, and food security). We can chart this shift in how the revised version of Limits discourse has surfaced through the reoccurring presence of certain images (post-"weather event" landscapes, abandoned cities, refugees, zombies, mutant animals, return to wilderness, and so on), metaphors (apocalypse, tipping point, ecological footprint), and environmental antagonisms (health of the commons vs.

business-as-usual growth). However, as we will see, television's ability to translate the underlying concerns of a "new" Limits discourse and the possibilities of more problem-solving discourses (such as Sustainable Development and Green Radicalism) have been successful only at a superficial level as character driven eco-entertainment and event programming that provide little actionable information have thrived, while a more instructive eco-conscious toolkit approach of green lifestyle television has struggled to find a sustainable place onscreen.

After Earth, Nature's Revenge, and the Zombie Apocalypse

On July 12, 2013, the U.S. cable channel Syfy debuted *Sharknado*, a film featuring sharks that invade the streets of Los Angeles, hitching a ride into the urban landscape thanks to a megastorm caused by global warming. The sharks were apparently seeking revenge for human over-exploitation of the ocean's bounty, illustrated most vividly in an opening scene wherein greedy and wasteful shark-fin fishermen are consumed by a swarm of storm-charged sharks.

This was bad TV by design. Vulgar kitsch with over-the-top acting and B-list "where have they been" film and television stars, the made-for-cable movie was created to stir up a reaction. And it worked. *Sharknado* was reportedly the "most tweeted" program in the history of the cable channel and generated enough buzz on national television for the network to rerun the program a week later. The July 19 rerun actually posted notable tweets from the week earlier throughout the cablecast: "Based on the Twitter attention it got, SHARKNADO is our Arab Spring #sharknado," "Can't wait to see how @MSNBC & @FoxNews cover this developing #Sharknado story," and Hollywood actress Mia Farrow's oddly articulate "Omg omg OMG #sharknado." Ironically, on the East Coast the rebroadcast actually ran a post-hurricane-Sandy promotional commercial for New Jersey Shore tourism, titled "Stronger than the Storm" and featuring Governor Chris Christie. The images of a wasted boardwalk with a Ferris wheel swept to sea, sans sharks falling from the skies and swimming through sewers and in the streets, matched much of *Sharknado*'s introductory storm scene. This piece of nature's-revenge programming is noteworthy because it managed to package, superficially at least, anthropogenic impacts and fears of climate change into a Survivalist story that would catch the attention of audiences now adapted to "multiscreen viewing" (say, watching TV while also online with a laptop or mobile phone) and would amplify its effect via the power of social media.

In fact, the over-the-top *Sharknado* drew so much attention and became such an iconic product for the channel that SyFy owners Comcast-Universal green lighted *Sharknado 2* (2014), which unfolded in New York City, and *Sharknado 3: Oh Hell No!* (2015), which along with its staple of flying sharks managed product placement of the Comcast Xfinity logo, promoted trips to the Universal Orlando theme park, inserted cameos by snarky, disgraced, and bizarre political figures (Ann Coulter, Anthony Weiner, Michelle Bachman), showcased the *Today Show* team, included music by the Ramones, and delivered the role of a lifetime for David Hasselhoff.

But beyond its achievements and campy, self-aware excesses, it should be clear to even the casual fan of cable TV that *Sharknado* is not the lone enviro-calamity franchise in the cable universe, and that Gaia's revenge and even eco-parody have become regular fodder (Simpson 2010; Stewart and Clark 2011). In fact, one can make a very strong case that cable and to a lesser extent public television have become key vehicles for Survivalism and related Earth discourses to take root within the otherwise broader Promethean entertainment landscape conjured up by transnational Western media companies. Consider, for instance, that along with the *Sharknado* movies, the SyFy network has become home to a diverse range of post-apocalyptic (*12 Monkeys*, *Z-Nation*) and alien invasion series (Arthur C. Clarke's *Childhood's End*) and those that blend both (*Defiance*).

Other cable-delivered channels such as Animal Planet, the Discovery Network, AMC, and TNT have developed similar fare, featuring "after people" shows, nature's revenge, disaster-survival docudramas and zombie melodramas. One of the more extreme examples is that the Disney Company and A&E Networks jointly owned the History Channel, which is offered in various forms in the United States, Canada, Europe, Scandinavia, Australia, India, Latin America, Africa, and the Middle East. In terms of shear enthusiasm for the end-days storytelling, this channel has no peer, presenting its now annual "Armageddon Week" of programs with post-apocalyptic themes. The 2011 UK promo for the week began with a view of Earth from space with the sun slowly rising and Louis Armstrong gently singing "I see skies of blue and clouds of white. . . ." This lyrical, poetic vision of Earth from outer space is quickly interrupted by the planet exploding and a voice-over announcing, "This week the Earth is history. Armageddon Week. Coming soon." The promo provides a pretty good taste of things to come. For example, the History Channel's highly anticipated pre-Mayan end-of-the-world prophecy program lineup for Armageddon Week 2012 was composed of *Apocalypse Island, After Armageddon, Seven Signs of the Apocalypse, Life After People:*

Wrath of God, Life After People: Bodies Left, The Bible Code: Apocalypse and Beyond, Nostradamus Effect: 2012 Extinction, and of course a special titled the *Mayan Doomsday Prophesy*. These programs played on "scientific" interpretations of prophetic visions and biblical warnings that predict how wars, plagues, fires, floods, earthquakes, droughts, solar storms, and other natural and human-made events would lay the earth bare.

End-of-the-world programming such as *Countdown to Armageddon, The Nostradamus Effect*, and *Revelation: End of Days* is also offered during the History Channel's regular schedule, particularly on H2, its second-tier cable channel. These types of cross-channel arrangements are what allow A&E, Disney, NatGeo, AMC, and others to develop original fare while also migrating programs among channels and even networks when needed to better tap into specialized audiences (often along gender lines) and expand the range of the content. This marshaling of resources is also what permits companies like A&E and Disney to create and bundle enough programming to realize conceptual ideas like Armageddon Week. The result is a viewing schedule defined by empty, decaying cities and icons (Paris and the Eiffel Tower, London and Big Ben, St. Louis and the Gateway Arch, New York City and the Statue of Liberty, Sydney and its Amphitheatre) being reclaimed by wilderness, underscoring what Jeff Lewis (2012, viii–ix) has called the amplification of crisis and the "profoundly human capacity for harm" as reoccurring tropes in today's global media sphere. In different ways these series play on nature's ability to "self-regulate," building on James Lovelock's (2007) thesis that Earth is a living, dynamic interconnected system, which he termed "Gaia" (drawn from Greek mythology), and does not long suffer organisms that do it harm.

Public television providers have also gotten in on the Gaia's revenge action as even PBS and the BBC have portfolios of "after-Earth" docudramas and post-apocalyptic dramatic series. One of the more interesting of these was the BBC 2005 docudrama "End Day," which presents Earth's demise with five different endings, "each predicted by scientists." "What's the worst that could happen in just one day?" asks the promotion's voiceover. The answer, apparently, is a global pandemic starting in the United Kingdom, a meteor storm crashing to earth in Berlin, a giant tsunami hitting the U.S. East Coast, the explosion of a supervolcano in Yellowstone Park, or a particle accelerator experiment gone wrong that creates an Earth-devouring black hole. The stories (plural, as there are five versions) follow a particular morning in the life of Dr. R. Howell, a scientist who wakes up in a London hotel prior to a controversial experiment that he and his team are set to conduct that, according to the news program playing in the background, "could cause the destruction of the Earth." Each twelve-minute segment of the docudrama presents in *Groundhog Day*-like fashion the same morning but casts the events in five different ways to profile how each one of the different Earth-ending disasters might unfold. These various versions all present the experts and officials who address the public during the unfolding crises as reassuring figures under pressure who are ultimately misguided, however, as they have greatly underestimated the true force and impact of what's in store. In each scenario, television plays a significant role for how the day's events are framed and interpreted.

Earth-in-peril programming that is more explicitly scientific has also established a presence on cable and public television, such the 2013 docudrama *Earth Underwater*. The program uses post-Katrina New Orleans and urban sprawl in the tidal estuaries of Bangladesh to frame how rising seas caused by climate change will affect the earth, and builds credibility through interviews with geologists, paleontologists, climatologists, oceanographers, and population scientists, scenes interwoven with special-effects visions of cities like Manhattan, Miami, Paris, and London underwater. The program highlights what kind of sea defenses will need to be erected to save cities, such as seawalls, levies, dams, pumps, and other engineering marvels, and how their mammoth costs will make them conceivable only for the Global North. *Earth Underwater* focuses much attention on how population density and loss of arable land will combine to create a global catastrophe, especially in South Asia, where much food production and most population centers are located in low-lying, highly fertile deltas. Created by National Geographic for its cable channels and DVD sales, the program also appeared on the History Channel and BBC channels, revealing again how such fare can end up in front of so many different audiences.

While grounded in legitimate science, programs like *Earth Underwater* typically come sandwiched within programming schedules that are much less driven by facts, or at least facts that are based on actual science. Consider, for instance, how programs like Animal Planet's *Mermaids: The Body Found*, a faux documentary about the existence of a race of aquatic humanoids in our oceans, Discovery's *Megalondon: The New Evidence*, a show that investigates the continuing presence of a thought-to-be-extinct fifty-foot prehistoric shark in our seas, or NatGeo's *When Aliens Attack* (2001), a program that uses NASA, UN, and Pentagon intelligence to frame the forthcoming alien threat, all employ "real science" as a means to manufacture legitimacy. The selective use of quotes from prominent scientists (Stephen Hawking, for instance, in *When Aliens Attack*) or the simple invention of experts when the voices of real scientists are not easily appropriated (as is the case with *Megalondon*'s "marine biologist" Colin Drake) have become discursive sleights of hand in the toolkits for how these programs claim veracity and draw in audiences. While both Animal Planet and Discovery received a backlash of criticism for such shows, the strong ratings they produced resulted in the production of follow-up pieces (*Mermaids: The New Evidence* was reportedly Animal Planet's strongest show in 2013 ratings). Part of the concern voiced by critics, many of them actual scientists, was that most audience members would not easily shift from factual fare to the more fantastical programming since they are both presented as scientifically driven—a concern that caused the National Oceanic and Atmospheric Administration to issue a statement after Animal Planet aired *Mermaids* (titled "Are Mermaids Real?") that "no evidence of aquatic humanoids has ever been found."[1]

But as the success of the *Sharknado* and *Mermaids* franchises suggests, scientific accuracy isn't necessarily the barometer that cable executives use to make decisions about the development of audience-pleasing TV. Case in point is the plethora of zombie shows, which has become its own paradigm of cable television, even invading the screens of such venerable networks as the BBC (*In the Flesh*) and National Geographic (*The Truth Behind Zombies*). Of special interest to media scholars and parents of teens alike would be the BBC's *I Survived a Zombie Apocalypse*, a survival game show played out in a Scottish shopping center where "survivor" contestants have to avoid the undead and exposure to smartphones, since these are what caused the outbreak. Other notable programs in the zombie-like cable lexicon include TNT's *The Last Ship* (2014–16), which follows the story of the scientists and crew of the *USS Nathan James* in their attempt to save humanity by finding a cure for a global viral pandemic; SyFy's *Helix* (2014–15), another "outbreak" series that followed a team of bioresearchers as they try to contain a gene-altering virus tied to corporate bioweapon development and an island-based religious community; and the network-saving series *iZombie*, on the struggling CW, a show whose promotional materials bill it as the story of an "overachieving medical student [Liv Moore] who is determined to pass as a human despite being a zombie."

Easily the most successful zombie TV series to date has been AMC's *The Walking Dead*, which has won critical acclaim and scored exceptionally high Nielsen ratings during its first six years. In many ways, the program follows the "classic" zombie formula, in that the story begins "post-event" with the characters already enmeshed in a world of empty cities, abandoned highways, looting bands of survivors, militarized safe zones, and, of course, the scavenging, flesh-eating undead. The storyline unfolds via how the characters negotiate issues of power, conflict, membership, and decision making in a world where the official rule of law no longer exists. Their ability to figure out how to create a community is central to their very survival, especially as the undead are not the only enemies they contend with. The protagonists progressively learn that cooperation—working as a team—is a requisite for survival; they move from an urban area, where this is more challenging, to a rural setting, where setting up defenses is more easily achieved. But life in the country brings its own complications, not the least of which continues to be social organization, authority, and individual versus group interests in a time of anarchy. By season 5, the survivors, who have now established some normative practices for shared decision making, have settled in the town of Alexandria, a "safe zone" led by a former Ohio congresswoman. However, in order to stay in the fortified town, the newcomers must become part of a new community and thus negotiate a new set of social expectations and adhere to more restrictive, even draconian terms of governance in return for an ostensibly safer, more permanent harbor from the zombie hordes.

Though these programs may not seem explicitly "environmental," beyond the occasional overachieving med-school zombie, as a rule they do more than just flirt with Limits themes by evoking powerful questions pertaining to control of the commons. Here, issues of authority, expertise, group dynamics, collectivity, self-interest, security, and freedom loom large, which in fact are of far greater concern than "what happened." In his brilliant and funny short book *Theories of International Politics and Zombies*, Daniel W. Drezner (2011) observes that "the greatest variation in zombie narratives is their origin story: what caused the dead to reanimate and prey upon the living?" (24). While this is a diverting question, Drezner asserts that issues of security and anarchy instead take precedence, especially as zombie outbreaks quickly become global. "The structure of anarchy is so powerful that it eventually forces all states into roughly similar policy preferences—maximizing security" (34). This reaction might initially create opportunities for multilateral problem solving and temporary accords to protect the public good, but eventually cooperation breaks down—"a common theme that permeates the zombie canon" (37). Within this context international regimes implode while powerful states develop stronger plans, engage in some ethical and moral activities, but for the most part protect their own interests. Lesser states suffer, face population uprisings, and serve as perpetual incubation sites for the zombie plague. Zones that are geographically protected and/or that have less population density are initially less affected, which feeds the survivors' inclinations to preserve the areas as safe zones through isolationism and tribalization. Within the many preserved cells, the remaining humans have to learn how to cooperate as a matter of self-interest to survive in a zombi-fied world, but success in these situations hinges on how well members of the group negotiate issues of authority, voice, and the rights of the individual in relation to the community.

Based on these narrative threads, it is clear that zombie shows present a couple of key elements of Survivalism as well as those associated with Demo-cratic Pragmatism. First, Survivalism's metaphor of the "lifeboat" (Hardin, 1977) lurks not so silently within many of the scenarios put forth in a world plagued by zombies, where states, represented by centralized control and elite decision making, as seen on *The Last Ship* (and by seasons 5 and 6 of *The Walking Dead*), control who gets to enter and who is excluded from the zombie-free lifeboat, with richer nations or more established authorities calling the tune and selecting the passengers. Solutions to combat the out-break, or at least strategies for its containment, come from elite mandarins. Alternatively, cooperation built on self-interest at the local level, such as portrayed on *The Walking Dead*, produces citizen-based collective problem solving—a dynamic that resonates with Democratic Pragmatism in that most zombie cable narratives move progressively toward practices of governance (as opposed to government) elaborated through consultation and consensus building that depend on dialogue and deliberation. But, as *The Walking Dead* and other ghoulfare clearly demonstrate, stability is ephemeral, as conflict over resources in the commons always threatens to bring ruin to all. These frames project their own versions of environmental antagonisms as related to the commons, but are played out in terms tied to human-centered sur-vival and the treatment of social power in relation to nature's self-regulating capacity in the form of zombies.

When cable and public television's stream of crisis, doom, and nature's-revenge programming is considered together as a whole, it suggests that, with the exception of some of the more science-driven shows, the problem facing the commons is not too many people, as was the explicit concern with Ehrlich's *The Population Bomb* (1969) or even Garret Hardin's more resource focused "The Tragedy of the Commons" (1968), but rather what people have done to themselves and their natural world and—if they survive—how they are now going to respond to new conditions. In fact, one of the main turns in most stories of crisis, doom, and nature's revenge is that, despite humans' best efforts, cooperation breaks down in the commons. Thus pursuing the greatest public good in a post-event context becomes virtually impossible as competing groups are unable to sustain even temporary accords. As such, cable's neo-Malthusian landscape is one driven by questions of post-event adaptation and survival in relation to nature's capacity to "bite back" (Gaia's revenge in the form of plagues, weather events, meteors, volcanoes, and animals) and how to avoid extinction, not strategies for pre-tipping-point prevention.

Green Lifestyle TV

As if offering a complementary alternative to cable's menu of crisis and doom entertainment, cable and public television have also become, over the past two decades, the home of green lifestyle television shows. While maintaining an underlying focus on scarcity (Limits discourse), in many ways these programs present more "practical" renderings of the Limits discourse and in fact in some instances suggest a closer alignment with Democratic Pragmatism (cooperation, shared governance, equality) and Green Radicalism (the local, activism, empowerment). This genre of programming has sprung up in various parts of the world—particularly in the West, but, thanks to cable and satellite, also in much of the Global South. The narrative thread that binds the genre together is typically the question of ethical consumption tied to eco-conscious decision making. New Zealand environmental media scholar Geoffrey Craig (2010) asserts that these "emblematic texts" articulate an underlying critique of global capitalism and a general distrust of consumption, and "offer insights into emerging enactments of individual agency and civic culture, within the contexts of capitalistic commodity culture, that derive from the ethical and affective potential of contemporary lifestyles" (176). These defining qualities of the genre work against the grain of the Promethean discourse by setting up a number of lifestyle questions: How does one live a "sustainable" lifestyle within a throwaway consumer society? What choices does a person make to minimize his or her ecological footprint? More progressively, how can one live "off the grid"? Still more progressive are questions about how can one confront a system that does damage to the earth and its nonhuman inhabitants.

Green-lifestyles television has taken up these questions in various creative ways through identifiable subgenres, ranging from green travel shows, local "low food miles" organic culinary programs, eco-fashion, gardening programs, and other sustainability lifestyle fare. They also include *Big Brother*–type survival shows, where members of a team that have been thrown together to live in the wilderness (in a mountain cabin, in a rainforest, or on a deserted island) must use their wits to live off the land, and "eco-make over" programs that follow the transformation of families from "normal" consumers to eco-conscious actors. Some are even more confrontational, such as the eco-adventure program *Whale Wars*, which showcases the need—in fact the urgency—to take whatever steps are necessary, even breaking international law, to enact change.

As the scope and trajectories of these programs suggest, "being green" on TV runs the gamut of advocacy for rather status quo adjustments (such as environmentally motivated consumer decision making) to paradigm-shifting eco-activism. In the latter case, entertainment programs reflect the more radical and profound ecological change associated with Deep Ecology's emphasis on the rights of nonhuman life (which discursively falls within Green Radicalism). But at the core of what has been generally conceived of as green lifestyle television is an instructional purpose; that is, the texts serve as public pedagogy in that they are designed to teach audiences how to enact a gentler, more thoughtful relationship with the commons (Craig 2010). As such, at their best these programs may serve in the role of what critical theorist Richard Kahn (2010) calls "ecopedagogy" and thus have an explicitly transformative goal.

THE CASE OF DISCOVERY'S PLANET GREEN

Within the universe of green television, no network or channel moved more purposefully into a no-holds-barred embrace of "ecopedagogy TV" than the Discovery Channel Network. The place of Discovery in the presentation of Earth discourses globally is important because, though headquartered in the United States just outside Washington, D.C., it is truly a transnational television company with an extensive presence in global markets. Its Web site boasts that Discovery Networks International reaches "3 billion global cumulative viewers in more than 220 countries and territories" composed of "five regional operations covering all major cable and satellite markets, including: Asia-Pacific; Central & Eastern Europe, Middle East and Africa (CEEMEA); Latin America/U.S. Hispanic; Northern Europe; and Southern Europe . . . [with] regional headquarters in Singapore, Warsaw, Miami, London and Milan. . . . [It] employs an extensive localization strategy by offering customized schedules and programming in 45 languages worldwide."[2]

Established in the United States in 1985, Discovery slowly built its reputation through the delivery of nonfiction content, particularly the documentary genre. Early on, it relied on content acquired from domestic and international producers, such as PBS, the BBC, and National Geographic. But by the late 1980s, understanding that it needed to take even greater advantage of a liberalized regulatory environment to better establish its own brand, the network moved to a more mixed model, developing its own programming and broadening its portfolio of channels, which by 1998 stood at eleven in the United States. With this web of interests taking shape, Discovery, a commercial cable network, was able to directly challenge PBS, the American public broadcasting network that had traditionally been associated with factual entertainment and documentaries. In his extensive study of the Discovery Channel Network, Ole J. Mjos (2010) charts how the network deliberately pursued a "public service model" more typically associated with public television. This agenda was articulated directly by Discovery founder John Hendricks, who stated, "We must focus on empowerment. We must not simply give people more information. We must give them news they can use and tools to help them make the most out of their lives, make wise business or lifestyle choices and even to improve their health" (52). The public-service image quickly became a defining element of the Discovery brand, shaping many of its subsequent moves.

In more recent years in the United States, the company has taken even more aggressive measures to situate itself atop the world of nonfiction television. For instance, Discovery established a "first look" partnership with BBC Worldwide for the exclusive distribution of all BBC factual programming in the United States. The agreement was secured so that Discovery could hobble its competition (namely, NatGeo and later Disney Channel) on U.S. cable screens. It also permitted Discovery to rework programming for a national audience by, for example, revising scripts and changing narrators, as was the case when they replaced David Attenborough's voice with that of Sigourney Weaver's in the eleven-part series *Planet Earth* (2006) for the U.S. market. But perhaps even more important is that the agreement served both the BBC and Discovery, as the two factual media firms could co-produce high-budget "mega" programs such as *Planet Earth*, *Frozen Planet*, and *Walking with Dinosaurs* through their shared resources and funding, to be distributed globally and, in turn, lead to spinoffs and other related projects. *Planet Earth*, for instance, reportedly cost an astonishing £1 million *per hour* to produce—a burden that was shared by the BBC, Discovery, and Japan's NKH, with the understanding that each would hold the rights in different parts of the world (Mjos 2010, 92).

This "branded" model of factual blockbuster programming development and distribution became a central strategy for Discovery as well as the BBC, primarily because the networks were able to attract large audiences and the attention of the press while crafting images that positively resonated with audiences (Mjos 2010, 93). And while it worked extremely well to further situate Discovery in the United States, Mjos reports that it also animated the company's larger intent, which was to grow its international interests, Discovery Networks International, to overtake those in the United States in terms of profitability (33).

As its relationship with the BBC Worldwide suggests, Discovery pursued its expansion primarily through partnership building, horizontal integration, and content development capable of generating links and echoes within the brand. The creation of a global network of interests and agreements within various markets allowed Discovery to search for funding opportunities and build partnerships outside of its national territory while extending its range for a broader, more diverse set of global audiences. Through this networked strategy, the company works like a "global television publisher" by commissioning, acquiring, and investing in programming based on a business model that "resembles [that of] other global enterprises . . . such as Nike, whose sole business is to develop the enterprise's trademarks, logos, and rights" (Mjos 2010, 79).

To push its brand deeper into "green" content, in 2007 Discovery announced its plans "take green to the mainstream" through the creation of a new channel dedicated to green lifestyles, Discovery Planet Green. This decision was inspired not only by the public reaction to Al Gore's lecture-film *An Inconvenient Truth* (2006), but even more so because of the phenomenal success of *Planet Earth*. What really got Discovery's attention, according to a senior executive at Planet Green, was how the series became a "global televisual event," drawing audiences by the millions from around the world and generating unprecedented DVD sales and other merchandise for Discovery (personal communication, March 23, 2012). The creation of Planet Green was therefore a calculation to build on the emerging "green market" while taking advantage of Discovery's resources and partnerships and its brand identification with nature and the environment. This point was made clear through various Planet Green pre-launch press releases and Discovery executive announcements. In 2007 Discovery Channel Network chief executive David Zaslav said, "The Earth has been central to Discovery since John Hendricks first chose the planet to represent our brand. The goal of Discovery Planet Green is to use Discovery's worldwide credibility to be the most comprehensive and trusted global resource for celebrating, preserving and protecting the planet" (DiCamillo 2007). Planet Green president and general manager Eileen O'Neill offered, "It really came from a groundswell of interest in the green movement," because other environmental programming and nature networks "left people with grave concern but not a lot of [answers to] 'What do we do now?'" (Owen 2008).

As these voices suggest, Discovery saw an opportunity to capture an audience through a movement and also the chance to marshal its many existing "factual television" resources, partnerships, and related subgenres of "natural history," "science," and "wildlife" programming from Discovery Channel, The Learning Channel (TLC), Animal Planet, and Science Channel into a singular product that would enhance its overall brand. As former Discovery chief operating officer Peter Liguori bluntly put it during a 2014 lecture at Temple University, "Scale provides leverage—with cable operators, with local channels, with audiences—and gives opportunities to do innovative programming" (Sherman Lectures, October 6).

The network was also very ambitious in what it hoped to achieve on its own, investing more than $50 million into Planet Green via the creation of original programming and user resources for audiences, such as online accessible materials, interactive tools, and "how-to" resources. To assure that it was grounded in sound environmental science and information, Discovery sought out partnerships with The Nature Conservancy, Grist, and TreeHugger .com. These partnerships were deemed crucial to the new channel's public profile as well as the plans to make it more than just a site for interesting, eco-driven programming. To push this effort forward, after some initial conversations about having TreeHugger.com work with Planet Green in an advisory capacity, Discovery decided instead to buy the online eco-news source and information site and hire key members of its staff as advisors and executives. In April 2013 I interviewed a top ex-TreeHugger-turned-Planet-Green-executive, who said,

> Discovery basically bought TreeHugger because they had this channel [Discovery Home] that wasn't working very well and they decided that they wanted to make it into a "green channel." And we brought some credibility, some knowledge, some skills and some ability to promote to the market that would be interested in that channel. So that's how I came on board. The website wasn't even established. Our mission was to push "green into the mainstream," and that's what Discovery was interested in.

He indicated that the vision for a coordinated, multiplatform delivery model was introduced during the planning stages of Planet Green, noting that there was a lot of excitement surrounding the creation of Planet Green, its new lineup of programming, and what the channel could represent in terms of green thinking. The idea was that the programming could inspire people to transform their lives and that they could find additional, more action-oriented material on the Planet Green / TreeHugger Web site. But there was also the recognition that the programming still needed to fit into Discovery's broader brand identity and draw from its strengths:

> There was no confusion for them [Discovery]. It's not like we were trying to launch a new channel out of thin air and there was no credibility from a creative perspective or a business perspective. Everyone knew what Discovery was about and therefore Planet Green could ride that very sincerely and very honestly. Also, as big an investment as Discovery made into content, there was no way that you could fill a full schedule of green content. It would have required an astronomical number of new programs. So, Planet Green made use of a lot of already existing content available from the Discovery Channel family that lent itself to Planet Green—past shows, specials, other series and environmentally themed shows. So there were a lot of existing shows that Planet Green could draw on from the Discovery stables. (Personal communication, May 1, 2013)

The channel was officially launched on June 4, 2008. Its first new special series was called *Ten Ways to Save the Planet*, and much of the early lineup of programs focused on "green" strategies for homes, cars, cooking, technology, and innovation. One of the higher-profile programs was "green celebrity" Leonardo DiCaprio's *Greensburg*, a narration-free documentary series that followed the environmentally progressive, energy-efficient rebuilding of Greensburg, Kansas, a town devastated by a tornado on May 4, 2007. It was an eco-recovery series and was also developed for the Science Channel. Other original content included *Emeril Green*, a program hosted by celebrity Chef Emeril Lagasse and shot mostly on location at Whole Foods, which instructed people on how to cook using sustainable, local organic food to promote a healthier lifestyle; *Focus Earth with Bob Woodruff*, hosted by ABC News anchor Bob Woodruff and billed as the "one-stop destination" for environmental impact stories (for example, climate issues and events, environmental policy, eco-news from around the world, environmental heroes); *Renovation Nation*, an on-location program that followed green restoration stories such as historic preservation in New Orleans, the Army's "greening" of a fort in Hawaii, or a family's insulation efforts in Boston, with green renovation solutions for homeowners and businesses posted online at PlanetGreen .com; and *Wa$ted!*—a series that examined how, in a three-week period, the average American home can go on a "green regime," to be changed from a "household full of eco-horrors" to a "clean, green haven, saving participants serious cash in the process" ("Planet Green Announces" 2009). To fill things out, the early lineup also included "encore" presentations of shows from Animal Planet, such as "green" episodes of *Dirty Jobs* and *American Chopper* (Kaufman 2007), as well as Planet Green weeklong specials, such as the Earth Day celebration "Turn Back the Temp: The Coolest Week on TV."

Following through with its multiplatform vision, each of the Planet Green shows had its own Web site with additional information about the program as well as a blog for fans and others to post comments and interact before, after, or even during an episode. Initially, this brought together Discovery fans and TreeHugger site users, creating a productive dynamic of exchange and dialogue. A member of the executive team remembered,

> People would see the sites and write in, often to discuss a green flaw in a show, as the audiences were very passionate about the content. And we had Tree-Hugger, so we were able to draw people to the Planet Green site. TreeHugger had a lot of knowledge content whereas Planet Green had a lot of "how to" content. A lot of that was to reflect back to the show content of Planet Green programs. (Personal communication, May 1, 2013)

Exciting as this was, it quickly became apparent that although the idea of a multiplatform green channel that provided post-weather-event recovery stories, green-dining shows, and ecological-footprint-reduction programming was "noble" (as one Discovery executive told me), it did not necessarily produce sizable audiences. In an effort to draw a larger audience, the channel continued to experiment with content by adding other notable shows, such as *TreeHugger TV*, *Planet Mechanics*, *Conviction Kitchen*, *The G Word*, *Gutted*, and *Living with Ed*. While several of these shows followed the "reality TV" format (*Living with Ed* and *Gutted* are two examples) and others more "how to" or informational (*The G Word* and *TreeHugger TV*, for example), the lineup of programs generally followed the same sorts of issues associated with early programming—namely, how to reduce, reuse, and live in a more environmentally sustainable way. In addition to utilizing these outsourced acquisitions, to fill up its time slots Discovery continued to recycle programs from its other channels, such as *Whale Wars*, *Blue Planet: Seas of Life*, *L.A. Ink*, *Lobster Wars*, *What Sank the Titanic*, and *Storm Chasers*.

By 2010 Planet Green added the reality show *The Fabulous Beekman Boys*, a program that was, in the words of a *New York Times* reviewer, "a gay 'Green Acres,'" that followed the adventures and mishaps of green gentleman farmers "Josh Kilmer-Purcell, a writer, advertising executive and former drag queen, and Brent Ridge, a physician and former 'vice president of healthy living' for Martha Stewart Living Omnimedia" (Hale 2010). By Planet Green standards, the show drew a sizeable audience along with a committed fan base, so the program was renewed for second year in 2011. However, in many respects *The Fabulous Beekman Boys* served as a barometer for changing ideas about programming for Planet Green. As one Discovery senior executive put it,

> We expanded with the idea that it could be about the environment, but it could also be a lot of other things—about nature, about business, about a whole broad range of things. It could be compelling. And you can have your characters. Like any extreme spectrum, you have your wild and woolly, eccentric, charismatic characters involved in the green movement. And those are the characters I wanted. I didn't want someone who was boring, dull and had no charisma. That's not going to rate on television. So we wanted shift our programming to great characters who are making change. That's how I like to think about it. And it didn't have to be about being green, but rather who embodied progressive ways of thinking. And that's a lot of what Discovery overall as a company believes in. It's about inspiring characters, inspired individuals who make us want to look at the world in a different way. (Personal communication, March 23, 2012)

As the shift to character-driven programming became more salient, the presence of informational "how to" content diminished significantly. Shows about reducing one's ecological footprint or a recovering commons were replaced with programs that just told a good story, programs markedly less "pedagogical." Given the commercial television industries' priorities, this was perhaps inevitable, as there was a sense that Planet Green's slot within the Discovery lineup was too valuable to the company to leave alone and just muddle along with a small audience. Since the channel reportedly was available to 60 million viewers in the United States but by 2011 was drawing only 76,000 viewers (ranking it seventy-sixth among all rated cable channels in the United States) (Schneider 2011; Seltzer 2012), they had to make a change. This translated into the introduction of less-green-hued and eventually not-green-at-all programming in the search for new potential audiences.

During this period of channel re-coloration, one of the more surprising moves was the partnership Planet Green developed that same year with General Motors in the form of the three-part documentary series, *Detroit in Overdrive*. According to a Planet Green press release, this series would be "the story of a diverse citizenry working together to overcome tremendous odds to rebuild their cherished Motor City—and create a 21st Century

Detroit" ("Planet Green Partners" 2011). Motivated in no small way by its desire to market its new electric car, the Volt, to an eco-conscious audience, General Motors added: "In addition to doing everything we can to support the city of Detroit, we also need to support the efforts to communicate the City's progress and positive stories. . . . Working with Planet Green, we are pleased to present this story about the great American spirit and the great stories behind the rebirth of this important American city" ("Planet Green Partners" 2011).

These content adjustments by Planet Green, the channel of *Emeril Green*, DiCaprio's *Greensburg*, and the more tongue-in-cheek *Hollywood Green*, were taken as signs of trouble by the entertainment press. Appropriating Kermit the Frog's famous tagline, *TV Guide* pithily reported, "It's not easy being green, as Discovery Communications has discovered," while quoting David Zaslav's message to investors: "We think we can probably do something else with that that would be more meaningful" (Schneider 2011). The *New York Times* entertainment reporter Brian Seltzer (2012) observed that while Planet Green had "turned a profit for Discovery each year since it was formed in 2008, . . . the company's executives have felt for a while now that the channel was a bust." While these observers were correct in their assessment, the channel was headed in a radically different direction: Destination America, a channel dedicated to American food culture and on-the-road adventure aimed at men ages twenty-five to fifty-four. In fact, even before the transition from Planet Green to Destination America was announced, the new channel's schedule had "already started to creep onto Planet Green's schedule, like 'BBQ Pitmasters,' which is an import from one of Discovery's other channels, TLC." "The channel will introduce 'Fast Food Mania,' an on-the-road show about comfort food, and 'Super-Duper Thrill Rides,' an hourlong series about roller coasters across the country" (Seltzer 2012). Seeing the end, the Mother Nature Network's Michael d'Estries (2012) wrote:

> Unfortunately, the ratings never really took off and with the exception of a few breakout hits (ie; "The Fabulous Beekman Boys"), the network struggled to provide content that would capture audiences while promoting a green message. Most recently, Planet Green has been dropping the eco-theme altogether with new shows such as "Midnight Snack" and "Suzilla: The Mouth That Roars," having nothing to do with the original focus. A release stated that the . . . two new programs "represent the first step in Planet Green's evolution, bridging its eco-centric roots into a destination for lifestyle and entertainment seekers." In other words, this is the beginning of the end for Discovery's big green experiment.

In the spring of 2012, Discovery's David Zaslav, the executive who originally pushed for the creation of the channel and pridefully announced its birth as a way for Discovery to use its "worldwide credibility . . . for celebrating, preserving and protecting the planet," (DiCamillo 2007) now announced, "We became convinced there was an opening there to build a channel based on middle America, strong values, behavior and customs" (Levin 2012). Hence the "rebranding" of Planet Green as Destination America, a channel stocked with programs that celebrated America's obsession with meat along with, evidently, hillbillies (*Hillbilly Blood*), wrestling (*Impact Wrestling*), ghosts (*Ghost Asylum* and *Ghost Stalker*), bigfoot (*Mountain Monsters* and *Killing Bigfoot*), and buying property in remote locations (*Buying Alaska* and *Buying the Bayou*). Discovery executive Henry Schleiff justified this new direction as a decision grounded in consumer research, indicating that "despite the existence of the Travel Channel and the Food Network," there was an audience for "programs about American travel and food," that "the format could be repeated in other countries, imagining a Destination Italy or a Destination United Kingdom" (Seltzer 2012).

From *Ten Ways to Save the Planet* to "America's obsession with meat," all in just under four years. The questions arise: What happened? Were shows about killing Bigfoot, chasing ghosts, and preparing meat really America's "destination"? Why was a channel that was so ambitious, so highly touted, so progressive in green vision and steeped multiplatform possibilities of eco-information delivery and exchange unable to survive? With its entire network of channels, partnerships, library of factual assets, and the leverage that this scale provided, if the Discovery Channel Network couldn't pull off such a vision, what network could?

According to some involved, Planet Green's failure may have been in its inability to take audiences to new places. By partnering with TreeHugger, it was assumed that an ecologically engaged audience would enthusiastically follow. But it was, perhaps more than anything else, programming "for the choir."

> The basic challenge was that, even if you're really into green you are not going to watch much green TV. And so what they were trying to do was to build the green and then try to get people to come to it. They were putting all of the green on this one channel and then trying to get people to come and watch it. And that's a really hard thing to do, no matter who you are. That's probably why we have not seen it be successful anywhere. Not that many people who are not interested in green are going to watch a green channel. So really your

market is greenies. And greenies maybe want to watch green stuff some of the time, you know, [but] they [also] want to watch *The Simpsons, Homeland, The Wire* . . . stuff just for relaxing. From time to time they might want to watch a documentary, but even if you are a hardcore greenie, most of the time when you sit down for TV is probably just to relax. So the better strategy is really to put green in the stuff where people are already going. You know, trying to integrate green into *Homeland*, into *The Simpsons*, into that stuff. You know people are already going there. (TreeHugger.com executive, personal communication, April 16, 2013)

One Planet Green executive shared that he thought Discovery learned what they already knew: that television needs to be entertaining, and this sort of science and technology has to be buried a little bit to make it interesting.

It either has to be buried behind beautiful visuals, like *Frozen Planet*, or it has to be buried within great stories. So, I often use the example of *Deadliest Catch*, the story of a crab fisherman in Alaska. People know a whole lot more about Alaska, the ocean, the weather, and geography of that part of the world because of this show. And that because those things are part of that show, but buried within the story telling. I think the same could be said of *Myth Busters* or other shows that are on Discovery. And I think that is what Discovery learned with Planet Green, that is the way to do it and that is what has worked in the past, that you can still get a message across while being true to the brand. Maybe it's just hard to do that in one dedicated channel. You need to appeal to other things, like their sense of nature, of fixing things, of adventure . . . other things than trying to appeal to their sense of green. (Discovery Digital executive and former TreeHugger.com executive, personal communication, May 1, 2013)

The Limits and Possibilities of Limits TV

So what does this mapping of Western cable and public TV's contemporary rendering of Survivalism and problem-solving Earth discourses tell us when zombies, vengeful sharks, and post-Earth scenarios make for more "sustainable" programming than a channel dedicated to environmental-stewardship fare featuring eco-conscious chefs, citified organic farmers, and off-the-grid families? If one accepts the in-the-trenches analysis from the staff at Planet Green and observations of the entertainment press, the failure in trying to "take green to the mainstream" was that it did not sufficiently anticipate the needs of the audience that the channel hoped to capture. That is, rather than taking a more engaging edutainment approach to eco-conscious living from the start, the channel made programming that basically preached to an already eco-conscious choir. And from an audience-share perspective the choir, as it turned out, was neither large enough nor mainstream enough to merit sustaining the "green" experiment within Discovery's portfolio of channels. Meanwhile, content like the kitschy cross-platform phenomenon *Sharknado*, the end-of-times viewing calendar event Armageddon Week, and the mega-hit *The Walking Dead* taught cable executives that, in different ways, death and survival before, during, and after the apocalypse have broad appeal and always seem to deliver an audience.

But regardless of how successful one might interpret these efforts to have or have not been in constituting an audience, it is clear that within the broader Promethean landscape of commercial media described in chapter 2, cable and public TV have become interesting barometers for Survivalism and other counter-discourses to take up residence within the public sphere and challenge the Promethean discourse's hegemonic status. However, in some important ways the challenges seem to ring hollow, as the cable-public formula points to what we might call the "limits" of commercial Limits TV and the inability for more progressive eco-conscious fare to gain traction.

This charge can be seen first and foremost in how the revised version of the Survivalism shifts emphasis away from overpopulation and carrying capacity, primary concerns in the 1960s and 1970s, and replaces it instead with the "anthropocene." This discursive recasting of a new geological age reshaped by human excesses is registered through a media combination of representations of post-event landscapes and Gaia's revenge. But instead of nuclear annihilation or crowded cities of starving people, the revised version of Limits is elaborated via the reoccurring iconography of empty cities, armed civilians, the highway of empty cars leading out of the city, zombies, vengeful or mutated animals, and urban posthuman wilderness. Beyond some lessons about postsurvivor rivalry, authority, conflict, and collectivity and what critical scholar Barry Vacker (2012) calls the preponderance of televisual models of "what nature will do after our disappearance" (110), the lessons for responding to ecological dilemmas are typically reactionary as opposed to anticipatory. Indeed, as the Planet Green case suggests, when commercial television has ventured into more progressive and anticipatory eco-conscious terrain, the results have not been good for capturing audiences. So the media-envisioned anthropocene has been defined largely by the prevalence of some metaphors (such as the apocalypse, tipping point,

lifeboat) with the faint resonance of others (ecological footprint or responsibility and sustainability in the commons, for instance).

What this archaeology of these enunciations tells us is that underlying
the discursive adjustment within television is the governing influence of the
market imperative—McChesney's (1999, 2004) "closed loop." That is, what
resonates with and draws in audiences within the media's already restricted
offerings comes to shape and define television's revised version of the Limits
discourse while those ideas and experiments that don't (eco-pedagogy, for
example) are relegated to the margins or even dropped altogether. As such, as
part of the broader global media sphere, cable and public TV provide a vision
of Survivalism that is compromised, and a conception of problem-solving
sustainability (Green Radicalism, Democratic Pragmatism) that comes and
goes, as all are pulled into and shaped by market logic.

These patterns recognized, it is apparent that Western "big media" entertainment television's ability to enunciate the underlying concerns of a revised
Limits discourse informed by the tragedy of the anthropocene as opposed
to the limits of growth has unfolded onscreen at only a superficial level. In
short, while perhaps smart and edgy (*Sharknado* notwithstanding), character-driven eco-entertainment and event programming that provide little
actionable information have thrived, while a more instructive eco-conscious
toolkit approach of green-lifestyle television—the stuff that articulates an
underlying critique of global capitalism—has largely failed.

Nevertheless, we should also take note of some of the important qualities
of cable and public television's revision of the Limits discourse, compromised
even as it may be. First, the Limits cablescape has offered openings for other,
more problem-solving and radical Earth discourses (for example, Democratic
Pragmatism and Green Radicalism) as some of the narratives in post-apocalyptic shows and reality series have shown (*The Walking Dead, Whale Wars*).
Second, while stories of doom, crisis, and nature's revenge may not provide
much by way of preventive strategies or actionable solutions for the planet's
ills, in many ways the cable and public TV programming described play the
role of ecological jeremiads. They are warnings, scenarios of what could be
and why we should be worried. In this way, while flawed, unchallenging,
and often even very silly (did audiences really need four *Sharknados*?), such
programs serve as important sites for conveying the message that there is a
need for social change in the commons. And if we don't make that change,
the message goes, then nature will for us.

4

Battle of the Blogosphere
Monsanto versus the World

The exercise of conditioning and privileging particular Earth discourses within the media commons is certainly not just the domain of powerful commercial media systems and their internal workings, as the elaboration of "corporate citizenship" has become embedded in the media commons by large corporations through their adoption of sophisticated communication strategies and new media platforms. Indeed, over the course of the past two decades corporate citizenship has come to occupy a central place in the cultivation of a brand identity for many corporations. Within this strategic projection of corporate self-regulation, the notion of environmental responsibility has become a key point of market positioning for big business, the result of growing consumer awareness about environmental problems and the perception that consumers want to support sustainable practices by selecting the products and services of eco-friendly companies (Cherian and Jacob 2012).

To capitalize on this turn toward green consumerism, many of the world's largest corporations have invested heavily in the elaboration of environmentally progressive profiles. For instance, to reduce its carbon footprint, Comcast, the planet's largest media conglomerate, has reportedly initiated such measures as recycling and reusing movie sets, experimenting with gas-saving stay-at-home e-commuting work schedules for its employees, promoting paperless billing, and implementing virtual (as opposed to physical) servers (Bushaus 2011). NBC Universal, Comcast's leading media company, launched an ad campaign during Earth Week 2012 called "One Small Act," linked to the Web site "Green Is Universal," featuring various television stars advocating eco-friendly practices and encouraging viewers to take the green pledge by changing a wasteful routine. Coca-Cola has worked hard to associate itself with sustainability, pointing to its role in protecting land rights for farmers in the developing world and its development of low-footprint "PlantBottle" technology in the United States and China. More visibly, its iconic polar bear Christmas advertising campaign was aligned with activism via a partnership with the World Wildlife Fund (WWF) to protect real polar bears and support other environmental initiatives. Google, perhaps the world's poster child of how to put your money where your mouth is when it comes to establishing a green corporate profile, has invested more than $1 billion in renewable energy, financing solar and wind power and actively looking for ways to create carbon-neutral data centers and efficient corporate campuses run on renewable energy (Carus 2013; Finley 2013; Knight 2009; Lacey 2013; Wang 2013).

For all of these global giants, information about these activities, their commitment to the environment, and assorted eco-accomplishments is readily available online through corporate Web sites linked to a stunning array of blogs, social media, videos, animation, journals, "webisodes," and the like, providing mission and vision statements, sustainability reports, overviews of environmental policies and practices, educational materials, and so forth. Though there is certainly variation, most efforts lean into the discourse of Ecological Modernization in that they project a sense that environmental challenges are in fact business challenges and thus can be overcome through coordinated interventions among motivated parties (industry, government, scientists, and citizens). But overall, most of the investment into green-hue-producing media operations is aimed at manufacturing a better "brand experience." For instance, Coca-Cola created separate pages for sustainability, water, and climate-protection activities on its Web site, but in 2013 the site's main attraction was a link to the animated short film, *The Polar Bears*, produced by noted British filmmaker Ridley Scott (Furrier 2013; O'Leary 2013).[1]

While laudable, these multiplatform-fueled efforts to go corporate green have not gone unchallenged. After receiving a cease-and-desist letter from ExxonMobil, Comcast pulled the satirical TV ad "Exxon Hates Your Children," scheduled to run in the United States prior to Obama's 2013 State of the Union address—an action that not only put the company's environmental commitment into question but also led to a petition by the activist group The Other 98% to run the commercial (Zara 2013b). Coca-Cola has been accused of greenwashing in Denmark for its misleading PlantBottle claims (Zara 2013a) and has come under scrutiny in India for its role in water shortages and contamination linked to its bottling operations (see "Case against

Coca-Cola"). And even Google, the corporate master of green, was admonished for its fundraising efforts in 2013 on the behalf of Oklahoma senator and climate-change denier James Mountain "Jim" Inhofe (Graves 2013; see Inhofe 2012).

The Case of Monsanto

These controversies expose fissures between moral positions, institutional practices, and brand building messages, presenting in stark relief the contradictory relationship between the business interests of these corporate "citizens" and the health of the global commons, revealing in the process the continuation of long-established "environmental antagonisms" (Cox 2013). While illustrative, the criticism that Comcast, Coke, Google, and others have tried to greenwash their way to an image of proactive environmental stewardship pales nevertheless in comparison to the sort of blowback that the U.S.-based multinational agricultural biotechnology corporation, Monsanto, has experienced. As one writer bluntly put it, "Monsanto is the agricultural world's prince of darkness, spreading its demonic genetically modified seeds in fields all over the earth. Or at least that's the case if you believe the likes of HBO talk-show host Bill Maher, the hazmat suit-wearing activists in Occupy Monsanto or any of a growing number of biotechnology haters" (Hopkinson 2013).

Keenly aware of its problematic international image but convinced of the value of—indeed, pressing need for—its visionary products' response to a world faced with massive population growth and global climate change, Monsanto has worked hard to re-brand itself as the global leader in sustainable agriculture. The company has operationalized this effort through a highly interlaced and responsive multiplatform media effort designed to project a corporate vision of sustainability and proactive environmentalism enabled through forward-thinking technological innovation. Monsanto elaborates its vision of sustainability through a blending of two core environmental discourses: the urgent and foreboding discourse of Survivalism coupled with the more entrepreneurial and innovative Promethean discourse. However, the firm also further complicates this articulation of environmental sustainability by selectively employing key terms from the problem-solving discourse of Sustainable Development (Dryzek 2005) as a means to provide cover for its Promethean moorings.

Monsanto has crafted this elaborate discursive structure as a sophisticated counter-position to those of its critics, who have largely employed discourses of Environmental Justice and Ecofeminism, along with elements of Democratic Pragmatism, to challenge the global giant's claims. In the next sections I map out the global range of these positions and then examine what kind of conceptualization of sustainability Monsanto privileges, how it is institutionally organized and projected through its media operations, and in whose interest.

Monsanto and Its Critics

According to its promotional materials, Monsanto is a chemical company turned food company. Though the company claims to be "new," its history actually dates back to 1901, when it was founded by John Francis Queeny, who gave the company his wife's maiden name. Monsanto's first product was saccharin, an artificial sweetener sold to the Coca-Cola Company, and by the 1920s the firm had established itself as one of the top ten industrial chemical companies of the United States. By the 1940s it expanded into plastics, and later its top products included aspartame (NutraSweet), PCBs, and dioxin—a toxic compound used in herbicides and, more infamously, in Agent Orange. During the course of the past quarter century, it has moved away from its chemical products and taken the lead in the commercialization of genetically modified (GM) seeds. Today, Monsanto largely controls the global market for row crops like corn, soybean, and cotton, while more recently moving into table fare such as tomatoes.

Proponents of GM seeds assert that they are a "gift to the developing world," designed to tackle world hunger and be a crucial response to the challenges of climate change (Reinhart 2008, 1), and the company credits its success to its commitment to scientific innovation and investment in technology, which allows it to take a global leadership role in producing "more food," "more security," and "a more stable, healthy, and prosperous future for everyone" (Monsanto 2011, 6). But despite the growth and widespread adoption of GM crops around the world, the public perception of agricultural biotechnology's engineering of drought- and insect-resistant seeds for feeding Earth's growing population is often more cautious than it is hopeful. In fact, GM opponents regard the technology as a form of "biological perversion" already eroding the planet's genetic diversity, with corporations playing the role of god (Reinhart 2008, 1), and Monsanto's critics hold a far less charitable view of the company's practices, asserting that its "success" is based on manipulative lobbying, meddling in policy, an aggressive legal department, media censorship, and "bio-piracy" (Frayssinet 2013; Mengel 2011; Pain 2013; Pollan 2006, 2008; Pringle 2003; Shiva 2000, 2004, 2013; Stock 2011; Warwick 1999).

These charges have been articulated in different ways by various parties, but much of the criticism toward Monsanto stems from the company's past development of chemical and synthetic products, like DDT, Agent Orange, rBGH, and aspartame, as well as one of its current core products, Roundup, a weed-control herbicide sold at home-improvement retail stores like Lowe's and Home Depot but that more notoriously was used in Plan Colombia as part of the U.S. "War on Drugs." More recently, Monsanto was the focus of the widely circulated *The World According to Monsanto*, a 2008 investigative documentary by French journalist Marie-Monique Robin. The film, which was translated into sixteen languages, detailed Monsanto's malpractice involving the development and defense of dioxin, PCBs, and bovine growth hormones, and provided a highly troubling case study of environmental racism in Anniston, Alabama, for which the company was directly responsible. The film's critique is grounded in the discourse of Environmental Justice via its rendering of key terms, tropes, and motives, which include toxic waste and dumping (NIMBY[2]), issues of risk and health tied to racial marginalization, and community and human rights.

Other, more sustained attacks on the company's current practices have come from higher-profile activists and image-defining events. For example, one of Monsanto's sharpest critics is food-movement guru Michael Pollan, author of *In Defense of Food*, *The Omnivore's Dilemma*, and *The Botany of Desire*. Through these books, related essays, and public lectures, Pollan has examined the ecological interrelationships between human societies and food systems. Much of his work has interrogated the imperatives of the food industries, tracing everything from the links among SUVs, ethanol production, and global food shortages to the consociation of GMO farming with the rise of meat consumption in China and India. Of course, residing within much of what Pollan writes and says, sometimes with exacting purpose but more often as implicit critique, is an unfavorable assessment of Monsanto's activities. For example, in a 2009 interview with Amy Goodman on the independent news program *Democracy Now*, Pollan plainly offered:

> Monsanto is very much on the attack right now, pushing its products, particularly in Africa, and making the case that the most sustainable agriculture will be intensive production on the land base we have. The argument is that there's only so much arable land in the world, we have ten billion people on the way, and that the only way to feed them is to get more productivity over the land we

have, to further intensify agriculture, using their genetically modified seeds. And the word "sustainable" is never far from their lips. (Goodman 2009)

Interestingly, in 2008 Pollan presented a more muted but no less critical perspective while participating in "Body 2.0: Creating a World that Can Feed Itself," a panel hosted by Google.org and featuring Monsanto CEO Hugh Grant. The exchange between the two, which was reserved and polite, revolved around changes in global food consumption and increasing food yields. But whereas Grant trained his focus on technology transfer (for example, between corporations and village farmers in India), Pollan argued that food problem solving needed to follow the Green Revolution's example of making "everything public" (transparent) to make an "honest assessment," where profit doesn't guide the conversation or decision making about sustainable food-production practices.[3]

In addition to these concerns, the purported superiority of GMO crops has raised doubts about the ideological nature of the science, particularly in terms of how the environmental narratives tied to that science negatively position people whose livelihoods rely on natural resources (Pearson 2006). This contentious debate has special resonance in India, where, according to the Center for Human Rights and Global Justice at the New York University School of Law, Monsanto's practices have been linked to "the largest wave of recorded suicides in human history" (Pain 2013). Critics claim that peasant farmers fell victim to Monsanto's aggressive marketing tactics, which promised increased yields and the road to better earnings, but delivered instead a vicious cycle of crop failure, forced debt, and mass suicide. However, others, such as Canada's conservative newspaper the *National Post*, have asserted that "the GM genocide" narrative is a "myth," noting that the rise of suicides among farmers was not the fault of GMO seeds, as cotton yields actually grew, and pesticide use decreased by nearly 40 percent (Abid 2013). Related to these ethical concerns are some of the more troubling charges, which include the assertion that GMO companies invest in crops like corn, soy, alfalfa, and canola because of the potential of these crops to be "contaminated" by wind pollination. That is, non-GMO plots of a particular crop will sooner or later be contaminated by the surrounding transgenetic plots, at which point Monsanto, asserting its ownership and as a means to protect its patents, can institute legal proceedings against those farmers who have not contracted to use its seeds. Along these lines if one follows the logic of a Monsanto contract, the seeds are not in fact purchased but rather "leased," in that they cannot be stored and used in the following planting season—a point that Pollan raised in *The Omnivore's Dilemma*.

Perhaps the company's most ardent critics have been those associated with antiglobalization movement. Foremost within these ranks is India's indigenous seed defender, eco-feminist and Nobel Peace Prize winner Vandana Shiva. Evoking Gandhi, Shiva has called for a "seed Satyagraha" of noncooperation in reaction to Monsanto's attempt to commoditize seeds through patents and global seed laws. At the center of her call is the notion of "seed sovereignty," which she asserts is essential, since the seed is the primary link in the food chain and so directly tied to farmers' rights, biodiversity, and the public good (Shiva 2005, 2013). This fight against genetic food engineering is animated by a broader political movement for peace, justice and sustainability, which she calls "Earth Democracy," a critical-action-based response against the "ownership society" privileged by corporate globalization and its media agents. Shiva argues instead for a return to a view of the planet as a commons that requires cultural knowledge, historical memory, dialogue, inclusion, diverse practices, and reciprocity if people are to realize peace and live with dignity (Shiva 2005)—ideas at the heart of Ecofeminism. For her, the future of the seed is therefore a matter that potentially threatens not only the future of food but also the future of democracy in an increasingly interconnected yet alarmingly disparate world.

This sense that control over seeds is a battle between self-organization and external power is progressively surfacing in many places around the world. For instance, in Mexico, the birthplace of maize and where native seed is a matter of cultural heritage and indigenous identity, there has been an explosion of anti-GMO activity in the past few years. At the grassroots level this has included efforts to establish seed banks, but the country has also witnessed an increase in cooperation between global and national NGOs, such as the *Sin Maíz No Hay País* movement ("without corn there is no country"), which has organized demonstrations and high-impact activities (Acedo 2013). On May 25, 2012, the street festival "Carnival of Corn" was held in Mexico City as a defense of native maize and as a show of resistance against the encroaching political influence of biotech companies like Pioneer, Syngenta, Dow, and especially Monsanto. Organized by young people, environmental organizations, and artists, the festival was planned as part of a worldwide "Occupy Monsanto" protest against President Obama's signing of "The Monsanto Protection Act" earlier that month. According to Alfredo Acedo, director of communication for the National Union of Regional Organizations of Autonomous Small Farmers in Mexico, participants created a "festive atmosphere, with drummers and street theater, music, performance and dance" and chanted "Queremos frijoles, queremos maíz, queremos a

Monsanto fuera del país" (We want beans, we want corn, we want Monsanto out of our country). To mobilize people through social media, they also created #FueraMonsanto (#MonsantoOut), the festival's most popular hash tag (Acedo 2013).

These examples of seed saving in India, the culture of corn in Mexico, middle-class food politics, and racialized environmental consciousness in the American South all call for resistance in some form or another. These calls are animated by questions of risk, the wisdom of the Earth, of cultural memory, of the Earth's own agency, of collective action, shared governance, equality, and voice. As such, they suggest that in different ways the capacity of counter discourses to articulate opposition, most prominently Ecofeminism (India's seed Satyagraha), Environmental Justice (communities of color in Alabama), and Democratic Pragmatism (Pollan and others), and a mixture of Green Radicalism and Democratic Pragmatism (Mexico's Occupy Monsanto).

Mexico's movement has been effective, as it has inspired the Mexican courts to block the cultivation of GMO soy in the states of Campeche and Yucatán and to uphold a countrywide ban on the planting of GMO corn (Chow 2015). But these battles are not always clear, nor do they necessarily produce thoughtful outcomes. One of the more vivid illustrations of how Monsanto's image as corporate environmental evildoer has led to confusion in what occurred in Haiti on June 4, 2010, when, in observance of World Environmental Day, approximately ten thousand peasant farmers reportedly took over four hundred tons of corn and tomato seeds and burned them all while chanting, "Long live the native maize seed!" (Stock 2011; see also Urfie 2010). The bold collective action was designed to send a message to Monsanto, which had donated the seeds to replenish the stocks of rural farmers who, after the catastrophic earthquake just some five months earlier, had exhausted their seed reserves feeding refugees. The spokesperson for Haiti's National Peasant Movement of the Congress of Papay called Monsanto's donation "a very strong attack on small agriculture, on farmers, on biodiversity, on Creole seeds . . ., and on what is left [of] our environment in Haiti" (Bell 2010). The response to Monsanto's donation was even harsher in the blog *Global Research*, through which writer Fr. Jean-Yves Urfie pithily asserted that the earthquake had been a "lucky business break for some," and that the "deadly gift of 475 tonnes of genetically modified (GM) seeds" had been provided by the same company that "made the 'Agent Orange' defoliant sprayed over Vietnam by US planes during the war there, poisoning both US soldiers and Vietnamese citizens" (Urfie 2010). Monsanto was quick to shoot back, challenging through its own blog the accuracy of such reports (Monsanto 2010a). Of central purpose for Monsanto was to make the points that first, what it donated was not GMO but rather hybrid seeds; second, that the donation was made to assist farmers in a time of need with seeds they could use to feed themselves—cabbage, carrot, melon, eggplant, onion, tomato, watermelon and spinach; and third, that the donation was administrated through the USAID-funded WINNER program, which controlled the distribution of seeds through Haitian farmer associations.

The way in which Monsanto's Haitian seed donation and the subsequent seed burning protest echoed throughout the blogosphere makes salient the passion and range of global anti-GMO proponents alongside Monsanto's own attempt to add its "voice" to the landscape of competing narratives, discursive frames, and the battle to control the "truth" about genetically modified seeds. But to get a fuller sense of how Monsanto's interests and activities have been interpreted around the world, one need only conduct a quick internet search using any combination of keywords such as "seeds," "GMO," or "food" with "Monsanto." The result yields a very telling mix of links to documentaries, interviews, reports, essays, videos, and specialized blogs. One of the most prominent of these is the "March against Monsanto" Web site,[4] a "global movement against Monsanto" available in five languages, with its accompanying links to a Facebook page, a Twitter account, and host of related media (Van Hook and Nagler 2013). Other randomly selected examples include the 2012 film, *The Seeds of Death: Unveiling the Lies of GMOs*, blog articles such as "Evil Monsanto Aggressively Sues Farmers for Saving Seeds,"[5] the 2013 public television documentary *Bitter Seeds*,[6] links to *Harvesting Justice: A Food Sovereignty Publication and Blog Series*,[7] the *Vanity Fair* expose "Monsanto's Harvest of Fear,"[8] articles in *The Guardian, Al Jazeera English*, and *India Today*, reports from *GM Watch*, the comic animated short "GMO-A-Go-Go,"[9] anti-GMO media alerts by the Panos Institute, and various takes on the "naked protestors" who objected to Bartle Bogle Hegarty's 1998 "life sciences" advertising campaign for Monsanto in the United Kingdom by holding a rooftop demonstration at the company's headquarters in Soho.[10] Even YouTube clips from Comedy Central's faux news program *The Daily Show with Jon Stewart* are available and have provided a comic "investigative" reframing of "Monsanto's heroic patent attorneys'" battle against "greedy farmers."[11]

While this is just a short list of English-language, Web-accessible responses aimed at Monsanto, it gives a fuller sense of the scope of the conversation in the blogosphere and how it has involved a broad collection of stakeholders ranging from watchdog groups and organic farmers to experts from the academy and industry. And as evidenced by the laundry list of image-defining controversies and unremitting interrogation on multiple fronts, the company continues to be seen as more Frankenseed than Johnny Appleseed, and one would be hard pressed to find another corporation that has become as contested and consistently vilified around the world as Monsanto. In fact, a Web search combining "evil" and "Monsanto" generates more than five million hits alone—and presents the stunning revelation that Monsanto was the winner of the 2013 "most evil corporation in the world" (an unwelcome prize, one would guess), easily beating out rivals BP, Halliburton, McDonald's, and Walmart by wide margins.[12]

Remaking Monsanto

To appear less like a lumbering monstrosity, feared and chased by the peasants of the global village for reasons ranging from charges of environmental injustice and bio-prospecting to being a merchant of a biological Pandora's box, the company has work hard to craft a new public image as a sustainable food producer. Monsanto actually began to pursue this path in earnest in the mid-1990s. According to Robert B. Shapiro, Monsanto's chairman and CEO from 1995 to 2000, the biotech company had a long history of considering environmental issues in its economic, technological, and competitive planning, but it wasn't until 1994, when an offsite meeting of a group of twenty-five "critical thinkers" led to a more deliberate focus on sustainable development (Magretta 1997). The embrace of sustainability created the opportunity for Monsanto to attempt to exorcize its ghosts, with the "original" industrial chemical and pharmaceutical Monsanto spinning off in 2000 to merge with Pfizer and Solutia to become "Pharmacia Corporation."[13] Through this reformation of the company, the agricultural and biotech assets, operations, and liabilities were transferred to the "new" Monsanto, which now concentrated on the development of hybrid corn and other row crops, along with its keystone product, Roundup herbicide. From 2008 through 2012, Monsanto's image makers made the decision to promote the company as a "new" "food company" dedicated to producing seed for farmers. That tagline has been subsequently revised, and Monsanto now defines itself as a "sustainable agricultural company" committed to meeting the "needs of a growing population, to protect and preserve the planet we all call home, and to help improve lives everywhere."[14] While the terminology has been adjusted over the past few years, and these semantic modifications will likely continue, the aim remains the same: recasting the company as a progressive problem solver serving humanity through biotechnology, while distancing itself from the "old" and controversial chemical company from days of yore.

Given the company's past product line, this is no small task and therefore perhaps no surprise that the new, sustainability-driven Monsanto has invested heavily in elaborating a sophisticated, interlaced media network to help re-shape its image. Like Coca-Cola, Comcast, and Google, information about Monsanto's activities and commitment to the environment is available online through a multiplatform universe of blogs, social media, videos, journals, "webisodes," and so forth. And like similar strategies of large corporations using media to reach out to its imagined publics, the Monsanto mediascape includes mission and vision statements, sustainability reports, educational materials, and overviews of environmental policies and practices. However, what separates Monsanto from most other companies attempting to attach their brand identity to environmental responsibility is that Monsanto's challenge isn't just about grafting its image onto progressive ecological activities; rather, they seek to establish a credible narrative that *what it actually makes is not only environmentally responsive but vital for a planet in crisis*. As I show in the rest of this chapter, Monsanto has done this by drawing heavily from the Limits discourse as well as the more problem-solving-centered Sustainable Development discourse to set up a Promethean solution.

Multiplatform Sustainability

Monsanto has performed its image-shaping project online through a truly impressive array of linked and networked Web pages, blogs, social media, YouTube videos, and other media-content sites. For instance, to get a sense of scope of the company's effort and how one might encounter it, in 2014 I conducted a common Google search of "Monsanto." This led me to the top selection, "Monsanto: A Sustainable Agricultural Company." The subtitle more than hints at what's in store. A click on this link, and the Monsanto Web site welcomes the visitor with a rotating panel of agro-imagery and exciting announcements: "Fighting Rural Hunger," "Monsanto Named One of the World's Best Multinational Workplaces," "Dr. Robb Fraley: 2013 World Food Prize Laureate," "Full-Scale Launch in Brazil: INTACA RR2 Pro." Selecting any of these panels leads to a separate page detailing the story. But to get a better sense of how the company's media operation is organized in relation to its mission, the "Who We Are" subhead at the top of the homepage is per-haps most revealing. A click on this title leads the site visitor to "Monsanto at a Glance," complete with a short video ("Monsanto Company: Committed to Sustainable Agriculture"). The video and other options within the "Who We Are" page of the Web site are designed to project the company's mission statement, instantiating an ethical code of conduct and standard of practice. The mission itself, which the company calls the "sustainable yield initiative," is founded on the motto "Producing More, Conserving More, and Improving Lives." The Web site presents and explicates this tripartite mission through an interlinked "rolling" interface to navigate through and clarify the company's guiding principles; users can access the material through either the "Improving Agriculture" or "Who We Are" pages within the site. Presented as "solutions," the parts of the motto's text read as follows:

> The Solution: Producing More. We are working to *double yields in our core crops* by 2030. These yield gains will come from a combination of advanced breeding, biotechnology, and improved farm-management practices.
>
> The Solution: Conserving More. We've strengthened our goal of doubling crop yields by committing to do it with *one-third fewer resources* such as land, water and energy per unit produced.
>
> The Solution: Improving Lives. We've been working to help famers achieve big increases in yield and productivity. And for all the world's farmers who raise themselves from poverty to prosperity, many more people will prosper.

While seemingly superficial, such statements are in fact extremely important sites for discourse analysis because they are powerful "carriers of the culture, ethos and ideology" (Swales and Rogers 1995, 226) of a given corporation, exposing the relationship between its historical vision, leadership, and communication in ways that make enunciations identifiable. Often penned by the CEO or other high-level executives, mission statements provide not only an indication of an "embedded social process" that reveals the intrinsic links between management and communication (they both shape and reflect organizational culture), but also, according to Swales and Rogers, how the company fosters employee "buy in" while communicating a corporate ethos to an external audience. Key characteristics of mission statements are that they tend to emphasize "*positive* behavior and guiding principals within the framework of the corporation's *announced* belief system and ideology" (227, emphasis in the original).

In such a way, Monsanto's mission—"Producing More. Conserving More. Improving Lives."—presents a textbook study of the links and practices outlined by Swales and Rogers. Indeed, until 2013 the statement was followed by "That's sustainable agriculture. And that's what Monsanto is about"—a subhead that provided a strong indicator that a process of ideological articulation was at work. The mission here isn't just about better crop yields, it's about finding better, more productive ways to serve a changing planet through a corporate vision. An earlier video (posted on the "Who We Are" page from 2009 through 2012) was somewhat more poetic in its rendering of this mission: "Feel the planet move beneath you. What you're feeling is a living planet; what you're feeling is our home." Then followed the reminder, "But the planet feels us, too. It feels the increasing weight of us, and the stress of supporting that weight." The video went on to describe the scope of the challenge and Monsanto's role in responding to it:

> Stand in the congested streets of a developing country and you'll see millions of people struggling to feed themselves. Stand in the Amazon or the Arctic and you'll see ancient rainforests and majestic shelves of ice disappearing. And stand in one of the many isolated villages around the world, and you'll see farmers with little access to technology or markets, unable to pull themselves out of poverty. These global challenges are complex, and there are no easy answers. But one thing is clear: Agricultural innovation holds a key solution. And we pledge to do our part.

The last minute of the video provided a montage of images of full green fields, rich yields of corn, cotton, and soybean, and contented, productive farmers from around the globe. Within this segment, the video's musical bed became more upbeat, and the narrator's voice shifted ever so subtly to a more optimistic tone:

> We are Monsanto, and we are working with farmers and partners worldwide to realize a vision for sustainable agriculture. It's a vision that strives to meet the needs of a rapidly growing population, to protect and preserve this planet we all call home, and to help improve lives everywhere. We are working with farmers to increase what they can grow on an acre of land, and we are making great progress. We are working to reduce the amount of land, water, and energy they'll need to grow those crops. And we are working to improve lives in the process. . . . Agriculture has always had a role in shaping the future of humanity, and we know it will take more than one company to shape the future of agriculture. So whatever the world looks like where you stand, the truth is, we are all in this together. And we believe, working together, we can create a brighter, sustainable world for all of us. That's the world we visualize at Monsanto, and we are working every day to make it reality."

The expository, voice-of-god narration and accompanying visuals that guided the viewer through this now-removed[15] video of Monsanto's vision for agro-sustainability relied on the tried-and-true advertising tropes of na-ture as backdrop, nature as product, and nature as outcome. Corbett (2006) explains that these frames are deployed by marketers to "green" their prod-ucts by associating them with sublime natural settings, a connection to the earth, and an eco-friendly footprint, respectively. Automakers and cereal companies, for instance, regularly employ such tactics in their advertise-ments, but typically just one, or perhaps two (for example, an SUV driving through a remote, forested road, or hiker enjoying a granola bar on a sunny mountaintop). But in its storytelling Monsanto manages to deftly squeeze all three frames into one short video by using backdrops of sun-drenched cornfields, working hands sensually sorting seeds, and farmers proudly dis-playing the bounty of their ("sustainably produced") harvest. These visuals are in turn framed by the rather sobering assertion, located just above the large "The Challenge" text on the "Who We Are" page, which reads, "Bil-lions of people depend upon what famers do. And so will billions more. In the next few decades, farmers will have to grow as much food as they have in the past 10,000 years—combined."

Interestingly, the more recent version of the Web site video, sans subheads, now relies primarily on the video to articulate the connection to nature via the soft fading in and out of instructive text, losing the gentle yet paternal voice-of-god storyteller. The newer presentation also celebrates Monsanto's achievements to a greater extent by focusing more deliberately on produc-tivity. But whether interpreting the older or newer versions of the "Who We Are" video, thematically the points of action—Producing More, Conserving More, Improving Lives—remain the same. As they represent the "Sustainable Yield Initiative" adopted in 2008, they are *the* defining terms of Monsanto's articulation of "sustainability" and can be traced directly to statements made by the company's former and current CEOs, thus giving a sense of their ori-gin and place within the corporation's culture over time. For instance, in a revealing interview published by the *Harvard Business Review* in 1997, Robert B. Shapiro argued:

> As many as 800 million people are so severely malnourished that they can neither work nor participate in family life. That's where we are today. And, as far as I know, no demographer questions that the world population will just about double by sometime around 2030.
>
> Without radical change, the kind of world implied by those numbers is unthinkable. It's a world of mass migrations and environmental degradation on an unimaginable scale. At best, it means the preservation of a few islands of privilege and prosperity in a sea of misery and violence. . . .

We're entering a time of perhaps unprecedented discontinuity. Businesses grounded in the old model will become obsolete and die. At Monsanto, we're trying to invent some new businesses around the concept of environmental sustainability. (Magretta 1997, 80–81)

More recently, in his plenary address at the 2010 Business Social Responsibility Conference, current CEO Hugh Grant said, "By 2025 it is estimated that we'll need about 50 percent more food than today; 2050, 70 percent more. So, we've been focusing on how you can do more with less. How can you increase yields on the same footprint and consume a third less stuff? And that's our definition of sustainability. We've been working really hard on making sustainability not just the center of our vision, but the center of what we do as a business."[16]

The public proclamations and the mission statement it has spawned serve the dual purpose of disassociating the company from its legacy issues (and the "old" Monsanto) while underscoring its more progressive, transformative, and, perhaps most important, empowering place within the field of agricultural biotechnology. And with any good social-responsibility effort, it is further punctuated with "Our Pledge," Monsanto's ethical code of conduct. Available in six languages, as part of the sustainable yield initiative the "Pledge" was originally composed of "Dialogue, Transparency, Respect, Sharing and Benefits," but over the course of the past few years they have added "Integrity," "Act as Owners to Achieve Results," and "Create a Great Place to Work." The reasons for creating this pledge are, again, tied to the company's desire to distance itself from highly controversial "legacy" products (Agent Orange used in Vietnam; Roundup Ultra used in Plan Colombia, and rBGH used in milk production), but according to its media team, the effort was driven even more so by Monsanto's need to be proactive and responsive to outside criticism through deliberate and engaged dialogue (personal communication, April 20, 2009).

Central to this effort to foster dialogue is Monsanto's desire to shape how the key term "sustainability" is understood by consumers and its own employees by challenging the perception that it is the domain of the organic-food movement. For example, the company's strategic model of "Promote, Respond, and Implement" focuses not on the science of, say, developing corn with an oil yield from 3 percent to 7 percent, but rather on why high-oil-yield corn is important. By shifting this emphasis, Monsanto is working to change the conversation from *what* Monsanto makes (and by association, what it used to make) to *why* what Monsanto does is important for a changing world. In this respect, the role of the Web site isn't conceptualized to be just a resource passively waiting to be discovered by the company's clients, critics, and a few curious academics. Rather, the biotech giant has deliberately positioned the Web site as the center of its efforts to pursue interaction through an institutionally coordinated and highly dynamic mediascape for its clients, employees, shareholders, critics, and others. This multiplatform effort is composed of the following[17]:

> *Newsroom*, an online news magazine, is the company's flagship media product dedicated to establishing an official record of Monsanto's activities and accomplishments. Accessible as a link on Monsanto's main corporate Web site, it provides informational links to specific issues and updated reports and news items ranging from news releases about particular products (such as sweet corn and sustainability) to opinion pieces penned by staff writers and Monsanto employees from around the world (for example, "The Seed Police?" or "The Challenge of Feeding 7 Billion People" by Monsanto's managing director in Brazil). *Newsroom* is also tied into "Social Media" and "Multimedia" pages (featuring, for instance, "infographics" and short videos such as "Honey Bee Pollination" and "Give it a Minute: Climate Change), as well as the anticipatory "Just Plain False" page featuring articles dedicated to pushing back against the "myths" about Monsanto (for example, "Myth: Monsanto Sells Terminator Seed"). It can also be set up to email reports, updates, and other information directly to investors.
>
> *Beyond the Rows* is the company's blog[18] and was created in no small part to "make employees ambassadors" by encouraging them to be involved in conversations about "chronic issues" (such as Indian farmer suicides, especially among cotton growers) as well as external critiques, such as Michael Pollan's *Omnivore's Dilemma*, or by tackling issues presented by groups most critical of Monsanto (for instance, the Center for Food Safety or GM Watch). The site is elegant, providing a link to an archive of almost one thousand articles from as far back as 2009, easy-to-navigate links to current information such as "News and Views," "From the Farm," "At Monsanto," as well as the invitation to ask a question at "Be a Part of the Conversation."
>
> **Improving Agriculture**—a main link on the Monsanto corporate Web site, this page serves as a showcase of the Sustainable Yield Initiative and the company's mission to Producing More, Conserving More, and Improving Lives. Significantly, it is also the location where Web site visitors will find a list of Monsanto's "Partnerships" (formerly

"Partnerships and Practices")—which includes reports on Tackling Climate Change, Conservation International in Brazil, "Project SHARE" in India, Water Efficient Maize for Africa (WEMA), Honeybee Health, and the Haitian Seed Donation. The site serves as both a means of damage control by directly addressing Monsanto-related controversies (honeybees, the plight of monarch butterflies) and a way to project the company's social and environmental responsibility (through scholarships, youth initiatives, partnerships, and the like).

America's Farmers Webisodes is linked both to the "News & Views" on Monsanto's homepage page as well as the standalone "America's Farmers" website.[19] This site is divided into "Community Outreach," "Learn about Farming," "Farm Blog," and "Meet the Families." Whichever entry point one selects, the guiding trope here is the farm family. Many of the "clicks" into the site lead the user to informational profiles of families or farm family "webisodes." Each webisode profiles a different theme about farm life. Titles include "The Sneed Family: Love the Land," and "Farm Wives, Farm Lives," the presentations feature farmers telling their own stories about their lives and values. In addition to the webisodes, links to Instagram and Twitter provide ways for farmers to post photos of everyday life on the farm and to "tweet" short messages, while YouTube, Facebook, and Pinterest are used to tie into a broader spectrum of farming-related content, ranging from agricultural humor and the best ways to use pumpkins, to "Ask a Farmer" videos and "popular uploads." Though the farmers profiled in the webisodes never directly state the connection to Monsanto, the connection is made salient, as the company's name and logo appear prominently at the end of each video as well as on the America's Farmers homepage. The webisodes are also supported by television advertising in the United States—thirty-second spots that celebrate farmers' connection to the land, production of food, and job creation, and which end by displaying the Monsanto name and logo, and the tagline "Brought to you on behalf of America's Farmers, by Monsanto."

Farm Show Coverage brings the Iowa and Illinois farm shows, via the Monsanto Web site, to audiences unable to attend them. This coverage is designed to "go beyond press releases" by using video, bloggers, and webcam coverage of events.

Monsanto TV is a news show created to be a "one-stop shop for information" about Monsanto for Monsanto employees but "without it sounding like corporate propaganda" (personal communication, April 20, 2009).

Social Media—whereas the Monsanto Web site has a "Social Media" section under the "Newsroom" page, its application of social media has actually been much more ambitious than meets the eye. In fact, since the inception of its "sustainable yield initiative" in 2008 the company has been an early adopter of various social media as tools for pursuing dialogue and as a way to direct people critical of and curious about Monsanto to visit the Web site for answers on various debates. To perform this function, the firm employs a host of "social media specialists," who are assigned to survey the internet and monitor blogs in order to engage the public and answer questions on Twitter, Instagram, and Facebook, as well as to get Monsanto "field advisors" and other employees to interact with "activists" and others. The company also posts their own YouTube videos, organized into "Featured Playlists," to help viewers identify key areas of conversation and issues of concern related to Monsanto and associated companies (for example, Seminis and Solaris).

This network of channels and forums allows readers, viewers, and participants in blog exchanges to learn about and engage in issues related to Monsanto's vision of sustainability. From Monsanto's point of view, this synergistic media model is justified as a necessary business investment necessary to "level the playing field" and add its own voice to the conversation about environmental stewardship and the future of food production (personal communication, April 20, 2009). Traditional 30-second television commercials further buttress the Monsanto message, some of which run nationally in the United States, but most are directed toward the Washington media market prior to important congressional votes that affect Monsanto interests. These typically resonate with the firm's chief talking points on sustainability, productivity, and conservation. The company also offers a more intimate opportunity to learn about its operations and guiding philosophy: the Monsanto tour at its corporate campus in St. Louis, Missouri (see Murphy 2013). In addition to these institutional activities, in 2012 Monsanto invested in media education, sponsoring the construction of the Monsanto Community Education Center at the University of Missouri St. Louis (UMSL). According to UMSL's chancellor, the center is envisioned to be a space "where the university and St. Louis Public Radio can offer community programming, classes in digital and new media and programs for a wider and diverse audience" (Zegel 2012).

Underlying Discourses

Through this review of Monsanto's multiplatform media operation, it is evident that the interlaced mediascape that emerges provides a rich case study of how a corporation manages its brand image by mobilizing a blend of new and traditional media to help shape and guide the contours of what is talked about and how. It is through the echoes within this network of newsletters, blogs, tweets, television advertisements, videos, and media-elaborated events that the company's deployment of a particular set of master terms, key images, and metaphors becomes detectable. These include productivity, cooperation, conservation, and, above all, sustainability through innovation, all cast against a backdrop of environmental stress, overpopulation, poverty and hunger, and the suggestion of ecological collapse in the commons.

Discursively what is most notable about this mixture of master terms and key images is that it draws from and extends oppositional sides of the radical-prosaic traditions of the "Earth discourses" (Dryzek 2005), pitting the looming tragedy of Survivalism against the innovative and entrepreneurial spirit of the Promethean response. To exercise this discursive shell game, the company first positions its "sustainable yield initiative" within the Survivalism discourse's simple but profoundly central pronouncement: today's global commons is in crisis because of concerns over population growth, famine, drought, depleted resources, and the planet's limited carrying capacity (Hardin 1968; Dryzek 2005). This launching point is articulated through the Monsanto media operations by deploying key Limits metaphors and associated imagery, such as exploding urban centers, excessive waste, overconsumption, and biospheres stressed by drought and flooding. Monsanto's role, the company informs us, is to help serve as an agent of change ("Producing More, Conserving More, Improving Lives"), responsive to the growing pressures of a world in flux, as the company's Web site says, by "offering better solutions to complex issues by developing better seeds and systems to help farmers with productivity."[20]

Herein lies the Promethean opening. To avert a catastrophe, we need better tools for our food producers (the farmer looms large here, a point I'll return to shortly) and smarter ways of growing food. Given the advancements in science, this of course is a matter of future-thinking stewardship through technological innovation. It is also what allows Monsanto to make its claim as a "food company" (as in the recent past) or a "sustainable agricultural company" (its current identity) and thus manufacture some distance from its chemical and biohazard pasts. Indeed, if food yields can be increased via innovative farming that requires less fertilizer and less water, it is also a matter of conservation as these technology-based solutions are then by definition more productive and responsive relationships with the earth.

By interlocking the two discourses—Limits and Promethean—the basic idea is that the world is urgently in need of solutions because it is overburdened by too many people and does not, given today's ecological and social challenges, provide productive ways to produce sufficient food to feed them. It is thus crucial to recognize that Monsanto's Promethean rendering of agricultural productivity is mediated as a matter of sound, scientifically informed environmental stewardship that would not be possible—or at least not convincing—without priming first an appropriate canvas of global challenges from which to depart. Thus Survivalism, with its ontology of environmental limits and focus on carrying capacity, ecosystem degradation, and food shortages, is paradoxically but nevertheless quite effectively relied on to seed the introduction of Monsanto's Promethean mission. In fact, one might argue, why is a Promethean response needed at all if not for the bleak horizon of human suffering and want prophesized by the Limits discourse?

Beyond this oppositional positioning of Survivalist dilemmas and Promethean solutions Monsanto's media strategy is given its "global meets local" texture by elements of Sustainable Development. The company elaborates this program by elements within its media messaging system that are interactive and even reflexive, allowing it to maintain a certain degree of discursive flexibility. For instance, through both messaging and utilization of social media Monsanto aligns itself with progress, public good, and social change in concert with participation, cooperation, and dialogue. They pursue this in two ways. First, Monsanto's narrative of how it can help communities take on Earth's coming environmental and social challenges is not as the rescuer of humanity but rather as a partner and participant willing and able to address the challenges with and through communities. Haunting this framing of relationships are Sustainable Development's goals of growth through cooperation and distributive justice. Indeed, Monsanto has worked hard to construct and project an image that it is working side by side with the Indian cotton grower, the African corn farmer, or the Canadian soybean sower, with its corporate hands in the dirt to bring in the harvest. This partnership only works because it relies on the heroic "global" farmer as guiding trope, since farmers are connected to the soil and subsequently understand at an existential level the direct and profound impacts precipitated by climate change. Through this vision of partnerships and on-the-ground agency, Monsanto manages to downplay its products' origins in the laboratory, conjuring up instead a communal and cooperative problem-solving effort that benefits from farmers' wisdom and Monsanto's innovative product line. Visually, this soil-bound rendering of agricultural cooperation is played out through the strategic deployment of cross-culturally recognizable iconography: fields, farms, livestock, tractors, and families tied to the land, be it in Africa, India, Brazil, or in the American heartland. When cities are shown, they are crowded, suffocating places, thus the cautionary codes of Survivalism that serve to place the collective productivity and cooperative elements of the farm into a perspective.

Second, the company asserts that it uses social media to invite dialogue, build partnerships, and engender public consideration of the issues. Monsanto achieves this not only through various blogs and other social-media outreach efforts but through its own employees, who become trained in the company's sustainability platform to serve as Monsanto "ambassadors" (personal communication, April 20, 2009). The public voice is thus heard and channeled in ways that Monsanto can control within the confines of the company's own brand identity and vision of innovative sustainability. Indeed, this vision of innovative sustainability is given even more capital by celebrating ideas directly from the Sustainable Development toolkit: participation, cooperation, empowered communities, and development. This cultivation of sustainability through locally grounded participation is exceptionally important, because it provides the company's Promethean foundation with a sympathetic human face—the farmer.

Together, this dual articulation of Sustainable Development—public good and collective/responsible decision making—allows the company to speak with greater "public" authority without the risk of losing its ideological bearings. Such a strategy also provides a point of defense against the charges of the company's critics by offering more "sober" counterpoints of discussion against what Monsanto would consider the more "ideological," less scientific, more passionate and hysterical of voices (what Cox [2013, 255] calls "indecorous voices"), such as those of ecofeminists, radical green activists, or other groups relying on discursive bearings that are not well established or do not have media support.

So, while the mediascape Monsanto has created seems flexible and open to external voices, critical debate, and dialogue, the coordinates of its central trope, *sustainability*, are firmly plotted in themes of technology, environmental stewardship, and corporate responsibility, all of which are evoked in terms of "innovation" and, interestingly, "collaboration." Promethean-like, "corporate responsibility" is thus articulated as innovation, and innovation thus the agent through which sustainability is not only possible, but through which a technology-driven vision of the future *is required* to respond to the needs of and challenges faced by the planet's inhabitants (Survivalism). It is, in the end, a platform founded on a market-based vision of food production grounded on the premise that sustainability is a product to be produced and delivered by a benevolent commercially driven agent.

5

Amazonian Indigenous Green
Media and the Ecologically Noble Savage

Few things seem to evoke as much first-world environmental anxiety and generate as much popular concern for ecological intervention as the Amazon rainforest. This should come as no surprise, as the massive jungle has long been understood in European and North American public spheres as one of the most ecologically diverse regions on Earth, occupying a prominent place in the Western environmental imagination, defined as much by natural abundance as by ecological crisis (Heise 2008; Hutchins and Wilson 2010). In fact, as Latin American environmental historian Shawn William Miller (2007) observes, "citizens of developed nations often appear more concerned about the ecological condition of the Amazon than they are about their own landscapes" (194). We can trace support for this observation through art, literature, travel writing, and scientific exploration, where it has emerged as a key trope in narratives about human depredation on the natural world and, after perhaps only the Arctic, the most iconic symbol of the need to take collective action to help save our ailing world and claim ecological redemption.

But in addition to the Amazon's prominence within literary, artistic, and geographic imaginaries, it is important to note that the region's symbolic weight is also in no small measure connected to how we earthlings have been able to *actually see* what has been happening to the Amazon from above and subsequently to think about its place within larger, more global environmental dilemmas. Miller reminds us that though humans were first able to have a "god's eye view" of Earth during Yuri Gagarin's 1961 orbit, it was the 1981 space shuttle images that provided a more penetrating and troubling vision.

Among the most captivating features were human marks on the earth's face, and the most apparent of these was the destruction of the world's largest tropical forest. At night, the shuttle crews exposed to film thousands of fires in Rondônia in Brazil's Western Amazon. By day, they measured a pall of smoke that spread over 3 million square kilometers. They also documented the unusual patterns of forest removal that followed the expanding highway networks punched into the forests by states eager to develop their jungle frontiers. In Rondônia, peasant and rancher clearings looked like zippers, roads whose borders were checked with rectangular clearings that extended from narrow frontages. (2007, 193)

This vision of an Amazon under attack resonated globally because of its association with paradise (the Pristine Myth; Eden), its mystique as a biological treasure trove of important medicinal plants, and with recent arguments that it served a special role as "Earth's lung" (Miller 2007, 194).

It is important that added to these associations and the portrayal of the Amazon as a vast and rich but ultimately fragile biosphere is the image of those who inhabit it. Body paint, feathered headdresses, lip plates, beads and bones, partial nudity, ritual dances, exotic pets, domed grass huts, and hammocks are the cultural codes of indigenous identity that have been important indexes for constructing a people who are "of" nature (Conklin 1997). For the West (and arguably now for the rest of the word) these exotic indigenous body images and primitive cultural practices have been used to project the notion of the "Ecologically Noble Savage,"[1] a being who dwells comfortably within the rules and rhythms of the forest and therefore outside the cosmopolitan, material world of consumer capitalism. This ecological nobility is aligned with the virtues of balance, simplicity, spirituality, and egalitarianism, reifying the sense that the Amazon and the beings who dwell there have a special status within the global commons.

The media commons has a rich tradition of trading on these narrative motifs. For instance, John Borman's 1985 film *The Emerald Forest* encapsulates these ideas, as his protagonist, an American hydroelectric-dam engineer, enters the forest from his deforested, soon-to-be-concrete-covered construction site to search for his son after he is abducted by the "Invisible People." Through his multiyear search he comes to question his role in destroying the forest, developing a deeper understanding of it and appreciation for the people who live there, especially as he discovers that his son has been adopted by a tribal chief. To protect his son and the tribe, the engineer blows up the dam, buying the forest dwellers a bit more time to remain invisible. Though supposedly based on a true story, this big-budget film's tale buttresses the (Western) notion that the Amazon is a place residing at the edge of the "modern" world yet free of its pollutants even as it is singularly susceptible to modern excesses. More recently, the January 2014 *National Geographic* digested and projected the essence of these converging ideas—tradition, preservation, defiance, exposure, vulnerability, and cultural authenticity—via its cover, which features a close-up of a young indigenous girl with a shaved head and plucked eyebrows, painted in tribal colors, gazing directly back at the reader. The cover reads, "Defenders of the Amazon: Taking on the Modern World. And Winning." The related article presents the picture of a Brazil whose ecological future resides in the hands of competing interests: most, like U.S. agro-businesses, a "progress"-oriented Brazilian state, and a hungry Chinese market, are more driven by consumer urges; but others, like Brazilian Amerindians and NGOs, are environmentally driven stakeholders using technology to preserve and defend this great eco-treasure from would-be plunderers.[2]

As these examples show, it is the symbolic construction of a place and its people that continues to imbue the Amazon with a particularly grounded quality of ecological purity and resistance at the same time it frames the region as "that most vulnerable of places" to a modernizing, insatiable outside world. This underlying tension supports American anthropologist Beth A. Conklin's (2010) view that, within "the dominant Western narrative of capitalist expansion into formerly nonmarket economies, there are only two story lines for indigenous cultures to follow: the well-trod narrative of alienation, cultural loss, corruption, and victimization, or the heroic narratives of rejection and resistance to capitalist domination" (130). As I examine at length in this chapter, thanks to a combination of media events, indigenous activism, and Western environmentalism, from the 1970s to the 1990s these renderings of the Amazon and its people were foundational in the elaboration of Green Radicalism, primarily in the form of Environmental Justice. More recently, however, the story of rainforest dwellers protecting their lands has resurfaced through a network of new communication technologies, mobile media applications, and the blogosphere, and have helped produce the discourse of Ecological Modernization that now defines Amazonian cultural survival in relation to perceived market value.

Eco-Indigenous Authenticity

It would be easy to dismiss recent past and current narrative arrangements about the Amazon and the Earth discourses they fuel as merely examples of Western cultural hegemony asserting a particularly polarizing "eco-othering"—that is, imposing a highly selective idea of what rainforest cultural authenticity should look like and the binary forces at work that shape and define it. However, it is important to recognize that the ingredients of recent discourses are produced in part from a longstanding reflexive, performative element of identity politics, tied intimately to Amazonian indigenous groups' quest for self-determination, negotiation of transnational discourses, intercultural encounters, and the selective appropriation of Western symbolic constructs and rhetoric for cultural survival.

According to anthropologists who have looked closely at contemporary indigenous cultural survival in the Amazon (Carneiro da Cunha and de Almedia 2000; Conklin 1997; Conklin and Graham 1995; Turner 1993, 1995), the rise of environmentalism in the 1980s and the ensuing explosion of international interest in the rainforest created a period for Amazonian Indians of increased intercultural exchange and relationship building. Much of this took place with more globally networked eco-conscious actors as indigenous nations forged alliances with new, nongovernmental interests, such as Cultural Survival, the World Wildlife Fund, the Nature Conservancy, GAIA Foundation, Rainforest Action Fund, and the Environmental Defense Fund to oppose environmentally destructive practices. The exchange also unfolded in relationship with progressive transnational companies that practiced "fair trade," most noticeably The Body Shop (cosmetics and skincare) and Ben & Jerry's (ice cream). These partnerships benefited both the "First World" and "Fourth World" actors involved in interrelated yet distinct ways. For the NGOs, environmentalists, and (eventually) marketers, the alliance with Amerindians helped such groups articulate a particular kind of ecological activism—one anchored in the myth that Native Americans were "natural conservationists," and so the preservation of biodiversity tied organically to indigenous knowledge and lifeways (Carneiro da Cunha and de Almedia 2000; Conklin and Graham 1995). Partnerships with Amazonian Indians thus permitted these Western interests to evoke a sense of eco-solidarity consistent with the tenets of Environmental Justice as it linked directly to indigenous rights and causes. This alignment added a sympathetic, environmentally rooted human face to their own conservation efforts—symbolic value of particular importance for NGOs, as they were highly dependent on the contributions of compassionate donors (Conklin and Graham 1995). More recently, as I will discuss later in this chapter but which the situation of the 1980s and '90s foreshadowed, the reliance on symbolism has assumed an even greater place within contemporary eco-stewardship efforts, especially for corporations as they are increasingly concerned with projecting a profile of social responsibility of which the environment is a major part.

For the Amazonian Indian, the alliances provided a level of recognition and legitimacy that, prior to these partnerships, they had struggled to achieve. Indeed, indigenous claims to land and natural-resource rights clearly predated the rise of environmentalism in the Amazon but were largely ignored by an unresponsive state that, for much of its history, was actively hostile toward native charges of outside incursions (Fisher 1994). However, through their increased experiences with powerful state and transnational interests, native Amazonian leaders began to recognize that in order for their populations to achieve greater political leverage, the road to self-determination would involve resuscitating an aesthetically identifiable "indigenousness." This began quietly at first within the confines of Brazil, most notably in late 1970s when the Xavante, an indigenous group from the state of Mato Grosso, began to challenge state corruption surrounding land-rights abuses by calling press conferences. According to Conklin and Graham (1995), this strategy was developed by the tribe's leader, Mario Juruna, who understood that media coverage of the community's grievances afforded the publicity they needed to insert themselves into the Brazilian public sphere. But Juruna was also savvy enough to realize that this attention could be cultivated through the power of images, and thus he deliberately elaborated camera-ready demonstrations.

> Armed with war clubs, bows, arrows, and the tape recordings of broken promises, Juruna and dozens of boldly painted Xavante men staged dramatic confrontations with high ranking government officials. Television and press photographers seized upon the images of Xavante wielding Western technology (the tape recorder) in theatrical protests and disseminated these images throughout Brazil. (699)

Despite Juruna's perspicacious understanding that media coverage could be manufactured via the tactical deployment of "native" symbolic capital, his culture-as-politics formula was too far ahead of the times to prove effective beyond Brazil. Nevertheless, he and the Xavante had pioneered a strategy of theatrical media politics—a strategy that would find its full potential with the global rise of environmentalism and the eco-activism that followed. Indeed, as has been well documented (Carneiro da Cunha and de Almedia 2000; Conklin 1997, 2010; Conklin and Graham 1995; Fisher 1994; Turner 1993), such performative practices took off in the late 1980s when indigenous leaders realized that the symbolic capital of "indigenousness" carried more weight in the West when it was married to environmentalism and human rights. This realization ignited a revival in native costume. Suddenly, "Native Amazonians who once took pains to hide external signs of indigenous identity behind mass-produced Western clothing now proclaim their cultural distinctiveness with headdresses, body paint, beads, and feathers" (Conklin 1997, 712).

Such articulations of "indigeneity" are a form of authentication taking place globally within various indigenous groups and can be understood as "an image self-constructed by the subordinate under restrictions set by the superordinate discourse" (Guenther et al., 2006, 24). But this does not mean that these presentations cannot lead to real gains. For many Amazonian tribes, the return to native dress was, on the one hand, motivated by the indigenous need to find a way to respond effectively to emerging transnational pressures and opportunities to better situate themselves, while, on the other hand, it was a response to the Western desire to have an indigenous face for a growing and increasingly global eco-politics. However, in the case of Amazonian indigeneity, it should be noted that the emerging trope of environmental nobility also fit neatly into the Brazilian state's new agenda of "development" (Carneiro da Cunha and de Almeida 2000). In fact, the indigenous-ecological coupling was in part fueled by Article 231 of Brazil's 1988 constitution, which clearly spelled out that indigenous lands were "originary"—that is, not just places for dwelling, but spaces for the "*preservation of environmental resources necessary of indigenous peoples' wellbeing as well as land necessary to their physical and cultural reproduction, according to their uses, customs, and traditions*" (Carneiro da Cunha and de Almeida 2000, 321, emphasis in the original). Ecological projects, at least in theory, were now supposed to take place with and through the indigenous residents of the forest, not by displacing them. Within this context, "authenticity," as Conklin (1997) points out, had "its rewards" (711).

During this time Amazonian indigenous activists also further transfigured the ways in which they presented their cultures to the world by adopting the language of environmentalism in concert with a better sense of how to use media to their advantage (Conklin and Graham 1995; Santos et al. 1997). Much of this language drew directly from concepts, metaphors, and key terms associated with Green Radicalism, especially Environmental Justice, as emphasis was placed on indigenous rights in relation to the land, community, cultural heritage, spirituality, and residence. In short, environmentalism provided indigenous agents with an identifiable platform through which they could translate their concerns to an external audience while still maintaining a level of native indexicality. So, whereas the revival of indigenous costume increased their ability to be "seen," the new "green" vocabulary gave the Amazonian community powerful discursive tools to be better "heard."

The Kayapó, Indigenous Eco-Activism, and the Media

It is clear that during this phase of Amazonian eco-politics, the indigenous communities that were the most media savvy and most adept at projecting their indigenous culture to the outside world were best able to mobilize transnational and pan-Indian support. No Amazonian tribe understood this better than the Kayapó, an indigenous nation from the Brazilian central state of Pará. The Kayapó attained international prominence during the 1980s and 1990s for their protests against megadevelopment rainforest projects, such as hydroelectric dams, as well as other issues that threatened their land and way of life. During this wave of indigenous eco-activism the Kayapó distinguished themselves through their political savvy and ability to create media events by seizing on opportunities for disruption. In no small way this involved marshaling their cultural capital and the language of environmentalism to effectively draw attention to issues of Amerindian cultural survival (Conklin 1997, 2010; Dewar 1995; Turner 1993, 1995). By explicitly coupling "culture" and "the environment," the Kayapó were able to speak to internal (Brazilian) considerations for the indigenous claims of originary legal status at the same time as they projected a sense of eco-mysticism and activism (the Ecologically Noble Savage) to the Global North. Moreover, the tribe's cultural theatrics resonated horizontally with other indigenous communities in the Amazon and beyond.

The Kayapó's capacity to elaborate effective demonstrations was perhaps best realized in February 1989, when they successfully organized a multitribe protest in the town of Altamira against the World Bank's and Brazilian government's plans to build two dams in the Xingú River valley. If completed, the dams were projected to flood thousands of hectares of rainforest and displace multiple indigenous communities from their ancestral lands. So the Kayapó and other river-basin tribes took a very public stand to alert the world of their struggle and to air their grievances. The show of resistance that unfolded was grounded in indigenous claims of cultural rights, biodiversity, and broader issues of environmentalism. However, by many accounts the effort was effective because the Kayapó knew how to capitalize on the media coverage to create a lasting cultural image (Conklin 1997, 2010; Fisher 1994; Rabben 2004). They were "experts" at self-objectification, as Terence Turner (2002), an anthropologist whose research on the Kayapó's media use is particularly extensive, has pointed out, and they possessed a deep understanding of the performative function of representation. As a result, the scope and impact of the Altamira media event was stunning by almost any measure. Not only were the Kayapó organizers able to mobilize broad indigenous participation (more than six hundred people showed up, with additional support from NGOs, politicians, celebrities, and citizen protestors) that lasted several days, but media reports of the protest were filled with traditionally adorned native Amazonians—an "indigenous" presentation of indigenous resistance made possible by the fact that the Kayapó evidently "urged other tribes to remove their western attire and decorate their bodies following their own customs" (Fisher 1994, 222).

This show of Amazonian resistance was seen and read about throughout the world, tapping into Western environmental anxieties and human rights concerns while reifying, in full tribal colors, the notion that native peoples were eco-conscious defenders of the forest. It also was credited with fostering the emergence of a pan-Amazonian indigenous identity (Conklin 1997, 2010; Fisher 1994). Most important for the peoples of the forest, it altered the plans of powerful interests. In fact, the Altamira protests reportedly generated "such intense political pressure that Brazil's government was forced to call a retreat in its plans for dam construction," and shortly after the protest "the World Bank announced that it was denying the Brazilian power sector loan" (Fisher 1994, 222).

Beyond this event, the Kayapó were able to draw on their indigenous Amazonian identity to penetrate networks of power, celebrity, and, eventually, conservation marketing, and a number of tribal leaders were propelled from local advocates for native land rights to global media stars of environmental activism and human rights (Conklin and Graham 1995; Conklin 1997; Graham 1998; Fisher 1994; Rabben 2004; Turner 1993, 1995). For instance, from 1988 to 1992 the Kayapó chief Paulinho Payakan (Payakã) "made a speaking tour of seven European countries, testified at the World Bank, met with French president François Mitterrand and former U.S. president Jimmy Carter, appeared on the Phil Donahue Show, was featured on the cover of *Parade* magazine" (Conklin and Graham 1995, 695). Payakan's cover image on *Parade* was particularly telling, as the accompanying headline announced, "A Man Who Would Save the World." Even more press worthy was the high-visibility relationship that Kayapó leader Rop ni Metuktire (more popularly known as Chief Raoni) established with British rock star Sting. The collaboration between the two men led to Raoni's accompanying Sting on a concert/fundraising tour in 1989, which included meetings with Pope John Paul II,

Brazil's president José Sarney, and (again) François Mitterrand, as well as the chief's honorary senior position in Sting's Rain Forest Foundation, which gathered concert proceeds and other funds to directly support Kayapó causes (Conklin 2010, 128).

Another advocate from the Global North, and in many ways the person from the metropolis who would have the most significant influence on the trajectory of Amazonian environmental politics into the global public sphere in the 1990s, was The Body Shop's Dame Anita Roddick. Roddick had attended the 1989 Altamira protests and became deeply involved in their struggle. She was interested in associating her company with green causes and the ethical, responsible treatment of the planet's resources. The relationship she established with the Kayapó was important, signaling a new kind of alliance between indigenous peoples of the forest and commercial interests (Turner 1995). Under Roddick's leadership the British cosmetics company adopted the "Rainforest Harvest" model of environmental defense through ecosystem yield. Developed by the Harvard-based NGO Cultural Survival, the basic idea was that, rather than turning to unreliable aid organizations or falling prey to unsustainable and damaging extraction opportunities (logging, mining), indigenous people could preserve their homelands and defend their cultures by tapping into more reliable and sustainable free-market opportunities. For forest dwellers, this involved identifying resources that could be harvested in nondestructive ways (Brazil nuts, for example) and marketed to the outside world as sustainable forest products. For The Body Shop, the idea manifested as the "Trade, Not Aid" project, a marketing campaign that peddled cosmetic lines grounded in "fair trade" principles and made with the sustainable, natural raw goods of the world's rainforests.

The relationship, as Turner (1995) put it, became a "test case" for "the effectiveness of the commercial marketing of forest products as a strategy for saving the forest and its native inhabitants from destruction and dispossession by development" (113). And indeed, this project placed a great deal of weight on how audiences would respond to a particular rendering of indigeneity. At the center of this framing of eco-indigenousness was the image of Chief Raoni and the person who was for a time to become the global face of Amazonian causes, Payakan. Both men had achieved the status of eco-indigenous royalty in political and popular-culture circles, and in the West their images as "real Indians" had become concomitant with cultural rights and environmental defense. Roddick was set on channeling the symbolic currency of these natural ecological actors toward The Body Shop. After the Altamira protest she enlisted Payakan to serve as The Body Shop's ambassador, while also helping the

Kayapó to create village nut-oil processing operations and establish fair-trade agreements for their products (Rabben 2004). To ensure Payakan's visibility and effectiveness, Roddick also reportedly purchased an airplane for him so that he could travel to participate in events around the world in defense of the rainforest (Dewar 1995; Turner 1995). In no short time, malls, magazines, and billboards throughout Europe and the United States were the promotional sites for the benefits of the rainforest, often via Payakan's image, and for a time the company "handed out copies of *Fight for the Forest*, a comic book that told the story of Roddick's support for the Kayapó" (Moberg 1997).

As Conklin and Graham observed, the visibility that this period of activism generated and the partnerships it produced made it "one of the most significant developments in the history of indigenous rights struggles" (1995, 697). However, it is also important to note that during this period the Kayapó's and other Amazonian indigenous groups' deliberate strategies to endow "indianness" with a natural environmentalism recognizable to the West was a tactical move that rooted their activism in culture rather than politics (Fisher 1994). This worked extremely well to help them put pressure on the state and achieve greater visibility, but it also made them vulnerable to the whims of "the market," the assumptions of their backers and the image politics that profoundly influenced how they were seen and heard.

Fissures in the Eco-Indigenous Imaginary

Indeed, despite the bonding, shared activities, and general sense of goodwill between north-south partners, it was not long before the indigenous-metropolis solidarity began to show a few cracks, largely because the alliances between indigenous actors and their cosmopolitan advocates were built on the erroneous assumption that all parties shared common values concerning environmental stewardship. While ostensibly eco-conscious and festooned with references to biodiversity, cultural rights, and fair trade, the environmentalists, NGOs, and activists had been operating through an underlying discourse of Green Radicalism, which assumed that the sustainable stewardship of the global commons could draw energy from the indigenous eco-mysticism of cultural survival. For these interests, eco-solidarity was moored to the Eurocentric notion that Native Americans were natural ecologists, and the sense that Amazonian Indians were "defenders of the forest" became a central trope in the mainstream media. As Conklin and Graham (1995) put it, the thinking was that "indigenous people are natural partners in the global ecological imaginary because of—not in spite of—their cultural difference" (697), thus reifying the idea that indigenous resource stewardship was "naturally" consistent with Western environmentalism. In fact, Conklin (1997) observed, "The ecological rationales for promoting Amazonian Indians' land rights and cultural survival that emerged in the late 1980s were premised on the idea of cultural continuity—the assumption that *past* traditions will orient *future* Indians to use natural resources in ways that are ecologically nondestructive. The eco-Indian alliance, in other words, hinges on a particular construction of indigenous authenticity" (721, emphasis in the original). In short, there was an underlying Western assumption that indigenous actors would not spoil the commons because they had spent centuries living in balance with nature. As "natural ecologists" (Fisher 1994, 220), the past, along with custom, would inform the future.

But this discursive alignment with Green Radicalism and one of its main corollaries, Environmental Justice, was eroded by the increasing knowledge that the Kayapó and other indigenous groups had in fact continued to profit from extractive practices such as gold mining and logging—activities once believed to be encroachments by outsiders but later revealed to be self-enrichment initiatives sought out by some tribal leaders and their families (Fisher 1994; Rabben 2004; Turner 1995). It also didn't help that some of the higher-profile relationships had soured with time, as Sting and Chief Raoni made public their growing mistrust of each other's motives (Conklin 2010). But most damning was the case of Payakan, whose symbolic value for "Rainforest Harvest" and other eco-defense initiatives quickly vanished just prior to the Earth Summit in 1992, when he was charged with rape (charges which were later dropped, and then revived for a controversial conviction in 1995). According to anthropologist and human-rights advocate Linda Rabben (2004), "news of the rape charge broke as an exclusive story in the weekly news magazine *Veja*, which plastered his glum visage on its cover, above the words, 'The Savage,' just before the Earth Summit began" (79–80). With this news Payakan became persona non grata for rainforest causes and was subsequently excused from NGOs worldwide; financing for his projects immediately dried up (Conklin and Graham 1995; Rabben 2004). Combined, these events, discoveries, and chilled relations ate into the West's eco-indigenous romanticism, feeding a sense that the Ecologically Noble Savage may not in fact be either that noble or that conservation minded, but rather, as the *Veja* cover title announced so unambiguously, just savage.

For their part, indigenous groups had invested in the relationships with interests from the metropolis for more pragmatic reasons, chief among these being self-determination and cultural rights. This should come as no surprise, given that Amazonian Indians had experienced firsthand what "moderniza-tion" meant for indigenous peoples in Brazil. Through his long-term study of the Kayapó, Turner (1993, 1995, 2002) has emphasized that they were in fact quite aware that a transformation in social relations was in order. They conceived culture as a dynamic tool, not simply an essence, of this transition, and by associating native identity with environmentalism indigenous com-munities were able to generate visibility in the global public sphere, which meant they could secure greater political traction. They pursued indigenous rights and self-determination through the identification of opportunities in which they could adjust and exercise culture to secure survival.

However, in acknowledging this instrumental investment in cultural iden-tity, within this period Amazonian indigenous groups also understood that they needed to rely on different and even contradictory strategies for self-determination and autonomy, some of which appeared environmentally destructive, unsustainable, and even against their own long-term interests (timber harvesting and mining are two examples). Given the long and painful history of institutional change and discontinuities in Brazilian state policy, intervention, and "development," Amazonian indigenous communities were reluctant to completely sever connections with local entrepreneurs and other interests in favor of international opportunities (Fisher 1994). In short, plac-ing long-term sustainability with distant partners over local agreements and immediate transactions seemed like a move that simply created a new, more global face of their dependency and one that gave tribes less direct control (Rabben 2004). Case in point, within the context of the Kayapó community, the experiment in green capitalism that took place under the banner of "Rain-forest Harvest" was uneven and caused its own share of problems. As Turner (2002) notes, despite the progressive goals of the some of the companies in-volved (for instance, Ben & Jerry's) and the Kayapó's enthusiasm in working with The Body Shop, the installation of capitalist projects in a noncapitalist community promoted the individual over the group and created wealth for some but not others. The resulting uneven distribution of wealth and rise in self-interest over tribal well-being caused deep schisms that still remain (Rabben 2004). Moreover, the project's true value itself was questioned, as reports surfaced that only a miniscule amount of forest materials were actu-ally used in The Body Shop's products, making the trade seem at best merely supplemental as opposed to productive over the long haul and at worst ex-ploitative and as promoting dependency (Corry 1993; Entine 1994; Rabben 2004). In addition to these charges was the assertion that the alliance did not fully compensate the Kayapó, as beyond the surface of the "Rainforest

Harvest"-inspired "Trade, Not Aid" slogan, the "real" product the Kayapó provided The Body Shop was "their photographic image" (Turner 1995).

Rise of the Techno-Indigenous Amazonian

Despite the rise and fall of an indigenous-infused "save the rainforest" era of eco-activism in the Amazon, of which the trope of the Ecologically Noble Savage was central in feeding the underlying discourse of Green Radicalism, it must be understood that this moment within the region's history was "created and maintained primarily through the circulation of media images and contacts with a small number of indigenous cultural mediators" (Conklin and Graham 1995, 703). Undoubtedly, during this period the Kayapó, along with the Yanomami, achieved a sort of special cultural currency within media networks and went on to develop strong media-production trajectories.[3]

But Amazonian indigenous groups that did not enjoy international media coverage, garner the attention of celebrities, or profit from fair-trade deals during the Rainforest Harvest era had to find different avenues to confront forces that were putting pressure on their survival. Here is where the availability of networked communication technologies and mobile media devices began to come into play, as access to these tools opened up pathways for a broader network of Amazonian communities to seek recognition, build partnerships, and register their cultures in the public sphere. Most noteworthy has been how Amazonian indigenous groups have used computers, the internet, and global positioning systems (GPS) to establish greater visibility and direct control over cultural defense. And as was the case in the past, nonprofit organizations have been highly involved this initiative. For example, the Amazon Conservation Team (ACT), founded by noted ethnobotanist Mark Plotkin, developed the idea that isolated indigenous communities could help achieve many of their goals of cultural survival if they were trained to employ geomapping technologies to register biodiversity, chart ancestral lands, and preserve their cultural knowledge of forest ecosystems. Partnering with local governments, ACT set up programs with indigenous communities in Colombia, Suriname, and Brazil to use GPS technology to monitor and conserve forest ecosystems and map and catalog their cultural territory.[4]

The Western press and related sources in the blogosphere took notice of this rise in the techno-indigenous Amazonian, especially in relation to its change agents. The article "Amazon Conservation Team Puts Indians on Google Earth to Save the Amazon" (Butler 2006), published by the online environmental science and conservation news site *Mongaby.com*, was among the first news sources to cover how these developments were unfolding. The journal's editor-in-chief, Rhett Butler (2006), observed that the initiatives provided a new form of defense in that community members could use the GPS and internet technology to monitor deforestation and other illegal incursions. He noticed also that "beyond the forest-monitoring capabilities, Google Earth and more generally the Internet, is also helping to strengthen bonds between indigenous children, hungry for technology, and their parents, who are interested in protecting their homeland." Beyond this astute observation, the primary focus of other news outlets, magazines, and newsletters has been on Amazonian conservation, technological responsiveness, and singular efforts of cultural defense. The vast majority of these place emphasis on how Google Earth or some similar GPS technology has enabled indigenous communities to patrol their lands via satellite and thus more easily identify illegal encroachments and take action to stop such environmentally destructive activities as gold mining (which causes river contamination, mercury pollution, and sedimentation) and logging (leading to deforestation). For instance, *Smithsonian* magazine's story "Rain Forest Rebel" (Hammer 2007) describes a team of Paiter-Suruí Indians, former military cartographers, and anthropologists working together to create a map designed to preserve the community's cultural, historical, and environmental memory. But much of the article is also focused on how Chief Almir, the "political activist, environmentalist and the first member of his tribe to attend a university" was "fighting to save his people and the rain forest they inhabit" (Hammer 2007). Later in 2007, the *San Francisco Chronicle* published the story "Google to Harness Satellite for an Amazon Tribe: When the Brazilian Government Failed to Defend His Tribe against Loggers and Miners, the Leader Found a High-Tech Ally" (Epstein 2007) and then followed up in 2009 with another piece titled "A Google Partnership to Save an Amazon Tribe and Rainforest" (Temple 2009). More recently, in 2010 *Spiegel Online International* issued the report, "Using the Internet to Save the Rainforest: How an Amazonian Tribe Is Mastering the Modern World" (von Mittelstaedt); in 2013 the *Washington Post* provided "Brazilian Chief Uses Technology to Help Save His Tribe and Curb Deforestation," which National Public Radio recast as "From Stone Age to the Digital Age in One Big Leap" (Forero 2013); and in 2014 *The Guardian* published an article titled, "Indigenous Leaders Empowering Communities through Social Enterprise."

As the titles and pitch of these reports reveal, agency shifts back and forth from external teachers and technology providers to the indigenous stewards of the forest armed with the technological tools and know-how to engage in cultural cartography. Judging from these media frames, achieving proficiency with communication technology—not the state or even NGOs—is the path that indigenous communities need to follow to not only protect their interests but "master the modern world." If there is any doubt about this, images that accompanied the reports generally relied on the predictable juxtaposition of key codes: a community member dressed in indigenous garb holding a laptop or some other high-tech communication device framed by a backdrop of lush forest. The Ecologically Noble Savage is resuscitated and now merged with and empowered by modern, portable communication technology. But as with the partnerships created and media narratives circulated during the Rainforest Harvest era in the 1980s and 1990s, the ties among cultural survival, politics, and environmentalism, and the motivations of those involved, is much more complex and multilayered than such imagery or cover stories about residents of the "stone age" leaping to the digital age suggest.

The Suruí Forest Carbon Project, 2007–2013

Few initiatives have the capacity to expose this underlying complexity as much as how the recent surge in indigenous ethnomapping has been used to pursue forest carbon-trading opportunities. Carbon trading is based on the notion that polluters who are either unable or unwilling to reduce their own carbon output can "offset" their emissions by investing in projects that sequester carbon. Outlined as part of the Kyoto Protocol, this process was conceptualized as an actionable international approach to mitigate global warming by permitting industrialized nations (what Kyoto labeled "Annex I" countries) to earn offset credits through projects realized in developing countries ("non-Annex I") (Gorte and Ramseur 2010). The protocol also considered the motivation of businesses in concert with the realities of anthropocentric climate change. The basic idea is that CO_2 emissions can be curbed globally if businesses are incentivized to voluntarily pay for carbon-management projects.[5]

Not surprisingly, large swaths of tropical forests were quickly identified as target areas for carbon market development because not only were they under assault from logging and other industries, but these ecosystems are also among the planet's largest carbon storehouses (Bonan 2008). Thus, investing in the world's tropical forests is an attractive offset option, especially when compared with more expensive investments (such as renewable energy or carbon capture) or the prospect of waiting for mandatory caps set by state agencies; they are inexpensive solutions that generate high-volume offsets.

Actors, typically Annex I countries, earn carbon credits by paying for forest ecosystems to be left alone, which are predominately in developing parts of the world. Significantly, investing in forest conservation not only keeps carbon "stored" (by halting deforestation) but also mandates that the "seller" develop a sustainability plan based on transparent and verifiable criteria that will keep forests standing as major carbon sinks as well as animate further reductions in deforestation and degradation (for example, afforestation and reforestation).

Reducing Emissions from Deforestation and Forest Degradation (REDD) is the pilot program that has since evolved into the center of this global initiative. In many ways, investing in REDD is a smart business move for companies interested in projecting values of social responsibility. Nature has value for an increasingly eco-curious public, and since many captains of industry have slowly come to the conclusion that there are profits to be made by associating oneself with sustainability, the protection of tropical forests seems like a more attractive investment than a business merely reducing its own pollution. However, the concern for many was how to make carbon more "charismatic" while at the same time trying to convince buyers of the non-timber value of forests (Daily and Ellison 2002). Here is where the presence of the Ecologically Noble Savage resurfaces with market value, because, as one carbon-trade observer put it, "not all carbon trading is created equal" (Zwick, personal communication, June 5, 2013). Put more plainly, "indigenous" carbon has special appeal in the international marketplace.

The most widely covered case involving ethnomapping and carbon trading—and at the center of most of the previously mentioned reports—is the story of the Paiter-Suruí and its college-educated leader, Chief Almir Suruí. The media attention this community has received is warranted, as the Suruí (as they are often more simply called), an Amazonian people whose territory is located within that northwestern Brazilian state of Rondônia (whose smoldering, deforested landscape was filmed by the space shuttle), was the first indigenous tribe to use cultural mapping as a direct method to earn the right to engage in the trade of sequestered forest carbon. To achieve its goal of earning REDD+ validation, the Suruí employed media tools such as the internet, Google Earth, Android phones, and YouTube, and developed partnerships with USAID, Google, Forest Trends, Amazon Conservation Team (ACT), Annenberg Foundation, Rainforest Fund, and others, as well as negotiated a more responsive relationship with FUNAI (Fundação Nacional do Índio)—the Brazilian government body that monitors indigenous policies and rights. These efforts allowed the community to establish greater visibility and craft a plan of eco-mitigation that would eventually permit them to earn carbon credits. The result was that on July 15, 2013, after almost ten years of work, the Suruí became the first indigenous tribe in the world to achieve REDD+ validation and thus be officially sanctioned to engage in carbon trading. And the first big sale did not take long: on September 10, 2013, the community completed a sale of 120,000 tons of carbon offsets to the Brazilian cosmetic giant Natura Cosmeticos ("Brazilian Cosmetics Giant" 2013).

Considering the broader historical forces that shaped and enabled the Suruí's turn toward eco-stewardship (such as the rise of indigenous rights in the late 1980s in Brazil; growing global concern for the Amazon in the 1980s and 1990s; and the emergence of portable, user-friendly media technology in the 1990s and beyond), this story has many possible beginnings. However, given the community's newfound status as "carbon seller" and as a global example of local-national-global conservation and indigenous rights, perhaps the most appropriate starting point is September 7, 1969—the date when the Suruí made "contato" (first contact) with westerners. Before 1969 the tribe was considered "uncontacted," having interacted only with the occasional rubber tapper who stumbled into their territory. But thanks to the construction of the two-thousand-mile World Bank-financed Trans-Amazon Highway, this isolation was quickly to end. To help facilitate the building of the highway and end Suruí warrior attacks on roadbuilders, the Brazilian government's Indian affairs agency initiated a plan to establish contact and build relations with the tribe. This was performed through the offering of machetes, pots, axes, mirrors, and other assorted goods to draw the Suruí from the forest. Once outsiders contacted the Suruí, the result was, in no uncertain terms, catastrophic for the community, decimating the tribe from five thousand to a few hundred, victims of age-old foes of indigenous peoples, such as measles, chickenpox, and tuberculosis (Butler 2009; Forero 2013a, 2013b; Hammer 2007). To make matters worse, the new highway brought with it easy access to the forest's bounty and thus a stream of settlers from the cities, fraudulent land titles in hand. In fact, because of these events the region devolved into the antithesis of what anyone would consider a realm of conservation, becoming rather "like the Wild West, a place where loggers and settlers penetrate Indian land, where traffickers smuggle cocaine and where hired pistoleros have killer Indians who were in the way of development" (Forero 2013). Not surprisingly, for the Suruí the period after the "first contact" became etched in their cultural memory as a time of suffering, marked by eroding community life caused by disease and loss of life, bloody conflicts with settlers, alcoholism, and ecological degradation (Butler 2009; Forero 2013a, 2013b).

But with time it also emerged as a period of learning and cultural recalibration. Speaking at the 20th Annual Bioneers Conference in San Rafael, California, Chief Almir offered:

> Today we are 1,300 Suruí. Before first contact, we were 5,000 and that really woke us up, because we knew if we didn't do anything our way of life could end. We became even more worried, when we saw that our forest would go with us. And so we had to find a way to create dialogue with the rest of the world, to find a way for our future. One of the ways we found we could communicate was through the Internet and through technology. (Temple 2009)

Since Almir's ascension as a village chief, which began while he was still a teenager, the community has organized itself to move away from the "post-contato" period of suffering and exploitation to purposefully pursue greater cultural sovereignty and the strategic defense of its lands. According to *Ecosystem Marketplace*, to do this, in 2007 Chief Almir approached Forest Trends (publisher of *Ecosystem Marketplace*), an environmental nonprofit organization based in Washington, D.C. It was through Forest Trends that he learned about REDD and the tribe's carbon-ownership rights. This was followed by a Suruí vote in 2009 to enact a moratorium on logging and establish a working relationship with IDESAM (*Instituto de Conservação e Desenvolvimento Sustentável do Amazonas* / Institute for the Conservation and Sustainable Development of Amazonas) to measure, verify, and report the impacts of the Suruí actions. In 2010 another Brazilian interest, FUNBIO (*Fundo Brasileiro da Biodiversidade* / Brazilian Biodiversity Fund) partnered with the community to establish the Suruí Trust Fund, created to ensure that income from the project is managed responsibly and transparently. Finally, FUNAI (*Fundação Nacional do Índio* / National Indian Foundation) endorsed the Suruí effort as a model project (Zwick, personal communication, June 5, 2013).

This period of relationship building and consultation has also been marked by the tribe's creation of a progressive vision of the future (the fifty-year "Plano de Vida"). The generation of this plan has involved convincing the tribe's members that the immediate financial benefit of selling off their forest resources was ultimately a road to cultural ruin (Petersen, personal communication, June 13, 2013). It also required splitting up the Surui into four different groups to live around the Sete de Setembro Reserve, the six-thousand-acre territory (three times larger than Manhattan) that the Brazilian government set aside for the tribe in 1983 (Hammer 2007). In addition, the Suruí employed more confrontational tactics, such as obstructing logging roads, chasing off miners and loggers, and calling out corrupt or lazy officials of the government agencies who are supposed to defend the tribe's indigenous rights. But arguably their most effective measures to move into a new phase of community life was realized through the utilization of new media technology to map their territory, register their (often fading) cultural knowledge, monitor their borders, and catalog illegal logging, all while projecting a progressive image of indigenous rights and resource stewardship.

This process has not been easy; evidently, some members of the tribe resented the plan and Almir's increasing status and emerging place as community's voice (Petersen, personal communication, June 13, 2013). These tensions notwithstanding, this approach, which Almir has characterized as "modernity through tradition" (Zwick, personal communication, May 6, 2013), has indeed helped the community establish global visibility and dialogue, thus situating the Paiter Suruí case as a replicable model for indigenous-led conservation.

From "Uninhabited" Forest to 3-D Ethnomap

By many accounts the embrace of communication technology as a path to greater visibility and dialogue, and eventually carbon trading, started with the Chief Almir's own curiosity. In the late 1990s, while still in his early twenties, the Suruí leader began to travel widely in order to attend environmental summits and meet with political leaders and conservation groups to discuss the plight of his people (Zwick, personal communication, June 5, 2013). Like the leaders of the Kayapó and Yanomani before him, Almir used these trips to meet with representatives of powerful government agencies and NGOs (the World Bank, the United Nations Environmental Programme, Annenberg Foundation) to connect with environmental groups like the Washington-based nonprofit Forest Trends, the Prince's Rainforest Project, and the Environmental Defense Fund, and to network with the likes of Al Gore, Jane Goodall, Prince Charles, Richard Attenborough, Michael Pollan, Bianca Jagger, and other luminaries of eco-activism (Zwick, personal communication, June 5, 2013).

Perhaps even more important, through these travels Almir took to visiting cybercafés and became familiar with a variety of online services. One of his favorites was Google Earth—a geographical mapping program he had become familiar with through ACT's indigenous mapping initiative (Zwick, personal communication, June 5, 2013) and pioneering initiative to train tribes in danger of extinction in the Amazon's most remote areas to use media technology for both cultural preservation and territorial defense. Set up in Brazil by ACT's Brazil program director, Vasco van Roosmalen, the basic idea was that, by establishing a living cartography of their lands via capturing fading generation knowledge, Indians were empowered to map, catalog, and monitor their ancestral territories (Butler 2006). Through the ACT workshops, Almir and Vasco had become friends. So in 2007, when Almir planned to travel to San Francisco for an environmental summit, the Suruí leader, now accustomed to access with important decision makers, asked Vasco to set up a meeting with Google. According to Steve Zwick, managing editor of Forest Trend's *Ecosystem Marketplace* and Chief Almir's biographer:

> Vasco got a meeting with Google's Rebecca Moore, and basically they initially gave him a half hour. Almir got very excited. Vasco warned him, "Well don't get your hopes up, they are probably just curious." Almir went in with his headdress on, which he always wears. He said that for him it's like wearing a suit; he doesn't do it for show but rather it makes him feel better, gives him a sense of formality. And he went in and he started giving this presentation saying, "I really like this Google Earth, this program you have. It's amazing." You know, kind of buttering them up. Showing them his village, getting them to zoom in on the village, and getting people coming in. They brought in the guy who lead the development team of Google Earth and had him look at it. And after he got all of the people in the room, Almir turned to the Google team and [said], "Now I have a question for you: How come it says 'uninhabited' here? Why aren't we on here?" And then he starts pushing them and pushing them . . . and doesn't let go. He hammered them on that and they got excited about it. (Zwick, personal communication, June 5, 2013)

From this meeting, which evidently started off as a courtesy to Almir, Google ended up sending a team to Rondônia in 2008 to train "ethnomappers." The idea was to take a previously created hand-drawn Suruí ethnomap of the 600,000-acre reserve and reproduce it as a Google map by having community members learn a whole range of Google mapping technologies. This process was also a means through which to literally chart the tribe's cultural memory by mapping information from interviews with Suruí elders about place-based knowledge on flora, fauna, events, spiritual sites, and other places of cultural significance. By 2009 Google was back in Brazil training the Suruí to go out into the forest to capture and upload images, document illegal activities, and chart an interactive map via the use of Android phones. These "rangers," as Google dubbed them, not only gathered the information for the creation of a 3-D visualization of the Suruí forest, but they also received a certification of course completion (Petersen, personal communication, June 13, 2013). In 2012 the Google team returned to the Amazon one last time to finish the cultural map. According to Google's blog "The Suruí Cultural Map,"

> Over three visits to the Suruí territory between 2008 and last month, our Google Earth Outreach team taught Suruí youth how to take photos and videos and to collect stories from their elders (such as from the time before first contact with the modern world). Then they learned how to upload these to the Google cloud using tools like Picasa, Docs, and YouTube. From there we used Spreadsheet Mapper 3 to bind it all together to create a Google Earth KML of their map, which contains almost 300 sites.[6]

This process has been incredibly important, allowing the Suruí to complete a number of interrelated objectives. First, it established a mechanism that now actively serves as a form of cultural defense. Early on, the move to "go virtual" was necessitated by the fact that the Brazilian government was largely unresponsive to Suruí charges that illegal logging was taking place on their land (Petersen, personal communication, June 13, 2013). The media technology, then, provided for a concrete starting point of cultural defense, in that they could produce undeniable documentation that incursions were taking place on their land. Thus the recording of images permitted the Suruí to generate a more responsive relationship with FUNAI and thereby illustrate that they needed immediate action from the state. Moreover, as *Cultural Survival* reported, the technology created a surveillance dynamic: "Those images not only give proof of incursions that can prompt action by the government, but they actually discourage incursions in the first place, because loggers and miners know they're being watched" (Camp 2010).

Second, it allowed the community to capture and encode tribal knowledge. Making the virtual map and its accompanying videos facilitated the preservation of the tribe's historical memory and cultural practices through the identification and charting of key geographic sites tied to hunting, battles, spirituality, food sources, and other natural resources. This allowed the Suruí to produce a cartographic interpretation of its ancestral lands in a way consistent with its cosmology, supporting ACT founder Mark Plotkin's observation: "Westerners map in three dimensions: longitude, latitude, and altitude. Indians think in six: longitude, latitude, altitude, historical context, sacred sites, and spiritual or mythological sites, where invisible creatures mark watersheds and areas of high biodiversity as off-limits to exploitation" (Butler 2006). Those who have worked with the community observed that this experience of ethnomapping also deepened generational bonds, as elders were tapped for their knowledge (which reified their status), while techno-hungry youth took leadership roles in documenting and translating the stories to virtual form (Petersen, personal communication, June 13, 2013; Zwick, personal communication, June 5, 2013).

Third, since earning REDD+ certification required a longitudinal plan for eco-mitigation, it obligated the tribe to develop a concrete plan of action for its future. According to Rachael Petersen, an environmental blogger and Environmental Defense Fund researcher who worked closely with the Suruí in 2013, this involved creating a climate for community buy in, especially as many Suruí had benefited directly from some of the earlier logging. Almir worked tirelessly to change the tribe's thinking, presenting the initiative as an "autonomous development project that involved the desire of the community coming together to literally not only map their lands but map their futures" (Petersen, personal communication, June 13, 2013). The process of creating the map and then "digitizing" it via Google directly fed the development of a "plano de vida," a requirement for carbon trading, which laid out how the community would create and manage a community action plan to be economically self-sustaining for the next fifty years. "This is much more than just carbon training. There's the marketing of Brazil nuts, the marketing of Suruí artisanal goods. But so much of this project was focused on how they would physically manage their land and resources" (Petersen, personal communication, June 13, 2013).

These are vital achievements because, as Plotkin notes, "you can't have rainforest Indians without the rainforest. The best way to protect ancestral rainforests is to help Indians hold onto their culture, and the best way to help them hold onto their culture is to help them protect the rainforest" (Butler 2006). In the case of the Suruí, the cultural map became the basis for their carbon project, and the carbon project a motivation for long-term community planning and cultural sharing. And while ACT came up with the methodology and Google provided the technology, it was the Suruí who furnished the knowledge.

From Environmental Justice to Ecological Modernization

Considering the long and exploitative history of extractivism in Latin America and the economic and political arrangements that still largely inform it (Acosta 2013; Latta and Wittman 2012; Miller 2007), the Rainforest Harvest and Carbon Trading periods (if it is not too early to call the latter a "period") of the Amazon are relatively progressive developments in that they have involved, in ways not seen in the past, indigenous organization, political agency, and environmental defense. Both periods have unfolded, albeit in different ways, by working through NGOs, multinational corporations, the services of the state (or lack thereof), the promise of multilateral agreements, and the logic of "the market." Interestingly, these periods also reveal that while nature continues to be a site of social struggle, media events and communication technologies can be leveraged to alter the existing "discursive formations" (Foucault 1972) through the inclusion of, and in some cases interruptions by, voices and images that have been largely kept silent or been absent in the past. So, despite some of their limitations and compromises, it is still worth considering some of the lessons learned from this rainforest experience, in which the figure of the Ecologically Noble Savage has had a reoccurring role.

While full of promise, the "Rainforest Harvest" period of Amazonian indigenous environmentalism in the 1980s and 1990s was marked by cultural misunderstanding, exploitation, greed, and miscalculation—a mixture that led to its "cancellation" in mainstream media and marketing circles. However, despite the movement's reliance on celebrities, transnational companies, and media coverage, the generation of a global, high-visibility Amazonian indigenous eco-politics was nevertheless grounded in very real concerns of environmental limits, community welfare, cultural autonomy, resource stewardship, and human rights. Indeed, before it crumbled due to its own internal inconsistencies and tensions, this moment of Amazonian environmentalism was truly global, and it did raise awareness about the plight of the Amazon, environmental justice, and indigenous struggles, and perhaps most broadly it presented openings for the respect and valuation of "place" and thus a deepening appreciation for environmental citizenship. As such, it presents an interesting case of how the assumptions and constructs of Green Radicalism momentarily pierced through the hegemonic landscape of the Promethean discourse to present an ethic of compassion and stewardship.

But in recognizing this dynamic, it must also be said that, as an articulation of Green Radicalism on a global scale, it played out as "radicalism" with a little "r." That is, this Amazonian moment might be understood as bioregional context that became internationalized, projected into a global public sphere via the guiding assumption that people could transform themselves and their thinking and take action to protect an existing ecosystem that had global significance. This effort was fostered, in no small way, through global-national-local partnerships and individual actors within a global community of concern based on human rights and enabled through media networks. The discourse was grounded in two kinds of agency. First, it was anchored in the normative (Western) assumption that indigenous communities were imbued with direct eco-agency, as it relied on the notion that indigenous actors (the Ecologically Noble Savage) were naturally connected to the earth and understood its limits. Indigenous activism was thus framed as *a priori* motivated by a sense that the natural balance of things had to be restored and that these agents were acting as defenders of the rainforest. Directly related to this was a secondary form of agency, which assumed that indigenous actors presented the West with distinct organic blueprints for eco-conscious living. This rendering of agency, while less normative, was in many ways more telling, as it relied on connecting cultural survival with an Amazon in peril and instilling cooperation through the practice of "fair trade"—a social obligation aligned with equality and Environmental Justice. Via this sense that "every person can be an agent" inherent in Green Radicalism (Dryzek 2005), "global" support and solidarity could be operationalized through the consumption of products (cosmetics and ice cream) tied to the forest and associated with indigenous struggles, an activity that had appeal due to its connection with progressive environmental subjectivities and action.

Looking back, we see the obvious weakness of these appeals, and indeed the idealism behind them, as solidarity seems like exploitation, charity masquerades as justice, and new ecological subjectivities cannot simply be cultivated through rainforest consumption. Nevertheless, as Brazilian Indians moved into the global public sphere and forged new international alliances, they were able to position themselves more strategically against a formerly unresponsive state and transnational interests. Thus, based on their activism and visibility, some Amazonian communities did witness change, such as greater understanding of indigenous struggles, and they did experience very real gains, such as land-right reforms, stoppage of destructive World Bank–funded megaprojects, and other forest "development" initiatives. And it is important to recognize that this period also led to a resuscitation of traditional Amazonian indigenous culture in relation to modernizing forces—what Latin American cultural critic Néstor García Canclini (1992) has dubbed "cultural reconversion," a strategy whereby the "symbolic patrimony" of cultural capital is transferred "in order to conserve it, increase its yield, and better the position of those who practice it" (31–32). In the Amazon of the 1980s and 1990s, the cultural reconversion of a particular aesthetic of indigenous authenticity and its association with Environmental Justice recharged native cultural expressions with greater political meaning.

Paradoxically, in many ways it also made this reinvestment in tradition captive to hegemonic ideas and visual codes, which positioned groups, even politically astute ones like the Kayapó, as vulnerable to the agendas of external interests. Within this contradictory landscape of the "Rainforest Harvest" stage of Amazonian environmental activism, the imaginistic qualities of native peoples and their assumed forest-caretaker role provided environmentalism and green-hued capitalism alike with both "weak" (change through eco-conscious consumption) and "strong" (environmental citizenship) variations of Green Radicalism, both of which were imbued with the struggle for human rights, the wisdom of Amerindian cosmology, and the ecological limits of an identifiable commons. These same qualities and identifying features helped the Kayapó achieve their visibility and voice and even some political potency within the global public sphere. But when there was a hint that the Kayapó didn't live up to these qualities and attributes, their symbolic value as environmental champions was immediately diminished. After all, what good is an Indian that fails to be "authentic"? Or, to put it another way, failure to maintain authenticity has its consequences.

Like the Kayapó before them, the Suruí are implicated in an ecological dilemma not of their own making. Their culture, or at least the external perception of what the "authentic" expression of their culture is and represents, is what gives them voice and visibility within the global public sphere, and perhaps more significant in their case, what gives their carbon "charisma." So, the Suruí are also reliant on, and in many ways ensnared by, the projection of a recognizable "indigenousness" that, because of its ties to organic balance and "natural" way of interacting with natural systems, "makes sense" to international human rights and environmentalism networks. The presence of these Western assumptions has not changed and, as with the Kayapó, despite their imposition (consider, for instance, Google's own patronizing characterization of "trading bows and arrows for laptops") they have allowed the Suruí to access, find voice within, and exercise political agency on a global stage. The Suruí have clearly understood this, and under Almir's leadership they have employed this symbolic currency along with their mastery of media technologies (as both performers and media makers) to chart a pragmatic path toward palpable goals: protecting resources from overexploitation, preserving cultural heritage, and achieving a sustainable future.

What makes the Suruí case noticeably different from the Kayapó's is the emphasis on anticipatory planning; cooperation among science, environmentalists, industry, and government; business incentives and leadership; and the marriage of environmental protection to economic progress. It is a situation also founded on the recognition of ecological crisis as ripe for a techno-institutional fix, albeit with an eco-cultural face. As I pointed out in chapter 1, these are the discursive signposts of Ecological Modernization, a "problem solving" discourse, which is much different than Green Radicalism's emphasis on changing society's and/or people's consciousness (Dryzek 2005). Consider, for instance, that while the Kayapó were understood as agents engaged in protests and media events to stimulate change—fodder ripe for the ranks of Green Radicalism—the Suruí have been positioned as the caretakers of a "forest carbon project"—a coordinated form of stewardship externally validated by a certifying body. Earning the status in the carbon offset marketplace is no easy chore, requiring the development of a longitudinal plan by community leaders to shift from logging to carbon capture in concert with the negotiation of a complex web of bureaucratic regimes and corruption, while often frustrated by unresponsive agencies and conflicting self-interests and cultural practices. To get there, as a "non-Annex I community" under the Kyoto Protocol and within the mandates of REDD+ policy, the tribe had to draft a scientifically verifiable plan, as well as go through a process of ethnomapping its biodiverse territory. Completing these tasks—all while mobilized by the community's desire to halt logging, preserve their resources for the future, register the cultural knowledge of the elders, and achieve cultural sovereignty—was nevertheless administrative and driven by the (externally "validated") objective of commodifying their forest as carbon credit.

Given the increased global emphasis on corporate social responsibility, it is clear why this crafting of a "carbon-zero" indigenous Amazonian commodity would have special value in the carbon-trading market. But it is hard not to shake the feeling that the Suruí have been positioned, via the same set of guiding assumptions about the Ecologically Noble Savage that shaped the Kayapó's place in global eco-politics, as Neolithic keepers of the global carbon storehouse. But in arguing this, it is important to acknowledge that while, like the Kayapó, the Suruí have invested in this image as a means for cultural survival, the expectations are radically different. That is, within the discourse of Green Radicalism the expectation was that, as natural agents of the forest, the Kayapó would enlighten the West through their eco-consciousness and save the rainforest through their activism—a moment of global ecological enlightenment that supporters could participate in via consumption-based solidarity. Conversely, the Suruí's path is not being charted through activism to force change but through community organization in relation to the kind of cooperation among government, scientists, and industry espoused by Ecological Modernization—a discourse, it should be noted, that historically has been strongly associated with the efficiencies of modern states (such as

Germany and the Netherlands), not indigenous communities. But to situate themselves within this discourse, the Suruí have had to work hard to mobilize the community and elaborate partnerships, along with interethnic support networks and horizontal mentoring programs through which other indigenous actors could earn mapping certificates and contractual agreements to "store" and "sell" their resources as a preserved eco-cultural product. Somewhat paradoxically, then, the forest thus depends on the preservation of culture more than commerce, as one sustains and nurtures the health and well-being of the other. Compared to the Kayapó's event-oriented activism, the Suruí's path is not particularly glamorous, but it is nevertheless still shaped by the Western appetite for authenticity, an authenticity commodifed and sold to the highest bidder for the benefit of the planet.

In both cases, the emergence of media-literate, technologically proficient, and eco-conscious Indians actually feed into Western assumptions. But they also complicated former semiotic arrangements by recasting the "Ecologically Noble Savage" not as children of the forest who could disappear "invisibly" into its canopy but rather as agents *for* the forest: activists (Kayapó) and caretakers (Suruí) highly capable of using communication and media tools to speak for themselves, engage in sophistical political negotiations, and register their culture, all while pushing for recognition and change (Kayapó) or organizing to identify problems and enact sustainable, market-registered solutions (Suruí). With the recent announcement that the Xingu River valley dams will now after all be built, it appears that the Kayapó's struggle for their cultural rights ends with a stunning defeat. Within the shadow of the Rainforest Harvest era, what remains to be seen is what kind of shelf life carbon trading will have, and as such its capacity to inform sustainable forest stewardship into the future. Clearly, as the first indigenous group in the world to sell carbon credits, the Suruí have benefited from their "first adopter" status. Will other indigenous communities be able to do the same? Or if the Suruí project fails, given the proclivities of "the market," or if the "indigeneity" of other forest communities is not authentic enough, will an activists' orientation of Green Radicalism need to be reimagined from these past efforts to give birth to a new wave of Amazonian activists to save the rainforest from the market?

Conclusion

Earth Discourses and the Question of Agency in the Media Commons

Marshall McLuhan once famously said, "There are no passengers on space-ship earth. We're all crew." The problem is that, whether one comes from privilege or lives a life of struggle, within today's media commons we are all invited to act like passengers, and most accept the invitation. And it is hard not to. I have tried to show in the preceding chapters that the structures and practices of our contemporary media systems are pervasive enough to assure that, even in the face of the profoundly troubling signs of ecological stress all around us, large segments of the world's population are encouraged to have market-driven relationships with the environment that rarely challenge audiences to think or act like crew.

This ecological ambivalence can be explained in no small measure by the fact that today's media institutions have not been leveraged in any meaningful way to break free from a cycle of passive recognition and weakly ecological, consumer-based action. Indeed, the discursive terrain of environmental messages that most media audiences find themselves enmeshed in is confusing, often contradictory, and obscured by mixed regimes of truth. I have attempted to diagnose these tendencies structurally through an analysis of institutional practices of production, representations, and the motives of actors in relation to wider changes in society and culture. While admittedly partial, I think it is evident from the case studies in this book that the media systems in place are in fact key producers of this very cycle.

The Market Will Solve the Problem

To get a fuller sense of the scope of things, in chapter 2 I surveyed the broader topography of the global media commons, arguing that the globally networked media work as a knowledge system designed to manufacture market subjectivities on a planetary scale. As institutions anchored in neoliberal ideology, they have been elaborated for the exercise of power and control of populations through the articulation of particular kinds of knowledge, a process increasingly obscured by the "glocalization" qualities of local/regional/national cultures. At the center of these structural practices is a discourse of perpetual growth expressed through the market, which, following Dryzek (2005), I referred to as the Promethean discourse. For the West, this cornucopian vision of the environment and its requisite free-market agent has been circulating for some time. For "the rest," whether the focus is Asia, Africa, Latin America, or Eastern Europe, in newly industrialized and post-communist countries alike, the marketization of subjectivities through commercial media systems has unfolded alongside the dual forces of consumerism and some version of democratization (even if only expressed as "voting" for a talent show contest).

The contradictions between some of these core ideas notwithstanding, the commercial media have thus evolved as a platform for neoliberalism's philosophical underpinnings, promoting "a claim that the market is better than the state at distributing public resources and . . . a return to a 'primitive form of individualism: an individualism which is "competitive," "possessive," and construed often in terms of the doctrine of "consumer sovereignty"'" (Ong 2007, 11)—ideas ideologically consistent with the Promethean discourse. In short, the global media system emphasizes individual agency, self-interest, and the invisible hand of the market while minimizing social-structural issues, thus marginalizing through its absence more collective, non-market-driven problem solving.

Through the evolution of the global neoliberal media landscape the Promethean discourse quietly but nevertheless quite convincingly (re)secured hegemonic status. Environmentally, the development of this discursive-philosophical bundling has been profound, as the resonance of the Promethean discourse across diverse nations and societies lies in the fact that it has become so globalized, so ubiquitous, that it is implicated in the very consequences it helps gives rise to—a quality that has enabled it to, evoking Foucault (1972, 49), "systematically form the objects of which it speaks." Moreover, since media systems are typically understood to be cultural, economic, and/or political institutions, not environmental ones, the production of Promethean logic does not stand out as particularly "environmental." This allows the discourse to shape audiences' relationships with the earth while somehow not seeming to be there at all—an ideological disappearing act that underscores Dryzek's (2005) observation that "political-economic discourse of liberal capitalist systems still generally floats free from any sense of environmental constraints" (52).

The naturalization of the Promethean discourse within the global media commons should be more than a little disconcerting because it is founded on the assumption that if a protectionist state merely gets out of the way, innovation, creativity, and problem solving will be abundant and thus sufficient to handle any problem on the horizon. As a regime of truth, it celebrates the role of citizens (or better yet, consumers) as powerful actors—an expression of agency that is empowering *as long as that agency is performed in market terms*. Concerns about environmental stewardship and questions about the limits of the Earth are thus individualized, and we are all potential problem solvers. While this might sound encouraging, the Promethean confidence in continual growth and innovation is born from the underlying belief that the marketplace of ideas, via its active entrepreneurs, will ultimately save the planet from any forthcoming challenges, such as climate-system disintegration. Scarcity, we should recall, is understood by the Built as an economic, not ecological, challenge (Garrard 2004) with new resources sought out, found, and tapped into only when they are needed (Dryzek 2005).

The Question of Agency

Within this confluence of neoliberal philosophy and cornucopian logic we need to ask, Who benefits from this rendering of agency—the individual so celebrated by the Built, or corporate "citizens"? Proponents of trade liberalization, such as the WTO, the World Bank, the IMF, many governments, and most political elites, take a Promethean tack, asserting that sustainable development will be the outcome of the innovation and natural-resource allocation efficiencies stimulated within less protectionist economies (Christoff and Eckersley 2013). But while economies have indeed been stimulated around the world since liberalization, most countries have experienced an increasing gap between the rich and the poor (Steger 2009; see also Kempf 2007). In addition, rather than generating greater efficiencies, the elimination of social-control mechanisms has often led to a weakening of global labor standards and ecological degradation through a "race to the bottom" (Klein 2007). Despite this track record, the globally networked media systems continue to help cultivate the notion that the best mechanism through which innovation can be incubated and problems creatively solved is an unencumbered, "free" market.

However, as I have also tried to demonstrate, the exercise of discursive power by media institutions is far from static, as these media spheres also possess their own internal contradictions, points of tension, and even divergent motivations. That is why, while the Promethean discourse may have achieved hegemonic status within the context of contemporary globalization, it continues to be profoundly conditioned by other discourses. Here, the notion of agency is the key entry point for understanding how discourses are co-produced and reliant on each other for self-definition, and even condition the terms through which competing or alternative discourses can find space.

Consider, for instance, that the Promethean's assertion that "agency is for everyone" is important in relation to what its discursive rivals offer or, perhaps more accurately, fail to offer. As examined in previous chapters, its most salient competitor in the global commons, Survivalism, frames agency as the domain of "the experts," not the unwashed masses, which it actually sees as one face of our current environmental ills. Superficially, when considered together the two tend to give the impression that they merely represent "free" versus "controlled" bookends for how environmental affairs might be pursued. However, the different conceptualizations of agency reveal more profoundly how, as "big picture" discourses, the Promethean discourse and Survivalism have co-authored the terms of agreement and dispute over the commons. These discourses have been pitted against each other since at least the 1970s, when the Club of Rome and other key works shifted public discourse in the West to environmental limits. Based on this shared history it should therefore not be surprising that the Limits discourse can survive within media spheres dominated by Promethean logic because it was the Survivalists who originally forced the Prometheans to articulate their assumptions. By default, this dialogical relationship also institutionalizes Survivalism as the alterative to cornucopian thought.

This dynamic of co-production has evolved to serve the interests of both. This point is perhaps best made, although unintentionally, by Bjorn Lomborg's "The Litany" (quoted in the introduction of this book) and his claim that the entertainment and news media help make the catastrophic familiar by presenting a vision of the environment that is in freefall. So, while global media spheres certainly do embrace practices that enunciate the doom and gloom of Survivalism, the presence of Survivalist tales helps give the impression that the Promethean-dominated global media system has room for competing discourses and is therefore open and flexible and thus non-ideological. Indeed, in some interesting ways the very notion of scarcity called out by the Survivalists helps Promethean logic blend into the background by creating discursive space through which the cornucopian innovators can, when needed, come to the rescue.

To be clear, this landscape of competing ideas and interests provides more than just discursive camouflage for the Promethean discourse as alternative discourses are reshaped through their articulation in global mediascapes. One of the more powerful forces at work on these alternatives is the market imperative, which refashions and/or squeezes out the more confrontational and pragmatic Earth discourses to serve its own interests. This is a point I make in chapter 3 by asserting that cable and public television have become, at least in the West, key sites for post-Earth and nature's-revenge narratives anchored in the Limits discourse. Here, there is no shortage of stories about human excess, prophesized disaster, extinction, and wilderness reclaimed by a self-regulating, living organism (Gaia). Cable and public TV's rendering of the Limits discourse has also moved audiences away from the Malthusian concern for overpopulation and scarcity of resources, placing the emphasis instead on twenty-first-century threats such as pandemics, migration, social unrest, and conflict—issues that share much in common with the "local" or community-based problem solving foci of Democratic Pragmatism and Green Radicalism (especially Environmental Justice and Ecofeminism).

But as cable and public channels themselves exist within a broader media system that is driven by market imperatives, entertainment value and programs' capacity to draw audiences override the impulse to tell more pragmatic, challenging, or potentially paradigm-shifting tales. When Discovery pulled the plug on Planet Green, the reaction of the channel's producers, even those passionately involved in the "noble" experiment, was that it failed because they needed more "character driven" shows. Perhaps this is true, and Discovery did in fact fail to understand the needs of an audience for Planet Green. But such ways of looking at how entertainment media present ideas and information about the environment continually place the canary, not the mine itself, at the center of attention. What the short life of Planet Green seems to teach us is that despite the best intentions by corporate media to development eco-conscious programming, the details about "the conflict" and the characters themselves will always demand more attention than the looming problems of the commons.

This state of "amusing ourselves to death" decision making, to borrow from Postman (1985), suggests that under the presumed demands of audience needs and the industry that ostensibly serves them, the environment becomes just another device through which to tell engaging stories, not an important topic in need of preventive strategies or actionable solutions. Within this corporate model, real environmental agency becomes a casualty, at best aligned with consumer adjustments for greener product choices, or more imaginatively perhaps, envisioned in relation to post-apocalyptic survival scenarios of zombies, tornado-charged sharks, and other nature's revenge and end-of-days tales that serve the role of ecological jeremiad but paradoxically without providing a call to action for real change. It is in the end an articulation of Survivalism, with discursive flirtations with Green Radicalism and Democratic Pragmatism, that does little to challenge the growth-forever lifestyles championed by the Promethean view of the world. In short, while there is room for Survivalism's focus on global issues, bleak as they might be, it does not translate into a space welcoming to more praxis-oriented, problem-solving discourses, at least not as a standalone material with a meaningful shelf life within commercial television.

Other sites of mediation present different versions of this discursive tug of war, in which the Protheans seem to hold home-field advantage. The case of Monsanto provides a lens through which we can better see how a large and controversial company has responded to external criticism by elaborating its own sophisticated multiplatform media operations to defend—indeed, rewrite—its public image. In my view this is an important case because not only does it reveal how, more and more, non-media companies have invested in their own highly networked and even "socialized" communication operations to reach out to the public, but also how such companies can use these media to strategically deploy multiple Earth discourses to shape their brand identity.

Monsanto presents us with a company's capacity to masterfully draw on and exploit key imagery, master terms, and a blend of metaphors across discourses to manufacture a brand that is, evidently and despite its controversial environmental history, highly responsive to Earth's challenges. To pursue this, Monsanto presents a classical rendering of Survivalism with its key concerns—overpopulation and scarcity—to underscore the need for a global Promethean response. But to make the global feel more local and thus ground the brand in the earth, the notion of partnership and locality (be it an African farm, an Indian village, or the American heartland) is delivered in the form of the farmer (or what Monsanto now calls the "grower"). This is a powerful symbolic endorsement in that it suggests that agency lies with those who work the soil—utopian visual cues of "membership" associated with Democratic Pragmatism, Sustainable Development, and Green Radicalism (Ecofeminism). It is in the end, however, a platform founded on a market-based vision of food production anchored on the premise that "sustainability" is produced through Promethean innovation, partnered with those who know the earth is alive but nevertheless a quality provided by an innovative, responsive commercial agent.

In many ways this case (and others like it that are tied to food, water, and the control of the commons and the natural resources we all depend on to sustain life) is about "voice," how various interests can be heard, and who or what controls the megaphone. Grassroots movements and citizen groups in Asia, Latin America, Canada, and Europe have been very good at mobilizing and using media horizontally to create community, organize, and challenge Monsanto's right to "engineer" nature. However, in this age of increasingly more personalized social media, this case clearly demonstrates that concern over voice and finding ways to shape public discourse through horizontal communication channels (Twitter, Instagram, Facebook, Youtube) to complement more traditional vertical approaches (such as print, television, or radio advertising) is also an area of deep investment by corporations, with companies developing their own nimble and highly responsive media operations to do so.

In terms of the personal as political and place-based activism and its people, the indigenous struggles to be seen and heard draw us even more deeply into the unfolding ecological drama between the local and the global and media as a discursive tool. At the center of the case of the Amazon, a place steeped in ecological symbolism in the West, is the image of Noble Savage as eco-interlocutor. Not only are the indigenous inhabitants of the Amazon *of the forest*, they are defined as its defenders. Amazonian indigenous communities, particularly the Xavante, Kayapó, and Paiter-Suruí, have benefitted from and have been taken advantage of through this "eco-othering," which anthropologists have characterized as tied to "Western narratives of alienation, cultural loss and victimization coupled with heroic narratives of resistance to capitalist domination" (Conklin 2010, 130). Indeed, the history of ecological activism and cultural defense through the performance of authenticity by the Xavante, Kayapó, and most recently the Paiter-Suruí underscores the degree to which indigenous communities have negotiated and continue to negotiate global and regional power networks to establish and exercise real agency with real local results. From the 1970s to the present they have achieved these gains through an activist orientation that relied on image events enabled by Western environmentalism to what is now a more market-driven, carbon-capturing path to cultural survival and indigenous resource stewardship made possible by new media technologies. While the experiences of the indigenous communities I examined are quite different among themselves, in order for local concerns to be made "visible" to the outside world in all of these cases, indigenous actors have had to invest, ironically, in Western ideas about what authentic Amazonian Indians are supposed to look like, act like, and even say.

This road to Amazonian environmentalism has thus unfolded via shifting discursive terrain driven in no small way by larger changes in global economics and political mood. The earlier articulations of cultural survival were motivated by the indigenous desire for political recognition and cultural rights and thus were pursued through tactics seen and heard within the context of Brazil. With the state's recognition that native Amazonians had constitutional rights, groups like the Xavante learned to invest in rather than dilute the more salient aspect of their culture. While these were marginally successful, once indigenous cultural survival was married to Western environmentalism through the Kayapó, such global visibility established a path for local-national agency. But the capacity for the Kayapó to achieve this level of political agency would not have happened if their strategies to create image events did not resonate—even if in ways that misunderstood and objectified them—with the Western appetite for the Ecologically Noble Savage. The relationships that opened up were intimately tied to their assumed role as "natural conservationists" and its connection to Green Radicalism (Environmental Justice) in ways that were not necessarily aligned with the Kayapó's own motivations. Once this gap between perception and reality became apparent, the Kayapó's status as the mascots of Western ecocentrism and ecological defense quickly faded, leaving parties on both sides feeling deceived and exploited.

The current historical chapter of Amazonian eco-politics involving the Suruí has followed a much different path but involves some of the same tensions. That is, the place of the Ecologically Noble Savage looms large, and the Suruí have in fact quite literally traded on this trope to give their carbon "charisma." Nevertheless, the ways in which the Suruí have mobilized their community to use new media tools to engage both young and old has been remarkable and led to increased participation and cooperation in long-term forest stewardship. Though (as with the Kayapó) this process is still highly dependent on "authentic indigeneity," it now combines anthropocentrism (carbon trading as a market activity) with elements of ecocentrism (the spiritual aspect of ethnomapping the forest), signaling a shift in the discourse from Green Radicalism to Ecological Modernization. Through this new discursive rendering of the Amazonian rainforest, its aboriginal dwellers must set goals and work together to protect the forest's resources from overexploitation to preserve cultural heritage for an imagined, albeit externally validated, sustainable future.

Collectively, the media spheres, institutional encasements, sponsors, and practices examined in this book underscore how environmental discourses are produced in contexts and thus co-produce one another in terms that are disruptive (in other words, challenges the established order), complementary (accepting of some of the basic ideas of another discourse but not others), or compliant (at the service of hegemonic power). They therefore serve as vital reminders of how discourse, to paraphrase Edward Said's take on Foucault, "fits into a network that has its own history and conditions of existence" and provides rules that serve as "epistemological enforcers" of what people think, live, and speak (Barrett 1991, 126–27). And while the cases provide some hopeful signs that different discourses are at play and in some cases even offer imaginative, problem-solving solutions, it is clear that the discursive formations described and mapped out in the global mediascapes I have identified are intimately tied to, in fact policed by, the liberal capitalist economy. This explains why multiple Earth discourses can circulate at the same time, even if one embodies more power and has a greater capacity to suppress. It also reveals why agency is consistently framed in economic and not ecological terms.

Limitations and Possibilities of Ecological Citizenship in the Media Commons

Yet within the media commons, alternative discourses have not provided clear or convincing paths of escape from this general framing of the economic over the ecological. Whereas the discourse of Survivalism draws attention to Earth's limited stocks yet prescribes draconian policies of control, environmental problem-solving discourses (Democratic Pragmatism, Sustainable Development, Ecological Modernization) see the need for better environmental stewardship but ultimately frame such efforts as tractable within existing economic and political models; discourses associated with Green

Radicalism are the least welcomed within global commercial mediascapes as they flatly reject the Promethean assumptions about the environment's ability to survive our market-driven appetites. As none of these disparate discourses hold center stage within the media commons, the key assertions and underlying ideas they produce are partial and thus generally experienced only in bits and pieces—discursive fragments that present audiences with incomplete articulations about the earth's care and treatment.

So, as sources of inspiration for better, more progressive ecological stewardship, these limitations and partialities hardly offer a roadmap for transformational eco-politics. This makes building oppositional movements and mobilizing citizens based on these discourses difficult, especially when the very media systems that might be charged with interrogating Promethean-neoliberal assumptions are actually those that have been designed to manufacture them. This explains why, at least in part, that despite protests and movements like Occupy Wall Street or the more environmentally driven 350.org and Earth Democracy, effective confrontations against market-driven globalization are difficult to organize and sustain, making the realization of more ecocentric, paradigm-shifting, non-market-driven visions about life on Earth hard to translate into policy or even broader, more progressive forms of ecological citizenship.

Despite this uninspiring discursive terrain, there are some positive signs from the periphery and even centers of power that other environmental imaginations are possible. For instance, not only did Pope Francis's spiritually anchored 2015 encyclical on the environment argue that humans have a moral imperative to protect the planet, but Latin America, as it did during the age of "modernization" with its critique of cultural imperialism, has also resurfaced as a site of intense debate and important critical thought regarding the politics of the Earth. South America, particularly Bolivia and Ecuador, has been at the epicenter of these activities, which have surfaced largely in response to new forms of extractivism produced by neoliberalism. The result has been what some describe as an "ecoterritorial shift" (Lang 2013, 10), as social justice movements have formed in defense of territory and natural resources. Within this context, one of the more interesting developments has been how *sumak kawsay* ("living well"), a concept that runs contrary to the materialist notion that "the good life" is found through consumption and leisure, proposes measuring life in terms of how well one lives in harmony with the Earth. This concept from Andean cosmology has become a site of intense discursive struggle between ecocentrism and anthropocentrism in the region (Pinto 2012; Viola 2014) and is now beginning to stir debate beyond Latin America.

Such voices and developments suggest that in order to gauge how the media commons is being reconditioned, we need to continue to track and make sense of media discourses through their horizontal, not just vertical, trajectories. From above (vertically), this should involve a continuing interrogation of power politics aimed at teasing out how commercial and political institutions embrace new media to articulate more eco-responsible discourses (such as Ecological Modernization and Sustainable Development). Questions to ask would include *What are the motives for this embrace, and in whose interest?* From below (in other words, from the grassroots level through horizontal channels), the key determination would seem to be how media are being used to create community, amplify voice, and engender greater visibility for more imaginative, cultural, spiritual, and even scientific ideas about the Earth, which too often seem to suffer from bad translation. In essence, this would be an investigative chore motivated by making sense of new, more radical, or previously marginalized discourses that suggest pathways for a different kind of society and inspire new articulations of agency. For instance, with regard to mass species extinction, in his 2016 book *Half-Earth: Our Planet's Fight for Life*, Pulitzer Prize–winning entomologist Edward O. Wilson makes a case for Green Radicalism, positing that we approach the planet's ills through a strategy modeled on the idea of an ark rather than a lifeboat. But instead of gearing any solution "for" humans, Wilson audaciously proposes that half the world be set aside in the name of biodiversity and nonhuman life in order to save it from human exploitation and despoliation. Wilson's primary assertion is that while extinction is a natural process, what's happening now is not. Here, the underlying emphasis is on moral issues, not economic ones, while underscoring that the very species responsible for the current state of things now needs to take radical action to stop it.

While such declarations and those like them might sound like quixotic undertakings, it is useful to recall that the Limits discourse surfaced in the 1960s and 1970s as precisely that: a radical discourse seeking, in Dryzek's words, "a wholesale redistribution of power within the industrial political economy, and a wholesale reorientation away from perpetual economic growth" (2005, 15). But regardless if the new visions are quixotic or merely pragmatically hopeful, what we need are discourses that challenge or break free from the market-dominated view of life on Earth. There simply need to be different motivations at work, different solutions being conjured up based on different ontologies. Given the state of the global commercial media and the discourses that circulate with the most force alongside the possibilities of new technologies and citizen-based action, this presents both a huge challenge and yet a requisite for real change, as more progressive, mediated Earth discourses could certainly offer blueprints for ecological intervention.

But this also seems like a problem that will require us to find ways to shape our media institutions rather than merely being satisfied with our institutions shaping us. Such an initiative, to quote Cox (2012), is necessarily part of the "challenge of building a more sustainable world in the face of disruptive or unsustainable social and economic systems" (51). Or, to put it into even more urgent terms, "In the course of history, there comes a time when humanity is called to shift to a new level of consciousness, to reach a higher moral ground. A time when we have to shed our fear and give hope to each other. That time is now."[1] Such a shift poses imaginative challenges. Chief among them: rendering invisible regimes of truth and their institutional encasements more visible so we can question their guiding ontological assumptions and break free from their underlying assumptions.

Notes

Introduction

1. *The Meatrix*, a parody of the film *The Matrix,* is an animated blog that challenges site visitors to "take the red pill" to confront "the lies we tell ourselves about where our meat and other animal products come from." Since its launch in 2003 it has been translated into thirty languages. It was "re-launched" in 2015 with new material. The Web site and its four videos are available at http://www.themeatrix.com.

2. This issue's author, J. Michael Straczynski, created the science fiction television series *Babylon 5*.

3. Indeed, an even more concentrated indicator of the place of environmental issues in international communication was the launching of the journal *Global Media and Communication* in April 2005. Of the twelve invited essays presented as part of the journal's inaugural forum, titled "What's global about global media?" only Oliver Boyd-Barrett (2005) took the opportunity to call for a vision of communication and globalization that takes into account the environment.

4. These visits included a 2009 site visit to Monsanto's corporate headquarters in St. Louis, Missouri, and interviews with key public relations and media personnel; site visits and interviews at Bolivian radio stations "Wayna Tambo" (El Alto) and "Mujeres Creando" (La Paz), as well as the Ministerio de Justicia Pueblos Indigenas y Empoderamiento, a governmental department headquartered in La Paz, Bolivia, in 2009 and 2011; interviews in New York City and via Skype with producers and executives of Discovery's now-defunct Planet Green channel and members of Treehugger.com 2012–13; interviews with producers and creative personnel involved in the "green" mediablog "The Meatrix" in 2013; site visit to BBC MediaAction headquarters in White City, England, and interviews with members of the Climate Asia staff in 2013; and Skype interviews with observers of the Paiter-Suruí Forest Carbon Project, 2012–13.

5. In his article "A Wilderness Environmentalism Manifesto: Contesting the Infinite Self-Absorption of Humans," DeLuca (2007) makes the compelling case that "on
the global level, nations repeatedly have asserted their local self-interests over global
interests. Paramount examples in this respect would be the U.S. refusal to ratify the
Kyoto Protocol on global warming and Brazil's refusal to heed international suggestions for protecting the Amazon rainforest. To idealize the local is a dangerous act
for environmental groups" (36).

Chapter 1. Earth Discourses

1. Dryzek's discussion of these "weak" and "strong" applications of Ecological Modernization draws directly from the work of Peter Christoff's 1996 article "Ecological
Modernization, Ecological Modernities," *Environmental Politics* 5 (3): 476–500; see
especially pp. 490–91.

2. Hajer (1995) also provides an analysis of how, despite a historical context of environmental concern in the 1970s through the 1990s and a government that in the
abstract endorsed the ideas of environmental modernism, the discourse was unable
to challenge the prevailing traditional-pragmatist approaches to policymaking that
shaped and guided institutional practices within the United Kingdom.

Chapter 2. Endless Growth

1. I write "seem" because there is a history of state intervention in various markets
when entrepreneurial freedoms and the invisible hand were evidently not enough.
For example, Dryzek (2005) notes that many ranchers, loggers, and natural-resource-
dependent industries have relied on subsidies in the form of free access to public
lands. Also, according to Kuttner (2000), "five times in the past two decades the great
powers have intervened in very significant ways to counteract the impulses—and
the damage—of speculative forces in capital markets. These included the concerted
intervention in late 1988 to prevent the yen from crashing and taking the Asian
economy with it; the Mexican rescues of 1983 and 1995; the Louvre Accord of 1988
to stabilise the dollar against the yen; and the Plaza Accord of 1985 which produced
a period of co-ordinated reductions in interest rates" (162). More recently, of course,
there are the cases in the United States of the 2007–2008 housing crisis / mortgage
subprime rate debacle and the subsequent "stimulus package" bailout of banks, and
the 2009 "cash for clunkers" government initiative to buoy the ailing auto industry,
and the bailouts of Greece and Ireland by the European Union.

Chapter 3. Neo-Malthusian Entertainment and the Limits of Green TV

1. The site can be found at http://oceanservice.noaa.gov/facts/mermaids.html.

2. See http://corporate.discovery.com/brands/international (accessed July 22, 2016).

Chapter 4. Battle of the Blogosphere

The genesis of this chapter stems from a site visit to Monsanto's U.S. corporate headquarters in St. Louis, Missouri, in 2009, which involved a tour of its facilities (labs and greenhouses) and interviews with key members of its Public Affairs office. I conducted onsite conversational interviews with Monsanto's director of issues and employee/electronic communication, the assistant director of public affairs, the director of public affairs, the director of internal news and communications, two social media specialists, the communications project manager, the R&D pipeline director, and the manager of tour coordinators on April 20, 2009. This experience at Monsanto informed my subsequent analysis of Monsanto's Web site, blogs, and other promotional and social media as well as charges levied by some of its chief critics.

1. See the link http://www.polarbearsmovie.com/?WT.mc_id=Holiday2013 to view the video.
2. Not In My Back Yard (NIMBY).
3. See the link http://www.youtube.com/watch?v=I9I1IkbcHNE to view the video.
4. See http://www.march-against-monsanto.com.
5. Available at http://www.alternet.org/food/monsantos-rural-police-state.
6. See the link http://www.itvs.org/films/bitter-seeds to view the video.
7. See http://www.osgata.org/2013/harvesting-justice.
8. Available at http://www.vanityfair.com/politics/features/2008/05/monsanto 200805.
9. See the link http://www.youtube.com/watch?v=KGqQV6ObFCQ to view the video from *Natural News*.
10. See http://www.campaignlive.co.uk/news/29693; and also http://frankenfood files.files.wordpress.com/2010/10/brunofinal.pdf.
11. See the link http://www.thedailyshow.com/watch/thu-september-12-2013/monsanto ---seed-patent-laws to view the video.
12. See www.ibtimes.com/monsanto-named-2013s-most-evil-corporation-new -poll-1300217 for *International Business Times* article on Monsanto's prize.
13. See http://www.monsanto.com/whoweare/Pages/monsanto-relationships -pfizer-solutia.aspx.
14. See http://www.monsanto.com/whoweare/Pages/our-commitment-to-sustainable -agriculture.aspx.
15. This video is available on YouTube at: https://www.youtube.com/watch?v =iZ9EiBgjQxs.
16. For the full address, see www.monsanto.com/newsviews/Pages/grant-2010-business -social-responsibility-conference.aspx.
17. Review of Monsanto Web site conducted on August 12, 2016.
18. Monsanto's blog can be located at http://monsantoblog.com.
19. See videos at http://americasfarmers.com.

20. Monsanto corporate website. Page can be located at http://www.monsanto.com/improvingagriculture/Pages/default.aspx.

Chapter 5. Amazonian Indigenous Green

1. "Ecologically Noble Savage" is a term Kent Redford coined (Redford 1991); Conklin (1997) employs it as well.

2. Oddly, the article never really explains how the "defenders of the Amazon" are "winning."

3. Even before most of the north-south partnerships cooled, these same tribes were among the first to invest in their own video production, as portable cameras made their way into the hands of rainforest communities in the 1990s. As has been well documented by anthropologists (Turner 2002), the Kayapó and Yanomami distinguished themselves through their ability to master media technology to document their culture and draw attention to their activities, and by 1995 the Xavante, one of the first tribes to adopt media-production technology, released the "first Amazonian music video" at the Native American Film Festival in New York (Santos et al. 1997, 560). These activities were early indicators of what became a percolation of indigenous media production, as tribes began shooting their own video as a means of cultural preservation and to pursue social justice.

4. For information about these programs, see http://amazonteam.org/programs.

5. Criticism of creating a carbon market includes the assertion that it is largely a market-driven shell game, allowing large polluters to conveniently buy their way out of the responsibility to cut their own emissions in the guise of cooperative action while leading to the dilemma of "leakage" (conservation efforts in one region merely shift deforestation to another). However, with the signing of the Waxman-Markey cap-and-trade bill in the United States in 2009 and the more recent development of the European Union's Emission Trading Scheme, as well as other state- and regionally sponsored initiatives and registries, the idea of carbon trading became grounded in more uniform standards and measures that helped boost its standing as an innovative solution for challenge of climate change and thus a commodity ripe for international trade (Gorte and Ramseur 2010).

6. See http://googleblog.blogspot.com/2012/06/surui-cultural-map.html (accessed June 18, 2012).

Conclusion

1. Wangari Maathai, winner of the 2004 Nobel Peace Prize: from her lecture before the Nobel committee, Oslo City Hall, Oslo, Norway, December 10, 2004. Text available at http://www.nobelprize.org/nobel_prizes/peace/laureates/2004/maathai-lecture-text.html.

Bibliography

Abel, Troy D., and Mark Stephan. 2008. "Tools of Environmental Justice and Meaningful Involvement." *Environmental Practice* 10 (4): 152–63.

Abid, Rubab. 2013. "The Myth of India's 'GM Genocide': Genetically Modified Cotton Blamed for Wave of Farmer Suicides." *National Post*, January 26. Accessed December 17, 2013, http://news.nationalpost.com/2013/01/26/the-myth-of-indias-gm -genocide-genetically-modified-cotton-blamed-for-wave-of-farmer-suicides/#__ federated=1.

Acedo, Alfredo. 2013. "Mexico Celebrates 'Carnival of Corn' and Rejects Monsanto. *Upside Down World*, June 10. Accessed on May 10, 2015, http://upsidedownworld .org/main/mexico-archives-79/4329-mexico-celebrates-carnival-of-corn-and -rejects-monsanto.

Acosta, Alberto. 2013. "Extractivism and Neoextractivism: Two Sides of the Same Curse." In *Beyond Development: Alternative Visions from Latin America*, edited by Miriam Lang and Dunia Mokrani, 61–86. Amsterdam, Neth.: Transnational Institute.

Agnew, John. 2005. *Hegemony: The New Shape of Global Power*. Philadelphia: Temple University Press.

Albarran, Alan B., and Sylvia M. Chan-Olmstead, eds. 1998. *Global Media Economics: Commercialization, Concentration, and Integration of World Media Markets*. Ames: Iowa State University Press.

Algan, Ece. 2003. "Privatization of Radio and Media Hegemony in Turkey." In Artz and Kamalipour 2003, 169–94.

Allan, Stuart, Barbara Adam, and Cynthia Carter, eds. 2000. *Environmental Risks and the Media*. London: Routledge.

Amaral, Roberto. 2002. "Mass Media in Brazil: Modernization to Prevent Change." In Fox and Waisbord 2002, 38–46.

Anderson, Alison. 1997. *Media, Culture and the Environment*. London: University College London Press.

Anderson, Terry L., and Donald R. Leal, eds. 1991. *Free Market Environmentalism*. Boulder, Colo.: Westview.

Appadurai, Arjun. 1996. *Modernity at Large: Cultural Dimensions of Globalization*. Minneapolis: Minnesota University Press.

Artz, Lee, and Yahya R. Kamalipour. 2003. *The Globalization of Corporate Media Hegemony*. Albany: SUNY Press.

Athique, Adrian. 2012. *Indian Media: Global Approaches*. Cambridge: Polity.

Avle, Seyram. 2011. "Global Flows, Media and Developing Democracies: The Ghanaian Case." *Journal of African Media Studies* 3 (1): 7–23.

Babe, Robert E. 1995. *Communication and the Transformation of Economics*. Boulder, Colo.: Westview.

Bagdikian, Ben H. 2004. *The New Media Monopoly*. Boston: Beacon.

Banda, Fackson. 2009. "China in the African Mediascape: A Critical Injection." *Journal of African Media Studies* 1 (3): 343–61.

Barrett, Michèle. 1991. *The Politics of Truth: From Marx to Foucault*. Stanford, Calif.: Stanford University Press.

Beck, Ulrich. 2000. "Living Your Own Life in a Runaway World: Individualisation, Globalisation and Politics." In *Global Capitalism*, edited by Will Hutton and Anthony Giddens, 164–74. New York: New Press.

Bell, Beverly. 2010. "Haitian Farmers Commit to Burning Monsanto Hybrid Seed." *World Post / Huffington Post*, May 17. Accessed July 5, 2016, http://www.huffingtonpost.com/beverly-bell/haitian-farmers-commit-to_b_578807.html.

Bettig, Ronald V., and Jeanne Lynn Hall. 2003. *Big Media, Big Money: Cultural Texts and Political Economics*. Lanham, Md.: Rowman and Littlefield.

Blankson, Isaac A. 2005. "Globalization, Pluralistic Media and Cultural Identity Transformation in Emerging African Democracies." *International Journal of Communication* 15 (1 and 2), 131–46.

———. 2007. "Media Independent and Pluralism in Africa: Opportunities and Challenges of Democratization and Liberalization." In Blankson and Murphy 2007, 15–34.

Blankson, Isaac A., and Patrick D. Murphy, eds. 2007. *Negotiating Democracy: Media Transformations in Emerging Democracies*. Albany: State University of New York Press.

Bonan, Gordon B. 2008. "Forests and Climate Change: Forcings, Feedbacks, and the Climate Benefits of Forests." *Science* 320 (5882): 1444–49.

Borenstein, Eliot. 2008. *Overkill: Sex and Violence in Contemporary Russian Culture*. Ithaca, N.Y.: Cornell University Press.

Bourgault, Louise M. 1995. *Mass Media in Sub-Saharan Africa*. Bloomington: Indiana University Press.

Bowers, Chet A. 2000. *Let Them Eat Data: How Computers Affect Education, Cultural Diversity, and the Prospects of Ecological Sustainability*. Athens: University of Georgia Press.

———. 2006. *Revitalizing the Commons: Cultural and Educational Sites of Resistance and Affirmation*. Lanham, Md.: Lexington.

Boyce, Tammy, and Justin Lewis, eds. 2009. *Climate Change and the Media*. London: Peter Lang.

Boyd-Barrett, Oliver. 2005. "A Different Scale of Difference." *Global Media and Communication* 1 (1): 15–19.

Branston, Gill. 2007. "The Planet at the End of the World: 'Event' Cinema and the Representability of Climate Change." *New Review of Film and Television Studies* 5 (2): 211–29.

"Brazilian Cosmetics Giant Buys First Indigenous REDD Credits." 2013. Ecosystem Marketplace, *Forest Carbon News*, September 10. Accessed March 4, 2014, http://www.ecosystemmarketplace.com/pages/dynamic/article.page.php?page_id=9932&section=home.

Brereton, Pat. 2005. *Hollywood Utopia: Ecology in Contemporary American Cinema*. Bristol, Eng.: Intellect.

Bruno, Kenny. 1998. "Monsanto's Failing PR Strategy." *The Ecologist* 28 (5): 287–93.

Budd, Mike, Steve Craig, and Clay Steinman. 1999. *Consuming Environments: Television and Commercial Culture*. New Brunswick, N.J.: Rutgers University Press.

Bullard, Robert D. 1996. "Environmental Justice: It's More than Waste Facility Siting." *Social Science Quarterly* 77 (3): 493–99.

Bushaus, Dawn. 2011. "Comcast Goes Green." *Tellabs Insight*, Q1, 14–15.

Butler, Rhett A. 2006. "Amazon Conservation Team Puts Indians on Google Earth to Save the Amazon." *Mongabay*. Accessed November 24, 2014, https://news.mongabay.com/2006/11/amazon-indians-use-google-earth-gps-to-protect-forest-home.

———. 2009. "Big REDD." *Washington Monthly*, July/August. Accessed November 24, 2014, https://www.unz.org/Pub/WashingtonMonthly-2009jul-2g00006.

Camp, Mark. 2010. "Forest Fighter." *Cultural Survival Quarterly* 34 (2). Accessed November 24, 2014, https://www.culturalsurvival.org/publications/cultural-survival-quarterly/brazil/forest-fighter.

Cantrill, James G., and Christine L. Oravec, eds. 1996. *The Symbolic Earth: Discourse and Our Creation of the Environment*. Lexington: University of Kentucky Press.

Carneiro da Cunha, Manuela, and Mauro W. B. de Almeida. 2000. "Indigenous People, Traditional People, and Conservation in the Amazon." *Daedalus* 129 (2): 315–38.

Carson, Rachel. 1962. *Silent Spring*. Boston: Houghton Mifflin; Cambridge, Mass.: Riverside.

Carus, Felicity. 2013. "Google—Leading the Way on Renewable Energy." *The Guardian*, August 5. Accessed November 20, 2013, http://www.theguardian.com/sustainable-business/google-renewable-green-energy.

"Case against Coca-Cola Kerala State: India." 2010. *Rights to Water and Sanitation*, August 20. Accessed April 27, 2015, http://www.righttowater.info/rights-in-practice/legal-approach-case-studies/case-against-coca-cola-kerala-state-india.

Castells, Manuel. 2000. *The Rise of the Network Society*. 2nd ed. Malden, Mass.: Blackwell.

Chang, Jack. 2007. "As Brazil's Rain Forest Burns Down, Planet Heats Up." *McClatchy Newspapers*, September 8. Accessed July 5, 2016, http://www.mcclatchydc.com/news/nation-world/world/article24469114.html.

Chávez, Daniel. 2006. "Globalizing Tequila: Mexican Television's Representations of the Neoliberal Reconversion of Land and Labor." *Arizona Journal of Hispanic Cultural Studies* 10 (1): 187–203.

Cherian, Jacob, and Jolly Jacob. 2012. "Green Marketing: A Study of Consumers' Attitudes Towards Environment Friendly Products." *Asian Social Science* 8 (12): 117–26.

Chopra, Anuj. 2009. "Debt Drives Farmers to Suicide." *The National*, January 20. Accessed July 5, 2016, http://vidarbhacrisis.blogspot.com/2009/01/debt-drives-vidarbha-farmers-to-suicide_20.html.

Chow, Lorraine. 2015. "Monsanto Handed 'Double Whammy' by Mexican Courts over Planting GMOs." *Eco Watch*, last modified November 9, 2015. Accessed April 10, 2016. http://ecowatch.com/2015/11/09/monsanto-mexican-court-gmos.

Christoff, Peter. 1996. "Ecological Modernization, Ecological Modernities," *Environmental Politics* 5 (3): 476–500.

Christoff, Peter, and Robyn Eckersley. 2013. *Globalization and the Environment*. Lanham, Md.: Rowman and Littlefield.

Comor, Edward A. 2008. *Consumption and the Globalization Project: International Hegemony and the Annihilation of Time*. New York: Palgrave Macmillan.

Conklin, Beth A. 1997. "Body Paint, Feathers, and VCRs: Aesthetics and Authenticity in Amazonian Activism." *American Ethnologist* 24 (4): 711–37.

———. 2010. "For Love or Money? Indigenous Realism and Humanitarian Agendas." In Hutchins and Wilson 2010, 127–50.

Conklin, Beth A., and Laura R. Graham. 1995. "The Shifting Middle Ground: Amazonian Indians and Eco-Politics." *American Anthropologist* 97 (4): 695–710.

Corbett, Julia B. 2006. *Communicating Nature: How We Create and Understand Environmental Messages*. Washington, D.C.: Island.

Corry, Stephen. 1993. "The Rainforest Harvest: Who Reaps the Benefit?" *The Ecologist* 23 (4): 148–53.

Couldry, Nick. 2003. "Passing Ethnographies." In *Global Media Studies: Ethnographic Perspectives*, edited by Patrick D. Murphy and Marwan M. Kraidy, 40–56. London: Routledge.

Cox, J. Robert. 2010. *Environmental Communication and the Public Sphere*. 2nd ed. Thousand Oaks, Calif.: Sage.

———. 2012. *Environmental Communication and the Public Sphere*. 3rd ed. Thousand Oaks, Calif.: Sage.

Craig, Geoffrey. 2010. "Everyday Epiphanies: Environmental Networks in Eco-Makeover Lifestyle Television." *Environmental Communication* 4 (2): 172–89.

Cubitt, Sean. 2005. *EcoMedia*. Amsterdam: Rodopi.

Curran, James, and Myung-Jin Park, eds. 2000. *De-Westernizing Media Studies*. London: Routledge.

Curtin, Michael. 2005. "Murdoch's Dilemma; or, 'What's the Price of TV in China?'" *Media, Culture and Society* 27 (2): 155–75.

———. 2010. "Comparing Media Capitals: Hong Kong and Mumbai." *Global Media and Communication* 6 (3): 263–70.

Daily, Gretchen C., and Katherine Ellison. 2002. *The New Economy of Nature: The Quest to Make Conservation Profitable.* Washington, D.C.: Island.

Darling-Wolf, Fabienne. 2015. *Imagining the Global: Transnational Media and Popular Culture Beyond East and West.* Ann Arbor: University of Michigan Press.

DeLuca, Kevin. 2006. *Image Politics: The New Rhetoric of Environmental Activism.* Mahwah, N.J.: Erlbaum.

———. 2007. "A Wilderness Environmentalism Manifesto: Contesting the Infinite Self-Absorption of Humans." In Sandler and Pezzullo 2007, 27–55.

Depoe, Stephen, and Celeste Michelle Condit. 1997. "Environmental Studies in Mass Communication." *Critical Studies in Mass Communication* 14 (4): 368–72.

d'Estries, Michael. 2012. "Discovery's Planet Green to Ride into the Sunset?" *Mother Nature Network*, January 17. Accessed July 5, 2016, http://www.mnn.com/lifestyle/arts-culture/blogs/discoverys-planet-green-to-ride-into-the-sunset.

Dewar, Elaine. 1995. *Cloak of Green: The Links between Key Environmental Groups, Government and Big Business.* Toronto: Lorimer.

DiCamillo, Kara. 2007. "Discovery Communications Announces New Network: PlanetGreen," *Treehugger.com*, April 6. Accessed July 5, 2016, http://www.treehugger.com/corporate-responsibility/discovery-communications-announces-new-network-planetgreen.html.

Dore, Mohammed H. I., and Jorge M. Nogueira. 1994. "The Amazon Rainforest, Sustainable Development and the Biodiversity Convention: A Political Economy Perspective." *Ambio* 23 (8): 491–96.

Dowell, Kristin. 2006. "Indigenous Media Gone Global: Strengthening Indigenous Identity On- and Offscreen at the First Nations/First Features Film Showcase." *American Anthropologist* 108 (2): 376–84.

Downey, John, and Sabina Mihelj, eds. 2012. *Central and Eastern European Media in Comparative Perspective: Politics, Economy and Culture.* Burlington, Vt.: Ashgate.

Downs, Peter. 1997. "Monsanto PR Mangles Language to Advance Genetic Engineering." *St. Louis Journalism Review* 28 (199): 9.

Drezner, Daniel W. 2011. *Theories of International Politics and Zombies.* Princeton, N.J.: University of Princeton Press.

Dryzek, John S. 2005. *The Politics of the Earth: Environmental Discourses.* 2nd ed. Oxford: Oxford University Press.

Economy, Elizabeth. 2004. *The River Runs Black: The Environmental Challenge to China's Future.* Ithaca, N.Y.: Cornell University Press.

Ehrlich, Paul R. 1968. *The Population Bomb.* New York: Ballantine.

Eko, Lyombe. 2003. "Globalization and the Mass Media in Africa." In Artz and Kamalipour 2003, 195–212.

Entine, Jon. 1994. "Shattered Image: Is the Body Shop Too Good to Be True?" *Business Ethics* 8 (5): 23–28.

Epstein, Jack. 2007. "Google to Harness Satellite Power for an Amazon Tribe." *San Francisco Chronicle*, June 10, 2007.

Escobar, Arturo. 1988. "Power and Visibility: Development and the Invention and Management of the Third World." *Cultural Anthropology* 3 (4): 428–43.

———. 1995. *Encountering Development: The Making and Unmaking of the Third World*. Princeton, N.J: Princeton University Press.

———. 1998. "Whose Knowledge, Whose Nature? Biodiversity, Conservation, and the Political Ecology of Social Movement." *Journal of Political Ecology* 5:53–82.

———. 2008. *Territories of Difference: Place, Movements, Life, Redes*. Durham, N.C.: Duke University Press.

Fairclough, Norman. 1995. *Media Discourse*. London: Arnold.

Featherstone, Mike, ed. 1990. *Global Culture: Nationalism, Globalization and Modernity*. London: Sage.

Finley, Klint. 2013. "Google Pushes for More Clean Energy in Land of Data Centers." *Wired*, November 15. Accessed November 20, 2013, http://www.wired.com/2013/11/green-source-rider.

Fisher, William H. 1994. "Megadevelopment, Environmentalism, and Resistance: The Institutional Context of Kayapó Indigenous Politics in Central Brazil." *Human Organization* 53 (3): 220–32.

Flieschli, Steve. 2006. "Mulch Madness." *New York Times*, October 12. Accessed October 12, 2006, http://www.nytimes.com/2006/10/12/opinion/12fleischli.html?_r=0.

Forero, Juan. 2013a. "Brazilian Tribal Chief Uses Technology to Help Save His People, and Curb Deforestation." *Washington Post*, May 27.

———. 2013b. "From Stone Age to Digital Age in One Big Leap." National Public Radio, March 28. Accessed November 24, 2014, http://www.npr.org/2013/03/28/175580980/from-the-stone-age-to-the-digital-age-in-one-big-leap.

Foucault, Michel. 1972. *The Archeology of Knowledge and the Discourse on Language*. Translated by A. M. Sheridan Smith. London: Routledge. Reprinted 2002.

Fox, Elizabeth. 1988. *Media and Politics in Latin America: The Struggle for Democracy*. London: Sage.

———. 1997. *Latin American Broadcasting: From Tango to Telenovela*. Luton, UK: University of Luton Press.

Fox, Elizabeth, and Silvio R. Waisbord, eds. 2002. *Latin Politics, Global Media*. Austin: University of Texas Press.

Frayssinet, Fabiana. 2013. "Argentine Protesters vs. Monsanto: 'The Monster is Right on Top of Us.'" *Nation of Change*, December 3. Accessed July 10, 2014, http://www.nationofchange.org/argentine-protesters-vs-monsanto-monster-right-top-us-1386086820.

Fuller, R. Buckminster. 1969. *Operating Manual for Spaceship Earth*. Carbondale: Southern Illinois University Press.

Fung, Anthony Y. H. 2008. *Global Capital, Local Culture: Transnational Media Corporations in China*. New York: Peter Lang.

Furrier, John. 2013. "Coca-Cola Leveraging Social to Drive Leadership in Social Media Marketing." *Forbes*, June 18, 2013. Accessed November 25, 2013, http://www.forbes.com/sites/siliconangle/2013/06/18/coca-cola-leveraging-social-to-drive-leadership-in-social-media-marketing.

Galperin, Hernan. 1999a. "Cultural Industries in the Age of Free-Trade Agreements." *Canadian Journal of Communication* 24 (1): 49–77.

———. 1999b. "Cultural Industries Policy in Regional Trade Agreements: The Cases of NAFTA, the European Union, and MERCOSUR." *Media, Culture and Society* 21 (5): 627–48.

———. 2000. "Regulatory Reform in the Broadcasting Industries of Brazil and Argentina in the 1990s." *Journal of Communication* 50 (4): 176–91.

García Canclini, Néstor. 1990. *Culturas híbridas: Estrategias para entrar y salir de la modernidad*. México, D.F.: Grijalbo / Consejo Nacional para la Cultura y las Artes.

———. 1992. "Cultural Reconversion." In *On Edge: The Crisis of Contemporary Latin American Culture*, edited by George Yúdice, Jean Franco, and Juan Flores, 29–44. Minneapolis: University of Minnesota Press.

———. 2000. *La Globalización Imaginada*. Paidós Estado y Sociedad, vol. 76. México: Paidós.

Garrard, Greg. 2004. *Ecocriticism*. New York: Routledge.

Gershon, Richard A. 1997. *The Transnational Media Corporation: Global Messages and Free Market Competition*. Mahwah, N.J.: Erlbaum.

———. 2000. "The Transnational Media Corporation: Environmental Scanning and Strategy Formulation." *Journal of Media Economics* 13 (2): 81–101.

———. 2005. "The Transnationals: Media Corporations, International TV Trade and Entertainment Flows." In *Global Entertainment Media: Content, Audiences, Issues*, edited by Anne Cooper-Chen, 2:17–35. Mahwah, N.J.: Erlbaum.

Gold, John R., and George Revill. 2004. *Representing the Environment*. London: Routledge.

Goldsmith, Zac. 1999. "The Monsanto Test." *The Ecologist* 29 (1): 5–8.

Goodman, Amy. 2009. "'Omnivore's Dilemma' Author Michael Pollan's New Advice on Buying Food: 'Don't Buy Any Food You've Ever Seen Advertised.'" *Democracy Now!* May 14. Accessed October 28, 2011, http://www.democracynow.org/2009/5/14/omnivores_dilemma_author_michael_pollans_new.

———. 2013. "Michael Pollan on How Reclaiming Cooking Can Save Our Food System, Make Us Healthy and Grow Democracy." *Democracy Now!* May 6. Accessed July 5, 2016. http://www.democracynow.org/2013/5/6/michael_pollan_on_how_reclaiming_cooking.

Gorte, Ross W., and Jonathan L. Ramseur. 2010. *Forest Carbon Markets: Potential and Drawbacks*. Washington, D.C.: Congressional Research Service.

Graham, Laura R. 1998. "Eye on the Amazon: Brazilian Indians, the State, and Global Culture." *American Anthropologist* 100 (1): 163–69.

Grantham, Bill, and Toby Miller. 2010. "The End of Neoliberalism." *Popular Communication* 8 (3): 174–77. doi:10.1080/15405702.2010.493433.

Grätz, Tilo. 2011. "Contemporary African Mediascapes: New Actors, Genres and Communication Spaces." *Journal of African Media Studies* 3 (2): 151–60. doi:10.1386/jams.3.2.151_7.

———. 2013. "Radio Advertising and Entrepreneurial Conjunctions in Benin: Producers, Styles and Technologies." *Journal of African Cultural Studies* 25 (1): 42–56. doi:10.1080/13696815.2013.749779.

Graves, Lucia. 2013. "Google Faces Environmentalist Wrath over Fundraiser for James Inhofe, Climate Change Denier." *Huffington Post*, July 11. Accessed November 20, 2013, http://www.huffingtonpost.com/2013/07/11/google-james-inhofe_n_3581216.html.

Gross, Peter, and Karol Jakubowicz, eds. 2013. *Media Transformations in the Post-Communist World: Eastern Europe's Tortured Path to Change*. Lanham, Md.: Lexington.

Guenther, Matthias, Justin Kenrick, Adam Kuper, Evie Plaice, Thomas Thuen, Patrick Wolfe, Werner Zips, and Alan Barnard. 2006. "The Concept of Indigeneity." *Social Anthropology* 14 (1): 17–32.

Hajer, Maarten A. 1995. *The Politics of Environmental Discourse Ecological Modernization and the Policy Process*. Oxford: Clarendon.

Hale, Mike. 2010. "Animal Husbandry, SoHo Style." *New York Times*, June 15. Accessed July 5, 2016, http://www.nytimes.com/2010/06/16/arts/television/16beekman.html?_r=0.

Hallin, Daniel C., and Paolo Mancini. 2004. *Comparing Media Systems: Three Models of Media and Politics*. Cambridge: Cambridge University Press.

Hallin, Daniel C., and Stylianos Papathanassopoulos. 2002. "Political Clientelism and the Media: Southern Europe and Latin America in Comparative Perspective." *Media, Culture and Society* 24 (2): 175–95.

Hammer, Joshua. 2007. "Rain Forest Rebel." *Smithsonian* 37 (12): 40–48.

Hannerz, Ulf. 1996. *Transnational Connections: Culture, People, Places*. London: Routledge.

Hansen, Anders. 1991. "The Media and the Social Construction of the Environment." *Media, Culture and Society* 13 (4): 443–58.

———. 1993. *The Mass Media and Environmental Issues*. London: Leicester University Press.

———. 2010. *Environment, Media and Communication*. London: Routledge.

Hardin, Garrett. 1968. "Tragedy of the Commons." *Science* 162 (3859): 1243–48.

———. 1977. "Living on a Lifeboat," In *Managing the Commons*, edited by Garrett Hardin and John Baden, 261–79. San Francisco: W. H. Freeman.

Harvey, David. 2005. *A Brief History of Neoliberalism*. Oxford: Oxford University Press.

Hattingh, Damian, Bill Russo, Ade Sun-Basorun, Arnd Van Wamelen. 2012. "The Rise of the African Consumer." McKinsey South Africa. Accessed July 5, 2016, http://www.mckinsey.com/industries/retail/our-insights/the-rise-of-the-african-consumer.

Heath, Carla W. 2001. "Regional Radio: A Response by the Ghana Broadcasting Corporation to Democratization and Competition." *Canadian Journal of Communication* 26 (1): 89–106.

Heise, Ursula K. 2008. *Sense of Place and Sense of Planet: The Environmental Imagination of the Global*. Oxford: Oxford University Press.

———. 2014. "Plasmatic Nature: Environmentalism and Animated Film." *Public Culture* 26 (2), 301–18.

Herman, Edward S., and Robert Waterman McChesney. 1997. *The Global Media: The New Missionaries of Corporate Capitalism*. London: Cassell.

Hernandez, Omar, and Emile McAnany. 2001. "Cultural Industries in the Age of Free Trade." In *Fragments of a Golden Age: The Politics of Culture in Mexico since 1940*, edited by Gilbert M. Joseph, Anne Rubenstein, and Eric Zolov, 389–414. Durham, N.C.: Duke University Press.

Herndl, Carl George, and Stuart C. Brown, eds. 1996. *Green Culture: Environmental Rhetoric in Contemporary America*. Madison: University of Wisconsin Press.

Hochman, Jhan. 1998. *Green Cultural Studies: Nature in Film, Novel, and Theory*. Moscow: University of Idaho Press.

Hopkinson, Jenny. 2013. "Monsanto's Makeover" (original title: "Monsanto Confronts Devilish Public Image Problem"). *Politico*, November 29. Accessed December 19, 2013, http://www.politico.com/story/2013/11/monsanto-agriculture-image-problem-100442.html.

Huang, Yu. 1994. "Peaceful Evolution: The Case of Television Reform in Post-Mao China." *Media, Culture and Society* 16 (2): 217–41.

Hughes, Sallie. 2008. "The Media in Mexico: From Authoritarian Institution to Hybrid System." In Lugo-Ocando 2008, 131–48.

Humphreys, Peter. 2002. "Europeanisation, Globalisation and Policy Transfer in the European Union: The Case of Telecommunications." *Convergence: The Journal of Research into New Media Technologies* 8 (2): 52–79.

Hutchins, Frank, and Patrick C. Wilson, eds. 2010. *Editing Eden: A Reconsideration of Identity, Politics, and Place in Amazonia*. Lincoln: University of Nebraska Press.

Ingram, David. 2000. *Green Screen: Environmentalism and Hollywood Cinema*. Exeter, Eng.: University of Exeter Press.

Inhofe, James M. 2012. *The Greatest Hoax: How the Global Warming Conspiracy Threatens Your Future*. Washington, D.C.: WND.

Jenkins, Henry. 2006. *Fans, Bloggers, and Gamers: Exploring Participatory Culture*. New York: New York University Press.

Johnson, Kirk. 2001. "Media and Social Change: The Modernizing Influences of Television in Rural India." *Media, Culture and Society* 23 (2): 147–69.

Juluri, Vamsee. 1999. "Global Weds Local: The Reception of Hum Apake Hain Koun." *European Journal of Cultural Studies* 2 (2): 231–48.

———. 2003. *Becoming a Global Audience: Longing and Belonging in Indian Music Television*. New York: Peter Lang.

Kahn, Richard. 2010. *Critical Pedagogy, Ecoliteracy, and Planetary Crisis: The Ecopedagogy Movement*. New York: Peter Lang.

Kaneva, Nadia, and Elza Ibroscheva. 2013. "Media and the Birth of the Post-Communist Consumer." In Gross and Jakubowicz 2013, 67–84.

Kasoma, Francis P. 1997. "The Independent Press and Politics in Africa." *Gazette: International Journal for Communication Studies* 59 (4): 295–310.

Kaufman, Debra. 2007. "Discovery Preps Planet Green." *Television Week* 26 (34): 48.

Kearins, Kate, and Babs Klyn. 1999. "The Body Shop International PLC: The Marketing of Principles along with Products." In *Greener Marketing: A Global Perspective on Green Marketing Practice*, edited by Martin Charter and Michael J. Polonsky, 285–99. Sheffield, Eng.: Greenleaf.

Kempf, Hervé. 2007. *How the Rich are Destroying the Earth*. White River Junction, Vt.: Chelsea Green.

King, Anthony D. 1997. *Culture, Globalization, and the World-System: Contemporary Conditions for the Representation of Identity*. Minneapolis: University of Minnesota Press.

Klein, Naomi. 2007. *The Shock Doctrine: The Rise of Disaster Capitalism*. New York: Holt.

Kleinman, Daniel Lee, and Jack Kloppenburg Jr. 1991. "Aiming for the Discursive High Ground: Monsanto and the Biotechnology Controversy." *Sociological Forum* 6 (3): 427–47.

Knight, William. 2009. "Google's Green Investments." *Computer Weekly*, February, 16–18.

Kraidy, Marwan M. 2005. *Hybridity; or, The Cultural Logic of Globalization*. Philadelphia: Temple University Press.

———. 2010. *Reality Television and Arab Politics: Contention in Public Life*. Cambridge: Cambridge University Press.

Kraidy, Marwan, and Patrick Murphy. 2008. "Shifting Geertz: Toward a Theory of Translocalism in Global Communication Studies." *Communication Theory* 18:335–55.

Kumar, Shanti. 2006. *Gandhi Meets Primetime: Globalization and Nationalism in Indian Television*. Urbana: University of Illinois.

Kuttner, Robert. 2000. "The Role of Governments in the Global Economy." In *Global Capitalism*, edited by Will Hutton and Anthony Giddens, 147–63. New York: New Press.

Lacey, Stephen. 2013. "A Timeline of Google's Clean Energy Investment." *Greentech-media*, November 15. Accessed November 20, 2013, http://www.greentechmedia.com/articles/read/A-Timeline-of-Googles-Surge-in-Clean-Energy-Investment.

Laferrière, Eric, and Peter J. Stoett. 1999. *International Relations Theory and Ecological Thought: Towards a Synthesis*. London: Routledge.

Latta, Alex, and Hannah Wittman, eds. 2012. *Environment and Citizenship in Latin America: Natures, Subjects and Struggles*. New York: Berghahn.

La Via Campesina. 2010. "Haitian Peasants March against Monsanto Company for Food and Seed Sovereignty." Accessed June 16, 2010, http://viacampesina.org/en/index.php/actions-and-events-mainmenu-26/stop-transnational-corporations-mainmenu-76/904-haitian-peasants-march-against-monsanto-company-for-food-and-seed-sovereignty.

Lerner, Daniel. 1964. *The Passing of Traditional Society: Modernizing the Middle East*. New York: Free Press.

Lester, Libby. 2010. *Media and Environment: Conflict, Politics and the News*. Cambridge: Polity.

Lester, Libby, and Brett Hutchins, eds. 2013. *Environmental Conflict and the Media*. New York: Peter Lang.

Levin, Gary. 2012. "Discovery Networks to Launch Destination America," *USA Today*, April 3. Accessed July 5, 2016, http://usatoday30.usatoday.com/life/television/news/story/2012-04-03/discovery-destination-america/53982082/1.

Lewis, Jeff. 2012. *Global Media Apocalypse: Pleasure, Violence and the Cultural Imaginings of Doom*. London: Palgrave McMillan.

Leyda, Julia, and Diane Negra, eds. 2015. *Extreme Weather and Global Media*. London: Routledge.

Li, Zhan, and John Dimmick. 2005. "Transnational Media Corporations' Strategies in Post-WTO China: Approaches of Three Global Leaders." *Journal of Media Business Studies* 2 (2): 35–59.

Lomborg, Bjørn. 2001. *The Skeptical Environmentalist: Measuring the Real State of the World*. Cambridge: Cambridge University Press.

Louv, Richard. 2008. *Last Child in the Woods: Saving Our Children from Nature-Deficit Disorder*. Chapel Hill, N.C.: Algonquin.

Lovelock, James. 1972. "Gaia as Seen through the Atmosphere." *Atmospheric Environment* 6 (8): 579–80.

———. 1979. *Gaia: A New Look at Life on Earth*. Oxford: Oxford University Press.

———. 2007. *Gaia's Revenge: Earth's Climate Crisis and the Fate of Humanity*. New York: Basic.

Lubold, Gordon. 2014. "Exclusive: The Pentagon Has a Plan to Stop the Zombie Apocalypse. Seriously." *Foreign Policy*, May 13. Accessed May 14, 2014, http://foreignpolicy.com/2014/05/13/exclusive-the-pentagon-has-a-plan-to-stop-the-zombie-apocalypse-seriously.

Ludwig, Mike. 2011. "Monsanto and the Gates Foundation Push GE Crops on Africa." *Truthout*, July 12. Accessed July 15, 2013, http://www.truth-out.org/news/item/2105:monsanto-and-gates-foundation-push-ge-crops-on-africa.

———. 2013a. "Monsanto Spends Millions to Defeat Washington GMO Labeling Initiative." *Truthout*, September 16. Accessed September 18, 2013, http://www.truth-out.org/news/item/18801-monsanto-spends-millions-to-defeat-washington-gmo-labeling-initiative.

———. 2013b. "Monsanto Wins Again: Voters Reject Washington GMO Labeling Initiative." *Truthout*, November 7. Accessed November 13, 2013, http://www.truth-out.org/news/item/19897-monsanto-wins-again-voters-reject-washington-gmo-labeling-initiative#.

Lugo-Ocando, Jairo, ed. 2008. *The Media in Latin America*. New York: Open University Press.

Luke, Timothy W. 1997. *Ecocritique: Contesting the Politics of Nature, Economy, and Culture*. Minneapolis: University of Minnesota Press.

Magretta, Joan. 1997. "Growth through Global Sustainability: An Interview with Monsanto's CEO, Robert B. Shapiro." *Harvard Business Review* 75 (1): 78–88.

Maher, T. Michael. 1996. "Media Framing and Public Perception of Environmental Causality." *Southwestern Mass Communication Journal* 12 (1): 61–73.

Martín-Barbero, Jesús. 1993. "Latin America: Cultures in the Communication Media." *Journalism of Communication* 43 (2): 18–30.

Mayobre, José Antonio. 2002. "Venezuela and the Media." In Fox and Waisbord 2002, 176–86.

McAnany, Emile G., and Kenton T. Wilkinson, eds. 1996. *Mass Media and Free Trade: NAFTA and the Cultural Industries*. Austin: University of Texas Press.

McCargo, Duncan. 2002. *Media and Politics in Pacific Asia*. London: Routledge.

McChesney, Robert W. 1999. "The New Global Media." *Nation* 269 (18): 11–15.

———. 2004. *The Problem of the Media: U.S. Communication Politics in the Twenty-First Century*. New York: Monthly Review Press.

McDaniel, Drew O. 2002. *Electronic Tigers of Southeast Asia: The Politics of Media, Technology, and National Development*. Ames: Iowa State University Press.

———. 2007. "An Awakening in Cambodia: From Failed State to a Media-Rich Society." In Blankson and Murphy 2007, 77–98.

Meadows, Donella H., Dennis L. Meadows, Jorgen Randers, and William W. Behrens III. 1972. *The Limits to Growth: A Report for the Club of Rome's Project on the Predicament of Mankind*. New York: Universe.

Mendelson, Joseph. 1998. "Roundup: The World's Biggest-Selling Herbicide." *The Ecologist* 28 (5): 270–75.

Mengel, Jimmy. 2011, February. "USDA Backs Monsanto, Caves under White House Pressure." *Green Chip Stocks*, February 2. Accessed July 5, 2016, http://www.greenchipstocks.com/archives/all/2011/02?page=2.

Merchant, Carolyn. 1989. *The Death of Nature: Women, Ecology, and the Scientific Revolution*. New York: Harper and Row.

Miller, Jade. 2012. "Global Nollywood: The Nigerian Movie Industry and Alternative Global Networks in Production and Distribution." *Global Media and Communication* 8 (2): 117–33.

Miller, Shawn William. 2007. *An Environmental History of Latin America*. New York: Cambridge University Press.

Mjos, Ole J. 2010. *Media Globalization and the Discovery Channel Networks*. New York: Routledge.

Moberg, David. 1997. "When Worlds Collide." *Chicago Reader*, October 2. Accessed September 19, 2014, http://www.chicagoreader.com/chicago/when-worlds-collide/Content?oid=894543.

Mohai, Paul, and Bunyan Bryant. 1995. "Demographic Studies Reveal a Pattern of Environmental Injustice." In *Environmental Justice*, edited by Jonathan S. Petrikin. San Diego: Greenhaven.

Monsanto Company. 2011. "Monsanto Corporate Brochure." Accessed July 5, 2016, http://www.monsanto.com/whoweare/documents/monsanto_corporate_brochure.pdf.

———. 2010a. "Five Answers on Monsanto's Haiti Seed Donation." *Beyond the Rows* [blog], May 20. Accessed January 5, 2011, http://monsantoblog.com/2010/05/20/five-answers-monsanto-haiti.

———. 2010b. "Monsanto Donates Maize and Vegetable Seed to Haiti." *Beyond the Rows* [blog], May 13. Accessed July 5, 2016, http://monsantoblog.com/2010/05/13/monsanto-donates-seed-to-haiti.

Monsiváis, Carlos. 1996. "Will Nationalism Be Bilingual?" In McAnany and Wilkinson 1996, 78–106.

Montague, Peter. 1998. "How Monsanto 'Listens' to Other Opinions." *The Ecologist* 28 (5): 299–300.

Moran, Albert. 2009. *New Flows in Global TV*. Bristol, UK: Intellect.

Morris, Nancy, and Silvio R. Waisbord. 2001. *Media and Globalization: Why the State Matters*. Lanham, Md.: Rowman and Littlefield.

Moss, Daniel. 2013. "Look Out Monsanto: The Global Food Movement is Rising." *Yes!*, April 10. Accessed April 20, 2013, http://www.yesmagazine.org/planet/look-out-monsanto-global-food-movement-is-rising.

Murdock, Graham, and Peter Golding. 1999. "Common Markets: Corporate Ambitions and Communication Trends in the UK and Europe." *Journal of Media Economics* 12 (2): 117–32.

Murphy, Patrick. 2013. "The Abbreviated Field Experience in Audience Ethnography." In *The International Encyclopedia of Media Studies: Audience and Interpretation in Media Studies (vol. 3)*, edited by A. N. Valdivia and R. Parameswaran. Oxford: Wiley-Blackwell.

Musa, Mohammed. 2011. "Media Flows, Domination and Discourse in Nigeria." *Journal of African Media Studies* 3 (3): 329–48.

Myerson, George, Yvonne Rydin, and Celeste Michelle Condit. 1997. "The Future of Environmental Rhetoric." *Critical Studies in Mass Communication* 14 (4): 376–79.

National Oceanic and Atmospheric Administration. 2012. *State of the Climate National Overview*. Accessed July 5, 2016, https://www.ncdc.noaa.gov/sotc/national/201213.

Nyamnjoh, Francis B. 2013. *Africa's Media: Democracy and the Politics of Belonging*. Pretoria, South Africa: Unisa.

Obeng-Quaidoo, Isaac. 1985. "Media Habits of Ghanaian Youth." In *Mass Communication, Culture, and Society in West Africa*, edited by Frank Okwu Ugboajah, 237–49. New York: Zell.

Oduro-Frimpong, Joseph. 2009. "Glocalization Trends: The Case of Hiplife Music in Contemporary Ghana." *International Journal of Communication* 3: 1085–106.

———. 2014. "Sakawa Rituals and Cyberfraud in Ghanaian Popular Video Movies." *African Studies Review* 57 (2): 131–47.

Okereke, Chukwumerije. 2008. *Global Justice and Neoliberal Environmental Governance: Ethics, Sustainable Development and International Cooperation*. London: Routledge.

O'Leary, Noreen. 2013. "How the World's Most Iconic Brand Was Saved from Itself." *AdWeek*, June 9. Accessed November 25, 2013, http://www.adweek.com/news/advertising-branding/how-worlds-most-iconic-brand-was-saved-itself-150127.

Ong, Aihwa. 2006. *Neoliberalism as Exception: Mutations in Citizenship and Sovereignty*. Durham N.C.: Duke University Press.

Onwumechili, Chukwuka. 2007. "Nigeria: Equivocating While Opening the Broadcast Liberalization Gates." In Blankson and Murphy 2007, 123–42.

Ophuls, William. 1977. *Ecology and the Politics of Scarcity: Prologue to a Political Theory of the Steady State*. San Francisco: Freeman.

Oravec, Christine. 1981. "John Muir, Yosemite, and the Sublime Response: A Study in the Rhetoric of Preservationism." *Quarterly Journal of Speech* 67 (3): 245–58.

Ó Siochrú, Seán. 2010. "Implementing Communication Rights." In *Media Divides: Communication Rights and the Right to Communicate in Canada*, edited by Marc Raboy and Jeremy Shtern, 41–61. Vancouver: University of British Columbia Press.

Ó Siochrú, Seán, Bruce Girard, and Amy Mahan. 2002. *Global Media Governance: A Beginner's Guide*. Lanham, Md.: Rowman and Littlefield.

Ostrom, Elinor. 1990. *Governing the Commons*. New York: Cambridge University Press.

Owen, Rob. 2008. "Planet Green Channels a Movement." *Pittsburgh Post-Gazette*, June 1.

Pace, David. 2005. "More Blacks Live with Pollution." *Associated Press*, December 13.

Padovani, Claudia, Francesca Musiani, and Elena Pavan. 2010. "Investigating Evolving Discourses on Human Rights in the Digital Age." *International Communication Gazette* 72 (4–5): 359–78.

Pain, Paromita. 2013. "Battling India's Monsanto Protection Act, Farmers Demand End to GMO." *Occupy.com*, August 19. Accessed December 11, 2013, http://www.occupy.com/article/battling-indias-monsanto-protection-act-farmers-demand-end-gmo.

Papathanassopoulos, Stylianos, and Ralph Negrine. 2011. *European Media: Structures, Policy and Identity*. Cambridge: Polity.

Pearce, Fred. 2005. "Forests Paying the Price for Biofuels." *New Scientist* 188 (2526): 19.

Pearson, Mark. 2006. "'Science,' Representation and Resistance: The Bt Cotton Debate in Andhra Pradesh, India." *Geographical Journal* 172 (4): 306–17.

Peeples, Jennifer, and Stephen Depoe, eds. 2014. *Voice and Environmental Communication*. Basingstoke: Palgrave Macmillan.

Pendakur, Manjunath. 1989. "Indian Television Comes of Age: Liberalization and the Rise of Consumer Culture." *Communication* 11: 177–97.

Pergams, Oliver, and Patricia Zaradic. 2008. "Evidence for a Fundamental and Pervasive Shift Away from Nature-Based Recreation." *Proceedings of the National Academy of Sciences of the United States of America* 105:2295–300. Accessed July 6, 2016, http://www.ncbi.nlm.nih.gov/pmc/articles/PMC2268130.

Perkins, John. 2006. *Confessions of an Economic Hit Man*. New York: Plume.

Perumatty Grama Panchayat v. State of Kerala [Coca-Cola groundwater exploitation case]. 2003. Accessed July 5, 2016, https://indiankanoon.org/doc/1161084.

Pickard, Victor. 2007. "Neoliberal Visions and Revisions in Global Communications Policy from NWICO to WSIS." *Journal of Communication Inquiry* 31 (2): 118–39.

Pieterse, Jan N. 2015. *Globalization and Culture: Global Mélange*. 2nd ed. Lanham, Md.: Rowman and Littlefield.

Pinto, Juliet. 2012. "Legislating 'Rights for Nature' in Ecuador: The Mediated Social Construction of Human/Nature Dualisms." In Latta and Wittman 2012, 227–43.

"Planet Green Announces Fan Favorite Returning Series Premiering in Second Quarter." 2009. *Futon Critic*, April 6. Accessed on October 12, 2014, http://www.thefuton critic.com/news/2009/04/06/planet-green-announces-fan-favorite-returning-series -premiering-in-second-quarter-30942/20090406planetgreen01.

"Planet Green Partners with General Motors on World Premiere Television Event: 'Detroit in Overdrive.'" 2011. *Futon Critic*, July 19. Accessed on December 1, 2013, http://www.thefutoncritic.com/news/2011/07/19/planet-green-partners-with-general -motors-on-world-premiere-television-event-detroit-in-overdrive-891102/20110719 planetgreen01.

Pollan, Michael. 2006. *The Omnivore's Dilemma: A Natural History of Four Meals*. New York: Penguin.

———. 2008. *In Defense of Food: An Eater's Manifesto*. New York: Penguin.

Postman, Neil. 1985. *Amusing Ourselves to Death: Public Discourse in the age of Show Business*. New York: Penguin.

Pringle, Peter. 2003. *Food, Inc.: Mendel to Monsanto—The Promises and Perils of the Biotech Harvest*. New York: Simon and Schuster.

Puckett, Jim, Sarah Westervelt, Richard Gutierrez, and Yuka Takamiya. 2005. *The Digital Dump: Exporting Re-use and Abuse to Africa*. Seattle, Wash.: Basel Action Network. Accessed July 6, 2016, http://archive.ban.org/library/TheDigitalDump.pdf.

Rabben, Linda. 2004. *Brazil's Indians and the Onslaught of Civilization: The Yanomami and the Kayapó*. Seattle: University of Washington Press.

Rajagopal, Arvind. 2000. "Mediating Modernity: Theorizing Reception in a Non-Western Society." In Curran and Park 2000, 293–304.

Redford, Kent H. 1991. "The Ecologically Noble Savage." *Cultural Survival Quarterly* 15: 46–48.

Reich, Robert B. 2011. *Aftershock: The Next Economy and America's Future.* New York: Vintage.

Reinhart, Hannah. 2008. "Framing Agricultural Biotechnology: A Case Study of Monsanto and the *St. Louis Post-Dispatch.*" Master's thesis, Southern Illinois University Edwardsville.

Reis, Raul. 2009. "Brazilian NGO Creates Innovative Social Carbon Methodology." *Environmental Communication* 3 (2): 270–75.

Reynolds, Mike. 2004. "How Does Monsanto Do It? An Ethnographic Case Study of an Advertising Campaign." *Text* 24 (3): 329–52.

Rogers, Everett M. 1962. *Diffusion of Innovation.* New York: Free Press.

Rogers, Everett M., and Lynne Svenning. 1969. *Modernization among Peasants: The Impact of Communication.* New York: Holt, Rinehart, and Winston.

Ross, Andrew. 1994. *The Chicago Gangster Theory of Life: Nature's Debt to Society.* London; New York: Verso.

Rust, Stephen. 2013. "Hollywood and Climate Change." In *Ecocinema Theory and Practice,* edited by Stephen Rust, Salma Monani and Sean Cubitt, 191–212. New York: Routledge.

Said, Edward W. 1993. *Culture and Imperialism.* New York: Knopf.

Sandler, Ronald L., and Phaedra C. Pezzullo, eds. 2007. *Environmental Justice and Environmentalism: The Social Justice Challenge to the Environmental Movement.* Cambridge, Mass.: MIT Press.

Santos, Ricardo V., Nancy M. Flowers, Carlos E. A. Coimbra, and Silvia A. Gugelmin. 1997. "Tapirs, Tractors, and Tapes: The Changing Economy and Ecology of the Xavánte Indians of Central Brazil." *Human Ecology* 25 (4): 545–66.

Schiller, Herbert I. 1976. *Communication and Cultural Domination.* Armonk, N.Y.: Sharpe.

Schneider, Michael. 2011. "Discovery Plans to Revamp Planet Green." *TV Guide,* February 12. Accessed July 5, 2016, http://www.tvguide.com/news/discovery-plans-revamp-1029235.

Schramm, Wilbur. 1964. *Mass Media and National Development: The Role of Information in the Developing Countries.* Stanford, Calif.: Stanford University Press.

Seltzer, Brian. 2012. "Discovery to Remake Planet Green Channel." Mediadecoder, a *New York Times* blog, April 4.

Semanti, Mehdi. 2007. "Media, the State, and the Pro-Democracy Movement in Iran." In Blankson and Murphy 2007, 143–60.

Shah, Hemant. 2011. *The Production of Modernization: Daniel Lerner, Mass Media, and the Passing of Traditional Society.* Philadelphia: Temple University Press.

Shahin, Saif. 2015. "Mediated Modernities: (Meta)narratives of Modern Nationhood in Indian and Pakistani Media, 1947–2007." *Global Media and Communication* 11 (2): 147–66.

Shiva, Vandana. 1991. "Biotechnology Development and Conservation of Biodiversity." *Economic and Political Weekly* 26 (48): 2740–46.

———. 2000. *Seeds of Suicide: The Ecological and Human Costs of Globalisation of Agriculture*. New Delhi: Research Foundation for Science, Technology, and Ecology.

———. 2004. "The Suicide Economy of Corporate Globalization." *Znet*, April 5. Accessed July 5, 2016, http://www.countercurrents.org/glo-shiva050404.htm.

———. 2005. *Earth Democracy: Justice, Sustainability, and Peace*. Cambridge, Mass.: South End.

———. 2013. "Reclaiming the Seed." *The Ecologist*, August 20. Accessed December 11, 2013, http://www.theecologist.org/News/news_analysis/1547185/reclaiming_the_seed.html.

Shohat, Ella, and Robert Stam. 1994. *Unthinking Eurocentrism: Multiculturalism and the Media*. London: Routledge.

Simon, Julian Lincoln, and Herman Kahn. 1984. *The Resourceful Earth: A Response to Global 2000*. New York: Blackwell.

Simpson, Catherine. 2010. "Australian Eco-Horror and Gaia's Revenge: Animals, Eco-Nationalism and the 'New Nature,'" *Studies in Australasian Cinema* 4 (1): 43–54.

Sinclair, John. 1999. *Latin American Television: A Global View*. Oxford: Oxford University Press.

Sinclair, John, Elizabeth Jacka, and Stuart Cunningham. 1996. *New Patterns in Global Television: Peripheral Vision*. Oxford: Oxford University Press.

Singhal, Arvind, and Everett M. Rogers. 1989. *India's Information Revolution*. Newbury Park, Calif.: Sage.

Sowards, Stacey K. 2003. "MTV Asia: Localizing the Global Media." In Artz and Kamalipour 2003, 229–43.

Sparks, Colin. 2009. "South African Media in Transition." *Journal of African Media Studies* 1 (2): 195–220. doi:10.1386/jams.1.2.195/1.

Starosielski, Nicole. 2011. "'Movements that are drawn': A History of Environmental Animation from *The Lorax* to *FernGully* to *Avatar*." *International Communication Gazette* 73 (1–2), 145–63.

Steger, Manfred B. 2005. "Ideologies of Globalization." *Journal of Political Ideologies* 10 (1): 11–30.

———. 2009. *Globalisms: The Great Ideological Struggle of the Twenty-First Century*. Lanham, Md.: Rowman and Littlefield.

Stewart, Julie, and Thomas Clark. 2011. "Lessons from *South Park*: A Comic Corrective to Environmental Puritanism." *Environmental Communication* 5 (3): 320–36.

Stiglitz, Joseph E. 2003. *Globalization and its Discontents*. New York: Norton.

———. 2012. *The Price of Inequality: How Today's Divided Society Endangers our Future*. New York: Norton.

Stock, Ryan. 2011. "Manifest Haiti: Monsanto's Destiny." *Truthout*, January 20. Accessed February 8, 2011, http://truth-out.org/archive/component/k2/item/93958:manifest-haiti-monsantos-destiny.

Straczynski, J. Michael. 2010. "Grounded." *Superman #701*, DC Comics. Saturday, July 17.

Straubhaar, Joseph D. 1982. "The Development of the Telenovela as the Pre-Eminent Form of Popular Culture in Brazil." *Studies in Latin American Popular Culture* 1:138–50.

———. 1991. "Beyond Media Imperialism: Asymmetrical Interdependence and Cultural Proximity." *Critical Studies in Mass Communication* 8 (1): 39–59.

Swales, John M., and Priscilla S. Rogers. 1995. "Discourse and the Projection of Corporate Culture: The Mission Statement." *Discourse and Society* 6 (2): 223–42. doi: 10.1177/0957926595006002005.

Tai, Zixue. 2006. *The Internet in China: Cyberspace and Civil Society*. New York: Routledge.

Takirambudde, Peter. 1995. "Media Freedom and the Transition to Democracy in Africa." *African Journal of International and Comparative Law* 7 (1): 18–53.

Takougang, Joseph. 1995. "The Press and the Democratization Process in Africa: The Case of the Republic of Cameroon." *Journal of Third World Studies* 12 (2): 326–49.

Tauxe, Caroline S. 1993. "Spirit of Christmas: Television and Commodity Hunger in a Brazilian Election." *Public Culture* 5 (3): 593–604.

Temple, J. 2009. "A Google Partnership to Save an Amazon Tribe and Rainforest." *San Francisco Chronicle*, October 18.

Thalén, Oliver. 2011. "Ghanaian Entertainment Brokers: Urban Change, and Afro-Cosmopolitanism, with Neo-Liberal Reform." *Journal of African Media Studies* 3 (2): 227–40.

Tomaselli, Keyan G. 2000. "South African Media, 1994–7: Globalizing via Political Economy." In Curran and Park 2000, 279–92.

Tomlinson, John. 1999. *Globalization and Culture*. Oxford: Polity.

Touré, Khadidia. 2007. "Telenovelas Reception by Women in Bouaké (Côte D'Ivoire) and Bamako (Mali)." *Visual Anthropology* 20 (1): 41–56. doi:10.1080/08949460600961596.

"Tracking Terrestrial Carbon." 2013. Ecosystem Marketplace, *Forest Carbon News*, September 10. Accessed on April 3, 2014, at http://www.forest-trends.org/documents/newsletters/forest_carbon_new.php?newsletterID=475.

Tunstall, Jeremy. 2008. *The Media Were American: U.S. Mass Media in Decline*. New York: Oxford University Press.

Turner, Terence. 1989. "Altamira: Paradigm for a New Politics?" Paper presented to the Annual Meeting of the American Anthropological Association, Washington, D.C.

———. 1993. "The Role of Indigenous Peoples in the Environmental Crisis: The Example of the Kayapó of the Brazilian Amazon." *Perspectives in Biology and Medicine* 36 (3): 526–45.

———. 1995. "Neoliberal Ecopolitics and Indigenous Peoples: The Kayapo, the 'Rainforest Harvest,' and the Body Shop." *Bulletin Series, Yale School of Forestry and Environmental Studies* 98:113–27.

———. 2002. "Representation, Politics, and Cultural Imagination in Indigenous Video: General Points and Kayapó Experience." In *Media Worlds: Anthropology on New Terrain*, edited by Faye D. Ginsburg, Lila Abu-Lughod, and Brian Larkin, 75–90. Berkeley: University of California Press.

University of Illinois at Chicago. 2009. "Scientists Agree Human-Induced Global Warming Is Real, Survey Says." *ScienceDaily*, January 21. Accessed May 3, 2010, http://www.sciencedaily.com/releases/2009/01/090119210532.htm.

Urfie, Jean-Yves. 2010. "A New Earthquake Hits Haiti: Monsanto's Deadly Gift of 475 Tons of Genetically-Modified Seeds to Haitian Farmers." *Global Research*, May 11. Accessed December 12, 2013, http://www.globalresearch.ca/a-new-earthquake -hits-haiti-monsanto-s-deadly-gift-of-475-tons-of-genetically-modified-seeds-to -haitian-farmers/19113.

Vacker, Barry. 2012. *The End of the World—Again: Why the Apocalypse Meme Replicates in Media, Science, and Culture*. Lindon, Utah: Center for Media and Destiny.

van Gelder, Sarah. 2013. "Vandana Shiva on Resisting GMOs: "Saving Seeds Is a Political Act." *Yes!* November 13. Accessed November 15, 2013, http://www.yesmagazine.org/issues/ how-to-eat-like-our-lives-depend-on-it/vandana-shiva-freedom-starts-with-a-seed.

Van Hook, Stephanie, and Michael Nagler. 2013. "Is the Monsanto Protest the Next Salt March?" *Truthout*, May 29. Accessed December 17, 2013, http://www.truth-out.org/ opinion/item/16633-is-the-monsanto-protest-the-next-salt-march.

Vialey, Patricia, Marcelo Belinche, and Christian Tovar. 2008. "The Media in Argentina: Democracy, Crisis and the Reconfiguration of Media Groups. In Lugo-Ocando 2008, 113–28.

Viola Recasens, Andreu. 2014. "'Pachamamista' Discourses versus Development Policies: The Debate over Sumak Kawsay in the Andes." *Íconos: Revista de Ciencias Sociales* 48: 55–72.

Vogler, John. 1995. *The Global Commons: A Regime Analysis*. New York: Wiley.

von Mittelstaedt, Juliane. 2010. "Using the Internet to Save the Rainforest: How an Amazonian Tribe Is Mastering the Modern World." *Spiegel Online International*, June 8. Accessed November 11, 2014, http://www.spiegel.de/international/world/ using-the-internet-to-save-the-rainforest-how-an-amazonian-tribe-is-mastering -the-modern-world-a-698511.html.

Waisbord, Silvio. 2001. "Family Tree of Theories, Methodologies and Strategies in Development Communication: Convergences and Differences." Prepared for The Rockefeller Foundation, New York. Available at http://www.communicationfor socialchange.org/pdf/familytree.pdf.

———. 2004. "McTV: Understanding the Global Popularity of Television Formats." *Television and New Media* 5 (4): 359–83.

Wallis, Cara. 2011. "New Media Practices in China: Youth Patterns, Processes, and Politics." *International Journal of Communication* 5:406–36.

Wang, Ucilia. 2013. "Google the Power Player Invests in Another Giant Solar Farm." *Forbes*, October 10. Accessed November 20, 2013, http://www.forbes.com/sites/ucilia wang/2013/10/10/google-the-power-player-invests-in-another-giant-solar-farm.

Warwick, Hugh. 1999. "The Next GM Threat: Frankenstein Forests." *The Ecologist* 29 (4): 250–51.

Wasserman, Herman. 2011. *Popular Media, Democracy and Development in Africa.* New York: Routledge.

Weisman, Alan. 2007. *The World without Us.* New York: St. Martin's.

Westra, Laura. 2008. *Environmental Justice and the Rights of Indigenous Peoples: International and Domestic Legal Perspectives.* London: Earthscan.

Wheeler, Mark. 2000. "Globalization of the Communications Marketplace." *International Journal of Press/Politics* 5 (3): 27–44.

White, Lynn, Jr. 1967. "The Historical Roots of Our Ecological Crisis." *Science* 155 (3767): 1203–7.

Wilkinson, Kenton. 2007. "Democracy Sponsored by NAFTA? Mexican Television in the Free Trade Ear." In Blankson and Murphy 2007, 199–218.

Wolfe, Dylan. 2008. "The Ecological Jeremiad, the American Myth, and the Vivid Force of Color in Dr. Seuss's *The Lorax.*" *Environmental Communication: A Journal of Nature and Culture* 2 (1): 3–24.

World Commission on Environment and Development. 1987. *Our Common Future.* Oxford: Oxford University Press.

Worster, Donald. 1979. *Nature's Economy: The Roots of Ecology.* Garden City, N.Y.: Anchor/Doubleday.

Zara, Christopher. 2013a. "Coca-Cola Company (KO) Busted for "Greenwashing": PlantBottle Marketing Exaggerated Environmental Benfeits, Says Consumer Report." *International Business Times*, September 3. Accessed November 25, 2013, http://www.ibtimes.com/coca-cola-company-ko-busted-greenwashing-plantbottle-marketing-exaggerated-environmental-benefits.

———. 2013b. "Comcast Yanks 'Exxon Hates Your Kids' TV Commercial: Online Petition Keeps It Alive." *International Business Times*, February 20. Accessed November 25, 2013, http://www.ibtimes.com/comcast-yanks-exxon-hates-your-children-tv-commercial-online-petition-keeps-it-alive-1094788.

Zegel, Maureen. 2012. "$1M Monsanto Gift to Fund Community Education Center." *UMSL Daily* [blog], May 4. Accessed on December 11, 2013, http://blogs.umsl.edu/news/2012/05/04/monsanto-gift.

Zhao, Yuezhi. 2000. "From Commercialization to Conglomeration: The Transformation of the Chinese Press within the Orbit of the Party State." *Journal of Communication* 50 (2): 3–26.

Zhu, Ying. 2012. *Two Billion Eyes: The Story of China Central Television.* New York: New Press.

Zwick, Steve. 2013. "Almir Surui: Perseverance under Pressure." *Ecosystems Marketplace*, September 18. Accessed June 3, 2014, http://www.ecosystemmarketplace.com/pages/dynamic/article.page.php?page_id=9956&section=news_articles&eod=1.

Index

Abbey, Edward: *The Monkey Wrench Gang*, 34

Administrative Rationalism: conservation movement in, 28, 29; ethnocentrism of, 31; natural relationships in, 29

advertising: green, 95–96, 108; on Indian television, 61, 62; Monsanto's, 112

Africa, sub-Saharan: consumerism in, 57; entrepreneurship in, 59; media commons of, 58–59; neoliberalism in, 56; political participation in, 57

agency, 34, 147–53; agricultural, 151; commercial media's articulation of, 9; in co-production of discourses, 148–49; corporate models of, 150; of Earth, 102; of Ecologically Noble Savage, 143; economic, 153; in Green Radicalism, 140; of indigenous Amazonians, 130, 151; Kayapó, 152; in neoliberalism, 68; in Promethean discourse, 42, 148; "prosumer," 28; in Survivalism, 148

Agent Orange (Monsanto), 98, 99, 102

Agnew, John, 44

agriculture: activism, 98–104; biotechnology of, 98; in Promethean discourse, 113. *See also* seeds, genetically modified; sustainability, agricultural

Alaba (Nigeria), electronics market of, 58

Almir Suruí, Chief, 132, 141; changing of attitudes, 138; environmental curiosity of, 135; meetings with ecological organizations, 135–36; technolgical advocacy of, 134

Altamira (Brazil), Kayapó protests at, 123–24

Amazon: biodiversity of, 117, 118; Earth discourses on, 119–20; ecological purity ethos of, 119; ecological symbolism of, 151; environmental abuses in, 35; in environmental imagination, 14, 117, 119, 126–29; Environmental Justice in, 119, 120, 122, 138; fragility of, 118; fraudulent land titles in, 133; global concern for, 133, 139; Green Radicalism in, 119, 122, 139, 143; megadevelopment projects in, 123–24, 140; NGO interest in, 120; view from space, 118. *See also* environmentalism, Amazonian; indigenous people, Amazonian

Amazon Conservation Team (ACT), 129; indigenous mapping initiative, 135–36

Anders, William: "Earthrise" photo of, 21

Animal Planet: faux documentaries of, 77, 78; green programming of, 87

animation, environmental themes in, 2, 21–22

Anthropocene era: Cold War terminology for, 71; media-envisioned, 92

anthropocentrism: in climate change, 131; conflict with ecocentrism, 154–55; of ecological problems, 34; in environmental discourses, 6; in environmental stewardship, 152–53

Apollo 17, "Blue Marble" photo of, 21
Athique, Adrian, 61
Attenborough, David, 83

Bartle Bogle Hegarty (firm), 103
BBC: Discovery Channel partnership, 83, 84; transition to market conditions, 51
Bible, environmental narratives of, 3, 18
biodiversity: of Amazon, 117, 118; geomapping of, 129
"Body 2.0: Creating a World that Can Feed Itself" (panel discussion, 2008), 100
The Body Shop: Kayapó work with, 128; promotion of dependency, 128; "Trade, Not Aid" project, 125–26, 128–29; use of Kayapó images, 128
Borman, John: The Emerald Forest, 118–19
Bowers, Chet A., 2
Boyd-Barrett, Oliver, 157n3
Brazil: development agenda of, 122; Kayapó protests in, 123–24; state corruption in, 121. See also indigenous people, Amazonian
Brundtland, Gro Harlem, 32
Butler, Rhett (Mongaby.com editor), 130

capitalism: Chinese, 63; consumer, 12; cultural hybridity of, 67; disorganized, 47; green, 128, 141; liberal, 147; neoliberalism relationships of, 47–48; in nonmarket economies, 119, 128; speculative forces in, 158n1
carbon trading: cultural survival through, 152; in Kyoto Protocol, 131, 142; as market activity, 153; polluters' use of, 160n5; Suruí people's, 131–35, 138, 142, 143, 152; sustainability and, 132
"Carnival of Corn" (street festival, Mexico), 101–2
Carson, Rachel: Silent Spring, 21, 71
Carter administration, Limits discourse of, 41
Castells, Manuel, 26
CEI-Telefonica (Argentine), 55
Center for Human Rights and Global Justice (New York University School of Law), 100
Chandra, Subhash, 61
change: root metaphors of, 19; social, 93. See also climate change
China: decentralization policies of, 65; environmental practice of, 65; fossil fuel use, 66; investment in African media, 57; market socialism of, 46–47, 65; media markets of, 63; TNMCs in, 63; in WTO, 63
China Central Television (CCTV): challenges to, 65; news programming of, 64
Chinese Communist Party, media policy of, 63, 64
Christie, Chris, 74
Christoff, Peter, 45
Cisneros (Venezuelan corporation), 54
citizenship: corporate, 95; entrepreneurial, 42; environmental, 139; market agency in, 147; pan-European, 50
citizenship, ecological, 34; in media commons, 153–56; progressive forms of, 154
Clarín (Argentinian newspaper corporation), 54, 55
climate change: anthropocentric, 131; citizen responses to, 1; human experience of, 37
Club of Rome: on environmental limits, 148; The Limits of Growth, 21, 71
Coca-Cola: greenwashing accusations against, 96, 97; sustainability campaign of, 96
Cold War: in ecological terminology, 71; Promethean discourse in, 45
colonialism, Promethean discourse in, 18, 42
Comcast: green initiatives of, 95; greenwashing accusations against, 97
commercial media, 12, 42, 49–50, 67; articulation of agency, 9; Chinese, 63; ecological collapse in, 71–73; environmental themes in, 21–22; Indian, 60, 62; Latin American, 54; neoliberalism in, 42; Promethean, 92; sub-Saharan African, 57–58
commons: control of, 151; cooperation breakdowns in, 80; corporate interst in, 97; disputes over, 148; Hardin's metaphor of, 4, 22–23, 24, 66, 71, 80; recovering, 88; social change in, 93; sustainable stewardship of, 126. See also media commons
communication: horizontal/vertical, 151; technology of, 45, 131, 139
communication networks: flexibility of, 26; indigenous people's use of, 129; as knowledge systems, 5. See also media systems
communication theory: environmental issues in, 6; information in, 45; technology in, 45
communities: environmental rights of, 35; key terms of, 40; master images of, 40; media in creation of, 155; root metaphors of, 40; in zombie melodramas, 80

Comprehensive Environmental Response, Compensation, and Liability Act (Superfund Law, 1980), 35
Conklin, Beth A., 119; on indigenous environmentalism, 126–27; on Xavante, 121
conservation: in ancient societies, 3; forest, 132; versus preservation, 7; professionalized strategy for, 28
consumerism: African, 57; choice in, 48–49; in commercial media systems, 146; in democratic modernity, 68; earth politics of, 1; Eastern European, 52–54; fuller life through, 68; gendered, 53; globalization and, 5–6; green, 95, 150; Indian, 62; sustainable lifestyle in, 81
consumption, mass, 44, 45; in Third World, 46
Corbett, Julia B., 66, 108
corporations: belief systems of, 106; earth politics of, 1; Ecological Modernization discourse, 96; environmental responsibility of, 3, 95–96; fair trade, 120; interest in global commons, 97; media presence of, 96; mission statements of, 106; multiplatform messages of, 3, 13, 96; social responsibility of, 7. See also institutions; Monsanto; transnational media corporations
cosmology, Amerindian, 137, 141
Cox, Robert, 4–5, 7, 156
Craig, Geoffrey, 81
creativity: ecological solutions through, 23–24; of Prometheus, 17
Crude (documentary film, 2009), 35
Cultural Survival (NGO), 125

The Daily Show with Jon Stewart, 103
The Day after Tomorrow (film, 2004), 72
"Decade of Development" (1960s), 46
DE Comics, environmental themes of, 2
"Defenders of the Amazon" (National Geographic, 2014), 119
deforestation, GPS monitoring of, 130
Deluca, Kevin: "A Wilderness Environmentalism Manifesto," 35–36, 158n5
democracy, consumer, 48–49
Democracy Now (news program), 99–100
Democratic Pragmatism, 24–28; collaborative possibilities of, 26, 38; consensus building in, 25; governance in, 25; in green-lifestyle television, 81; information exchange in, 26; "membership" in, 151; networked mediascape of, 28; opportunities in, 25; pluralism in, 27; pragmatist

philosophy in, 24–25; problem-solving in, 153; public consultation in, 25; public-private partnerships in, 26; in television, 73; in zombie narratives, 80
Deng Xiaoping: market policy of, 65; media policy of, 63
Destination America. See Discovery Planet Green
d'Estries, Michael, 89
deterioration, environmental: litany of, 3–4; and neoliberalism, 147–48
Detroit in Overdrive (Discovery Planet Green), 88–89
DiCaprio, Leonardo: Greensburg, 86, 89
discourses: complementary, 8; epistemological enforcers of, 153; as site of power, 7–8; underlying assumptions of, 9. See also Earth discourses; environmental discourses
discovery, military practice of, 18
Discovery Channel: BBC partnership, 83, 84; challenges to PBS, 83; DVD sales, 84; eco-pedagogy on, 82; faux documentaries of, 78; "mega" programs of, 83–84; partnerships of, 84, 85; programming of, 82–83, 90; public service model of, 83; reputation of, 82
Discovery Networks International: audiences of, 82; profitability of, 84
Discovery Planet Green, 84–91; audience of, 85, 87; creation of, 84; failure of, 89–92; goals of, 84–86; multiplatform delivery model, 85, 87, 90; partnership with General Motors, 88; profitability of, 89; programming of, 85, 86–90; rebranding of, 89–90
Disney Channel, 83
Doordarshan (public broadcaster, India), 59; Hindi programming of, 60; Hum Log, 60; sponsorship for, 61
Drezner, Daniel W.: Theories of International Politics and Zombies, 79
Dryzek, John S.: on Administrative Rationalism, 28, 29; on Democratic Pragmatism, 24; on Earth discourses, 12; on Ecological Modernization, 30, 31, 158n1; on green consciousness, 34; on liberal capitalism, 147; The Politics of the Earth, 7–8, 17; on Promethean discourse, 19, 37–38, 40; on public consultation, 25; on public land access, 158n1; on redistribution of power, 155; on social networks, 26–27; on Sustainable Development, 32

Earth: agency of, 102; carrying capacity of, 21, 71; exploitation of, 18; images from space, 20, 117–18; living in harmony with, 154; politics of, 1, 39
Earth Day, 20, 44
Earth Democracy (organization), 154
Earth discourses, 12, 17; alternative, 15; on Amazon, 119–20; analytical frameworks for, 10; choice of, 37–38, 40; coexistence of, 153; co-production of, 15, 148–49, 153; cultural metaphors of, 40; ecological intervention in, 156; fieldwork on, 10; in green-lifestyle television, 81, 91; institutional analysis of, 9–10; interpretation of, 9; market imperatives in, 149; in media commons, 9, 69; media events in, 10; privileging of, 95; problem-solving, 72, 91, 93, 105, 142, 150, 153; radical, 93, 113; shaping of identities, 150; summary of, 37–38, 39, 40; textual analysis of, 10. *See also* environmental discourses
Earth Underwater (National Geographic docudrama, 2013), 77
Eckersley, Robyn, 45
eco-activism, Kayapó people's, 123–26, 142, 143
ecocentrism: conflict with anthropocentrism, 154–55; in environmental discourses, 6
eco-criticism, tropes of, 6
Ecofeminism, 34, 35, 151; challenges to corporate globalization, 37; in film, 72; food systems and, 101, 102; of Global South, 37; in Green Radicalism, 36–37; view of technology, 36–37
ecological collapse: in commercial entertainment, 71–73; in films, 21
Ecologically Noble Savage, 118, 160n1; agency for forest, 143; in Green Radicalism discourse, 129; Kayapó evocation of, 123; market value of, 132; Suruí people as, 142; use of technology, 131; Western appetite for, 152
Ecological Modernization, 15, 30–32; Amazonian, 138–43; business-government cooperation in, 30; corporatism in, 33–34, 96; criticisms of, 31; cultural authority in, 30; ethnocentrism of, 31; European, 32; incentives for, 30; media embrace of, 155; problem-solving in, 142, 153; production

and consumption in, 31; shift from Green Radicalism, 119, 153; social engineering in, 30; storylines of, 31; Suruí people and, 142–43; weak/strong applications of, 158n1
ecology: deep, 34, 35, 82; media commons for, 4
economics: Keynesian, 43, 44, 46; libertarian, 41. *See also* markets
Economy, Elizabeth, 65
eco-pedagogy, 82
eco-politics: spokespersons for, 3; transformational, 154
Ehrlich, Paul: *The Population Bomb*, 21, 71, 80
electronic culture, leisure society of, 27
Emeril Green (Discovery Planet Green), 86, 89
"End Day" (BBC, 2005), 76–77
entertainment: commercial, 71–73; Limits discourse in, 71; neo-Malthusian visions in, 71, 81
environment: alternative visions for, 20; antagonisms over, 7; contradictory messages concerning, 2–3; cornucopian vision of, 146; corporate responsibility of, 3, 95–96; discourse approach to, 5–8; effect of globalization on, 2; empirical materials for, 8–11; expert management of, 29; human relationships with, 1, 7, 35–36; impact of media systems on, 2, 5; institutional arrangements for, 40; interactive policy-making for, 26; knowledge systems of, 5; market-driven relationships in, 46, 145; and media culture, 5; media messages on, 1, 2; narratives of improvement, 3–4; public consciousness about, 20; sites of inquiry for, 8–11; social imagination about, 1; symbolic treatment of, 5, 6–7; techno-institutional fixes for, 30, 31, 32
environmental discourses: anthropocentric, 6; challenge to market, 155; citizen responses to, 4–5; competing, 4, 5, 8; complementary, 153; core and periphery in, 11; of defense, 3; ecocentric, 6; ethnocentric, 6; incomplete articulations of, 154; neoliberalism and, 43; shaping of public perception, 40. *See also* Earth discourses
environmental imagination: Amazon in, 14, 117, 119, 126–29; media production of, 11; politics of, 40; rights in, 11

environmentalism: Cold War terminology in, 22; dawn of, 21; global, 121; media and, 9; political agency in, 34; professional class of, 29; rise of, 8–9; Western truths of, 37

environmentalism, Amazonian: celebrities in, 139; cultural misunderstanding in, 139; discursive terrain of, 152; Ecological Modernization in, 138–43; exploitation of, 139; global aspects of, 139; indigenousness and, 121–22, 126; language of, 122; media coverage of, 139; rise of, 121; of Suruí people, 131–38; Western narratives of, 151. *See also* Amazon; indigenous people, Amazonian

Environmental Justice, 7, 11, 34–36; activism for, 34–35; in Amazon, 119, 120, 122, 138; anti-GMO, 102; concerning Monsanto, 99; in film, 72; global, 35; in Green Radicalism, 34–36, 119; and indigenous culture, 140; U.S. movement for, 35

environmental policy, interpretive school of, 7, 17, 26

Environmental Protection Agency, 44

environmental stewardship: anthropocentric, 152–53; of forest, 152–53; in Green Radicalism, 126; individual concerns for, 147; Monsanto's narratives of, 115; Suruí people's, 133; symbolism of, 120–21

equality, biocentric, 34

ethnography, media, 10

ethno-mapping, indigenous, 129–31, 132; Suruí people's, 135–38

Europe, Eastern: consumerism in, 52–54; Western influence in, 52, 53

European Commission, on over-regulation, 50

European Union, markets of, 50

extinction, moral issues of, 155

extractivism: Latin America, 138; neoliberal, 154

The Fabulous Beekman Boys (Discovery Planet Green), 87–88, 89

Fairclough, Norman, 9–10

Farrow, Mia, 74

fertilizer, creation of dead zones, 1

Fight for the Forest (comic book), 126

films: apocalyptic, 38; Ecofeminism in, 72; ecological collapse in, 21; Environmental Justice in, 72; environmental themes of, 2; "nature's revenge" in, 72; Survivalism in, 38, 71–73; "tipping point" scenarios in, 72; zombie, 71–72

films, Indian, 60; Bollywood, 38; regional-language, 61

First World, indigenous alliances with, 14–15

Focus Earth with Bob Woodruff (Discovery Planet Green), 86

food systems: Ecofeminism and, 101, 102; human societies and, 99–100; market-based vision of, 116; politics of, 102

forests: conservation of, 132; environmental stewardship of, 152–53. *See also* rainforests

Forest Trends (nonprofit): Chief Almir and, 134; *Ecosystem Marketplace*, 134, 136

Foucault, Michel: on discourse, 7, 8; on object formation, 146

"Fragile Planet" (Al-Jazeera series), 2

Francis, Pope: encyclical on the environment, 154

free market ideology: effect on environmental governance, 46; in global media, 15; media promotion of, 67; in neoliberalism, 43, 146. *See also* markets

Friedman, Milton, 41

Fuller, R. Buckminster: use of Limits discourse, 21

FUNAI (Fundação Nacional do Índio), 132; Suruí relationship with, 134, 137

FUNBIO (*Fundo Brasileiro da Biodiversidade*), Suruí partnership with, 134

Gagarian, Yuri, 117

Gaia hypothesis, 20, 149

Gandhi, Indira: television policy of, 59

García Canclini, Néstor, 140

Garrard, Greg, 5, 18

Geertz, Clifford, 66

General Agreement on Tariffs and Trade (GATT), 50

General Motors, partnership with Discovery Planet Green, 88

Genesis, Book of: nature in, 18

genetically modified (GMO) crops: banning in Mexico, 102; contamination of non-GMO crops, 100; environmental narratives concerning, 98, 100; Mexican activism against, 101–2. *See also* seeds, genetically modified geomapping, indigenous people's use of, 129

geopolitics, media coverage of, 72

glacier melt, 1

globalization: consumer culture and, 5–6; corporate, 37; discourse approach to, 5–8; effect of media on, 9; effect on environment, 2; neoliberal, 46–47, 66

Global Media and Communication (journal), 157n3

global positioning systems (GPS): indigenous people's use of, 129, 130; monitoring of deforestation, 130

Global South: ecofeminism of, 37; green-lifestyle television in, 81; markets of, 68; media saturation of, 2

"glocalization," 146

GM Watch (United Kingdom), 25

Golding, Peter, 50

Goodman, Amy, 99–100

Google: characterization of Suruí, 141; Chief Almir and, 135–36; greenwashing accusations against, 97

Google Earth: indigenous people's use of, 130; Rondônia mapping project, 136–37. *See also* ethno-mapping, indigenous

Gore, Al: *An Inconvenient Truth*, 72, 84

governance: in Democratic Pragmatism, 25; environmental, 46

government, limited, 12

Graham, Laura R., 121; on indigenous environmentalism, 126–27

Grant, Hugh (Monsanto CEO), 100, 109

Grantham, Bill, 42

Grassroots movements, media use by, 151

"Green Is Universal" Website, 95

green-lifestyle television, 73, 81–91, 149; Deep Ecology in, 82; Discovery Planet Green, 84–91; Earth discourses in, 81, 91; eco-make overs, 82; in Global South, 81; storylines of, 150; survival shows, 74, 81–82, 91. *See also* television programming

green politics, 34

Green Radicalism, 15, 33–34; agency in, 140; in Amazon, 119, 122, 139, 143; anti-status quo of, 34; ecofeminism in, 36–37; Ecologically Noble Savage in, 129; environmental justice in, 34–36, 119; extinction and, 155; global, 139; in green-lifestyle television, 81, 82; "membership" in, 151; rejection of, 153–54; shift to Ecological

Modernization, 119, 153; social change in, 34; sustainable stewardship in, 126

Green Revolution, 100

Greensburg (Discovery Planet Green), 86, 89

Gross, Peter, 52

Haiti, protest against Monsanto in, 102–3

Hajer, Maarten, 30, 31, 158n2

Hardin, Garrett: "The Tragedy of the Commons," 4, 22–23, 24, 66, 71, 80

Harvey, David, 43–44

Hawking, Stephen, 77

Hayek, Friedrich, 41

Heise, Ursula K., 11, 20

Helix (SyFy Channel), 78

History Channel, "Armageddon Week," 75–76

Hollywood Green (Discovery Planet Green), 89

Ibroscheva, Elza, 52, 53

ideas, mass delivery of, 42

IDESAM (*Instituto de Conservação e Desenvolvimento Sustentável do Amazonas*), 134

Imhofe, James Mountain, 97

India: consumerism in, 62; "GM genocide" in, 100; media-related entrepreneurship in, 60; modernity of, 59; nation-building in, 59; neoliberalism in, 62; satellite technology in, 59; seed saving in, 102; water problems in, 96

indigeneity: and Amazonian environmentalism, 121–22, 126; authentication through, 122, 140, 141; performative practices of, 121

indigenous people: eco-agency of, 140; Eurocentric assumptions about, 126–27; First World alliances of, 14–15; Western assumptions concerning, 127, 140, 143

indigenous people, Amazonian: activism of, 14; agency of, 130, 151; autonomy for, 128; in blogosphere, 129–30; cultural continuity of, 120, 127, 140; cultural rights of, 127; eco-indigenous authenticity of, 119–23, 127, 140, 141, 151–52; "eco-othering" of, 151; in eco-politics, 120–26; eco-solidarity with, 120; effect of modernization on, 128; ethno-mapping by, 129–31, 132, 135–38; fair trade partnerships of, 120, 140; GPS use, 129, 130; intercultural exchange with, 120; land rights of, 140; native costume use, 122–23, 124, 131; as natural ecologists, 126–27; pan-Amazonian identity of, 124; reinvestment in tradition, 140–41; self-determination for, 121, 127, 128; state recognition of, 152; techno-indigeneity of, 119, 129–31; threats of extinction for, 135; ties to entrepreneurs, 128; transnational pressures on, 122; use of Google Earth, 130; use of mobile media, 129; video productions by, 160n3; visibility to West, 152; Western assumptions concerning, 143. *See also* Amazon

Industrial Revolution, Promethean discourse in, 18

information: in communication theory, 45; in Democratic Pragmatism, 26; free flow of, 49

innovation: discourse of, 12; globalizing discourse of, 41; in Promethean discourse, 19, 37, 43, 147; by rational economic subject, 36

institutions: discourse-rendering, 1; key terms of, 40; master images of, 40; root metaphors of, 40. *See also* corporations

Interagency Working Group on Environmental Justice (IWG), 35

International Monetary Fund (IMF): good governance programs of, 57; neoliberalism of, 46

In the Flesh (BBC), 78

iZombie (CW Channel), 78

Jakubowisc, Karol, 52

Johnson, Kirl, 62

Juluri, Vamsee, 62

Juruna, Mario, 121

Kahn, Richard, 82

Kaneva, Nadia, 52, 53

Kayapó people, 122; cultural activism of, 14, 126; cultural capital of, 123, 129; divisions among, 128; eco-activism of, 123–26, 142, 143; "eco-othering" of, 151; external interests affecting, 141; fair-trade agreements with, 126; global visibility of, 128; "indianness" of, 126; media use, 123–25, 142; megadevelopment protests, 123–24, 142; nut-oil processing, 126; political agency of, 152; resource extraction practices, 127; social awareness of, 128; and Suruí experience, 141–42; use of indigenous cos-

tume, 124; use of media, 160n3; in Western marketing strategies, 125–26

Kraidy, Marwan, 67

Kuttner, Robert, 158n1

Kyoto Protocol: carbon trading in, 131, 142; U.S. rejection of, 158n5

Lagasse, Emeril, 86

The Last Ship (TNT), 78, 80

Latin America: clientelism in, 54; extractivism in, 138; media conglomeration in, 54–56; media/politics collusion in, 56; privatization in, 54. *See also* Amazon

Lerner, Daniel: *The Passing of Traditional Society*, 45

Lewis, Jeff, 76

liberalism: embedded, 43; market, 44, 46

liberalization: Latin American, 55; in Promethean discourse, 13

libertarianism, economic, 41

Liguori, Peter, 85

Limits discourse, 12; agents of, 24; in cable/public television, 72; in entertainment, 71; on environmental exhaustion, 23; on maximum good, 23; in media commons, 13, 148; Monsanto's use of, 105, 113, 114; quality of life in, 23; reception of, 23–24; redistribution of power in, 155; revised version of, 73–74, 93; Survivalism in, 21–24; in television programming, 73–74, 91–93

Lomborg, Bjørn, 148; *The Skeptical Environmentalist*, 3–4

Lopez, Barry, 34

Lovelock, James: Gaia hypothesis of, 20, 149

Maher, Bill, 97

"mandarins," ecological, 24

"March against Monsanto" Web site, 103

markets: challenge of environmental discourses to, 155; in Earth discourses, 149; of Global South, 68; invisible hand of, 19; pan-European, 50; personal empowerment through, 68; as problem solvers, 146–47; replacement of state institutions, 44; state interventions in, 158n1. *See also* free market ideology

Martín-Barbero, Jésus, 47

Mato Grosso (Brazil), state corruption in, 121

McChesney, Robert, 48–49

McLuhan, Marshall, 145

The Meatrix (blog), 2, 157n1, 157n4
media: bio-piracy charges against, 99; commercial restructuring of, 49–50; contradictory messages from, 40; control over content, 28; in creation of communities, 155; discourse approach to, 5–8; discursive power of, 148; ecological ambivalence in, 145; effect on globalization, 9; effect on public culture, 1; environmentally responsive, 2, 11; environmental messages of, 1, 145; evolutionary trajectories of, 9; extreme weather coverage, 72; free market ideology in, 15; Indian market for, 61; Kayapó use of, 123–25, 142; mobile, 129; multiplatform, 3, 9, 13, 27, 32, 51, 105–23; political arena of, 27; and politics of the earth, 39; production of environmental imagination, 11; Promethean discourse in, 15, 42–43, 68–69, 146, 149; public policy issues in, 5; regimes of truth in, 9; in regional trade agreements, 49–50; role in neoliberalism, 42. *See also* commercial media; social media; transnational media corporations
media commons: corporate citizenship in, 95; Earth discourses in, 9, 69; ecological citizenship in, 153–56; for ecology, 4; Limits discourse in, 13, 148; metaphor of, 9; non-ecological norms of, 15; passenger metaphor for, 145; Promethean discourse in, 15, 147; reconditioning of, 155; sub-Saharan African, 58–59. *See also* commons
media culture, environment and, 5
mediascape: Ecological Modernization in, 32; environmental advocacy in, 28; global, 15, 66, 149; Monsanto's, 105, 113, 115; neoliberal, 50, 146; neo-Malthusian, 71, 81; participants in, 28; Promethean discourse in, 66; "prosumer" agency in, 28; Survivalist perspective in, 66. *See also* television
mediascape, Central/Eastern European: civilizing narratives in, 53; female body in, 53; neoliberal-Promethean, 53–54; transitions in, 52; transnational forces in, 52–53
mediascape, Chinese, 62–66; commercial, 63; enlightenment through, 63; environmental coverage of, 65; external actors in, 63–64; mobilization through, 64; neoliberal globalization of, 65; private, 65; relationships with state, 63
mediascape, European: deregulation of, 50–51; marketization of, 51, 52; public-private aspects of, 51–52

mediascape, Indian, 59–62; commercialization of, 60, 62; diversity in, 61; entrepreneurship in, 60; nationalistic, 62; neoliberalism transformation of, 59; non-state, 60
mediascape, Latin American, 54–56; commercialization in, 54; deregulation of, 54, 56; internationalization of, 55; market orientation of, 55–56; neoliberalism in, 55, 56; radio in, 58
mediascape, sub-Saharan African, 56–59; Chinese investment in, 57; commercial, 57–58; marketization of, 56; pan-African markets for, 57–58; privization of, 56
media studies: environment in, 6; global, 6
media systems: audience needs in, 150; commercial, 42, 67, 146, 156; environmental impact of, 2, 5; global, 67, 69; institutions of, 9; justification of market, 68; as knowledge systems, 5; market imperatives of, 149; market subjectivities of, 68; networked, 28, 68, 148; production of cyclical change, 145; Promethean, 146–47; structural changes to, 66. *See also* communication networks
megafires, 1
Merchant, Carolyn, 36
Mermaids (Animal Planet), 77, 78
Mexico: seed activism in, 14, 101–2; television, 54, 55, 56
Mijos, Ole J., 83
Miller, Jade, 58
Miller, Shawn William, 117
Miller, Toby, 42
modernism, environmental, 158n2
Mongaby.com (conservation news site), 129–30
Monsanto: advertising campaigns, 103; as agent of change, 113; Agent Orange, 98, 99, 102; agricultural cooperation narrative of, 115; "ambassadors" of, 115; antiglobalization critique of, 101; blogosphere on, 102–4; brand identity of, 13, 97, 115–16; challenges to, 151; chemical products of, 98, 99, 113, 114; code of conduct, 109; connection-to-nature narrative of, 108; corporate campus tours, 112; corporate responsibility narratives, 115; critics of, 97, 98–104, 109, 150; discourse analysis of, 106; Earth discourses of, 14; Environmental Justice discourse concerning, 99; environmental stewardship

narratives of, 115; as food company, 113–14; GM seeds of, 98–104; Haitian protest against, 102–3; hybrid seed distribution, 103; image-shaping campaigns, 13, 97, 104–5, 109–10, 150; key images of, 113; legal practices, 98; Limits discourse of, 105, 113, 114; lobbying practices, 98; marketing practices, 100; master terms used by, 113, 150; metaphors of, 113; motto of, 106; multiplatform media messages, 97, 105–12, 113; negative image of, 97, 102, 104; Promethean discourse of, 14, 97, 105, 113, 114, 115, 150; "Promote, Respond, and Implement" model, 109; promotional media of, 98, 159; public good discourse, 115; racial incidents involving, 99; rebranding efforts of, 13, 97; response to controversies, 111; Survivalism discourse of, 14, 113, 114, 115, 116, 150; sustainability advocacy, 14, 104–12, 113, 114, 115; Sustainable Development discourse of, 97–98, 114; "Sustainable Yield Initiative" of, 108, 112; television commercials of, 112; Web responses to, 102–4
Monsanto Community Education Center (University of Missouri St. Louis), 112
"Monsanto Company: Committed to Sustainable Agriculture" (video), 105–6
"Monsanto Protection Act" (2012), 101
Monsanto Web site: *America's Farmers Webisodes*, 111; *Beyond the Rows* blog, 110; blog exchanges of, 112; Farm Show Coverage, 111; Improving Agriculture section, 106, 110–11; mission statement on, 106–7; Monsanto TV, 111–12; mutiplatform, 105–6; *Newsroom* magazine, 110; "Our Pledge" page, 109; on productivity, 113; promotional videos on, 105–8; Social Media section, 112; sustainability discourse on, 105–12, 114; synergistic media model of, 112; underlying discourses of, 113–16; "Who We Are" page, 105–8
Monsiváis, Carlos, 56
Moore, Rebecca, 136
Muir, John, 19, 20; wilderness preservation of, 28–29
multimedia systems, corporate interests in, 27
Murdoch, Rupert, 61
Murdock, Graham, 50

NatGeo Channel, 83

National Environmental Justice Advisory council (NEJAC), 35
national identity: Eastern European, 53; in European media, 51; in interventionist state, 43–44
Native Americans, as natural ecologists, 126. *See also* indigenous people
NATPE conventions (2011–2012), 10
Natura Cosmeticos (Brazil), carbon offsets for, 133
nature: coexistence with human systems, 32; as cultural construct, 36; human depredation of, 117; as human resource, 31; public perception of, 7; social struggle over, 139; subordination to humanity, 18
NBC Universal, green advertising by, 95–96
Negrine, Ralph, 50–51
Nehru, Jawaharlal, 59
neoliberalism, 12; African, 56; in capital relationships, 47–48; in Chinese mediascape, 65; in commercial media, 42; and ecological degradation, 147–48; as economic philosophy, 46; environment discourse and, 43; extractivism in, 154; in free market ideology, 43, 146; global, 42, 46, 66; Indian, 62; individual agency in, 68; mediascapes of, 50, 146; Promethean discourse in, 42, 43–47, 68–69; in public imagination, 42; rejection of protectionism, 71; rich-poor divide in, 147; role of media in, 42
Nollywood (West Africa), 38, 58
nonhuman world, rights of, 11
nuclear power, European: public consultation in, 25

Obama, Barack, 101
Occupy Monsanto protest, 97, 101, 102
Occupy Wall Street movement, 154
O'Neill, Eileen, 84–85
Ophuls, William, 24
Organizações Globo (Brazil), 54
Ostrom, Elinor, 24
The Other 98% (activist group), 96
overpopulation: market solutions for, 23; technological solutions for, 23

Paiter-Suruí people: cultural-survival efforts of, 14; eco-mitigation plans of, 133; "ecoothering" of, 151; GPS use by, 130; media tools of, 132. *See also* Suruí people
Papathanassopoulos, Stylianos, 50–51

Payakan, Paulinho: meetings with world leaders, 124–25; rape charges against, 127; work with The Body Shop, 125–26
Petersen, Rachel, 138
Pharmacia Corporation, 104. *See also* Monsanto
Pickard, Victor, 49
Pinchot, Gifford, 19–20; Administrative Rationalism of, 28; conservation goals of, 29
Planet Earth (Discovery Channel series), 83, 84
Planet Green. *See* Discovery Planet Green
"PlantBottle" technology, 96
Plotkin, Mark, 129, 137, 138
The Polar Bears (Coca-Cola film), 96
Pollan, Michael, 99–100; *The Omnivore's Dilemma*, 99, 100
Postman, Neil, 150
power: discourse as site of, 7–8; links to knowledge, 7, 8; of Promethean discourse, 69; redistribution of, 155
preservation, versus conservation, 7
privatization: Latin American, 54; in Promethean discourse, 13; replacement of protectionist initiatives, 42
production, Fordist, 45
progress: in Promethean discourse, 18; public scrutiny of, 20; root metaphor of, 19
Promethean discourse: abundance in, 43; agency in, 42, 148; agricultural productivity in, 113; challenges to, 19–20, 42, 92; in Cold War, 45; in colonialism, 18, 42; in commercial media, 92; competition in, 43; continuing power of, 69; cornuopian mentality of, 18, 42, 45, 146; defense of, 20; in European mediascape, 52; in global media, 15, 66, 148; hegemonic, 92; innovation in, 19, 37, 43, 147; market orientation of, 13; media articulation of, 15, 42–43, 68–69, 146–47; in media commons, 15, 147; Monsanto's, 14, 97, 105, 113, 114, 115, 150; in neoliberalism, 42, 43–47, 68–69; opportunity in, 19; perpetual growth in, 146, 150; progress in, 18; of Reagan administration, 41; scarcity in, 147; Survivalism and, 148–49; sustainable development in, 147; technological progress in, 19; tenets of, 12–13; unarticulated, 17–20; wilderness in, 42
Prometheus (titan), creativity of, 17
prosumerism, 28; green, 38
protectionism: neoliberal rejection of, 71; in Western governments, 41–42

Queeny, John Francis, 98

Rabben, Linda, 127
Rainforest Harvest initiative (Amazon), 125, 127, 128–29, 138, 141, 142
"Rain Forest Rebel" (*Smithsonian* magazine), 130
rainforests, 14; carbon of, 131–32. *See also* Amazon; carbon trading; forests
Ramayan (Doordarshan television series), 60
Raoni, Chief (Rop ni Metuktire), 124, 125
Reagan administration, Promethean discourse of, 41
reality shows, eco-makeover, 2
Redford, Kent, 160n1
Reducing Emissions from Deforestation and Forest Degradation (REDD), 132; Suruí certification with, 133, 134, 138, 142. *See also* carbon trading
Renovation Nation (Discovery Planet Green), 86
resource management: Eurocentric, 19; morality of, 23; role of state in, 46
rhetorical criticism, environmental discourse model of, 6
risk, environmental, 34
Robin, Marie-Monique: *The World According to Monsanto*, 99
Roddick, Dame Anita: Amazonian activism of, 125, 126–27
Rogers, Priscilla S., 106
Rondônia (Brazil), cultural mapping of, 132, 136–27
Roosmalen, Vasco van, 136
Ross, Andrew, 8–9
Roundup herbicide (Monsanto), 99, 104
Russia, Promethean discourse of, 47

Said, Edward, 153
San Francisco Chronicle, on techno-indigenous Amazonians, 130
"save the rainforest" movement, 14
scarcity: as economic phenomenon, 18; Malthusian concept of, 149; in Promethean discourse, 147; in survivalism, 149
Schiller, Herbert: *Communication and Cultural Domination*, 49
Schleiff, Henry, 90
Scott, Ridley: *The Polar Bears*, 96
seas: dead zones of, 1; pollution of, 11
seed activism: in India, 102; Mexican, 14, 101–2; "seed Satyagraha," 101

seeds: commoditization of, 101; control over, 100–3; hybrid, 103

seeds, genetically modified (GM): Monsanto's, 98–104; proponents of, 98. *See also* genetically modified (GMO) crops

The Seeds of Death (film, 2012), 103

Seltzer, Brian, 89

Shapiro, Robert B., 104; on sustainability, 108–9

Sharknado (Syfy channel), 74–75, 78, 92, 150; Survivalism in, 74

Shiva, Vandana, 13–14, 36–37, 101

Sinclair, John, 54

Sin Maíz No Hay País (Mexico), 101

Smith, Adam, 19

social control, mechanisms of, 147

social media: articulation of agency, 9; shaping of public discourse, 150. *See also* media

social networks, environmental communication in, 26–27

South, American: environmental consciousness in, 102

Spiegel Online International, on techno-indigenous Amazonians, 130

Steger, Manfred B., 47

Sting (rock star): Kayapó activism of, 124; Rain Forest Foundation of, 125

Straczynski, J. Michael, 157n2

Super Girl (Hunan Satellite TV), 64, 67

Superman (character), environmental storyline of, 2

Super PACs, 27

"The Suruí Cultural Map" (Google blog), 137

Suruí people: artisanal goods of, 138; authentic indigeneity of, 153; community activism of, 142; conceptualization of maps, 137; confrontational tactics of, 134–35; contact with West, 133–34; cosmology of, 137; cultural memory of, 136–37, 142; Ecological Modernization and, 142–43; as Ecologically Noble Savages, 142; eco-mitigation plans, 138; eco-politics of, 152; environmentalism of, 131–38; ethno-mapping project of, 135–38; first adopter status of, 143; forest carbon project, 131–35, 138, 142, 143, 152; generational bonds of, 137–38; government unresponsiveness to, 137; impact of Trans-Amazon Highway on, 133; and Kayapó experience, 141–42; media technology use, 135–38, 141, 152; moratorium on logging, 134; "Plano da Vida," 134, 138; population losses, 134; REDD+ certification status, 133, 134, 138, 142; relationship with FUNAI, 134, 137; resource management by, 138; support networks of, 143; symbolic currency of, 141; Trust Fund of, 134; youth leadership among, 138. *See also* Paiter-Suruí people

Survivalism: agency in, 148; alternatives to, 24, 148; carrying capacity in, 71; commons metaphor of, 22; draconian policies of, 153; in films, 38, 71–73; in green-lifestyle television, 74, 81–82, 91; hierarchical authority of, 26; lifeboat metaphor of, 80, 93; "Limits" discourse of, 21–24; in mediascapes, 66; Monsanto's discourse of, 14, 113, 114, 115, 116, 150; overconsumption in, 22; population growth in, 22, 23; Promethean discourse and, 148–49; resurgence of, 13; revised version of, 92; scarcity in, 149; in zombie narratives, 80

sustainability: carbon trading and, 132; in Promethean discourse, 147

sustainability, agricultural, 97; Monsanto's advocacy of, 14, 104–12, 113, 114, 115

Sustainable Development, 32–33; contextual flexibility of, 32; cooperation in, 114; counterdiscourse of, 20; media embrace of, 155; Monsanto's discourse of, 97–98, 105; origins of, 32; private interests in, 32; problem-solving in, 153; state interests in, 32; subordination to human needs, 32; in television, 73; ties to IGOs, 32

Swales, John M., 106

systems: key terms of, 40; master images of, 40; root metaphors of, 40. *See also* media systems

technology: communication, 45, 131, 139; ecofeminism on, 36–37; indigenous Amazonians' use of, 119, 129–31; myth of progress, 2; "PlantBottle," 96; in Promethean discourse, 19; vision of future, 116. *See also* global positioning systems (GPS)

telenovelas, 56; environmental themes of, 2

Televia (Mexico): corporate missteps of, 55; monopoly status of, 54; tequila novelas of, 56

television: corporate decisions in, 9; defensive strategies of, 67; discursive adjustment within, 93; homogenized sensibilities in, 67. *See also* commercial media; Discovery Channel; green-lifestyle television; mediascape television, commercial: adjustable models of, 67; Chinese, 64; environmental themes in, 21–22

television, Indian, 59–62; advertising on, 61, 62; effect on village life, 62; Music, 62; regional, 61

television programming: "After Earth," 73; bundled, 76, 77; cross-channel arrangement, 76, 77; Democratic Pragmatism in, 73; earth-in-peril, 77; eco-horror, 73; ecologically themed, 13, 149; eco-parody, 75; end-of-the-world, 76–77, 92, 150; faux documentary, 77–78; Gaia's revenge, 76, 81, 92; Limits discourse in, 72, 73–74, 91–93; localized, 66–67; "nature's revenge" in, 73, 74–75, 80, 150; post-apocalyptic, 75–76, 92, 93, 150; Sustainable Development in, 73; "tipping point" scenarios in, 92; variety in, 91; zombie, 75, 78–80

Ten Ways to Save the Planet (Discovery Planet Green), 86, 90

Texico/Chevron, environmental abuses of, 35

Thatcher, Margaret, 41

Third World: mass consumption in, 46; in modernization theory, 45–46

350.org, 154

Trans-Amazon Highway, impact on Suruí, 133

transnational media corporations (TNMCs), 12; in China, 63; creation of consumers, 48; in U.S., 48–49. *See also* media, global

TreeHugger.com, Discovery Channel purchase of, 85–86

The Truth Behind Zombies (National Geographic Channel), 78

Tunstall, Jeremy, 60, 61–62; on Chinese media, 64

Turner, Terence, 128

TV Azteca (Mexico), 55; tequila novelas of, 56

UNESCO, New World Information and Communication Order debates (NWICO), 49

Urfie, Fr. Jean-Yves: *Global Research* blog, 102

U.S. Environmental Protection Agency, 25

Vacker, Barry, 92

Veja (news magazine), 127

Vietnam, market socialism of, 47

Volt (electric car), 89

Waisbord, Silvio R., 67

The Walking Dead (AMC), 78–79, 80, 92

Wall-E (animated film), environmental theme of, 2, 3

Wasted! (Discovery Planet Green), 86–87

Waxman-Markey bill (U.S., 2009), 160n5

weather, extreme: media coverage of, 72

Weibo (Chinese microblog), 64–65

Weisman, Alan: *The World Without Us*, 72

welfare states, public broadcasting in, 51

Whale Wars (eco-adventure program), 82

When Aliens Attack (NatGeo, 2001), 77

wilderness: conquest of, 12; versus culture, 18; in Promethean discourse, 42

Wilson, Edward O.: *Half-Earth*, 155

WINNER program (USAID), 103

The World According to Monsanto (documentary, 2008), 99

World Bank: good governance programs of, 57; Kayapó protests against, 123–24; megadevelopment projects of, 123, 140; neoliberalism of, 46

World Commission on Environment and Development, *Our Common Future*, 32, 33

World Trade Organization (WTO): China in, 63; media landscapes and, 50; opening of markets, 12–13; regulatory reforms of, 55

World Wildlife Fund (WWF), partnership with Coca-Cola, 96

Xavante people (Brazil): challenge to state corruption, 121; cultural-survival efforts of, 14; "eco-othering" of, 151; media coverage of, 121; use of media, 160n3

Xingú River Valley, dam projects for, 123–24, 143

Yanomami people: cultural currency of, 129; use of media, 160n3

Ying Zhu, *Two Billion Eyes*, 64

Zaslav, David, 84, 89, 90

ZEE TV (Hindi television), 61

zombie melodramas, 150; communities in, 80; in film, 71–72; storylines of, 79; televised, 75, 78–80

Zwick, Steve, 136

PATRICK D. MURPHY is an associate professor in the department of media studies and production at Temple University. Murphy is a co-editor of *Negotiating Democracy: Media Transformation in Emerging Democracies* and *Global Media Studies: Ethnographic Perspectives.*

THE GEOPOLITICS OF INFORMATION

Digital Depression: Information Technology and Economic Crisis   *Dan Schiller*
Signal Traffic: Critical Studies of Media Infrastructures   *Edited by Lisa Parks and Nicole Starosielski*
Media in New Turkey: The Origins of an Authoritarian Neoliberal State   *Bilge Yesil*
Goodbye iSlave: A Manifesto for Digital Abolition   *Jack Linchuan Qiu*
Networking China: The Digital Transformation of the Chinese Economy   *Yu Hong*
The Media Commons: Globalization and Environmental Discourses   *Patrick D. Murphy*

The University of Illinois Press
is a founding member of the
Association of American University Presses.

University of Illinois Press
1325 South Oak Street
Champaign, IL 61820-6903
www.press.uillinois.edu